Lecture Notes in Computer Science 4300

Commenced Publication in 1973
Founding and Former Series Editors:
Gerhard Goos, Juris Hartmanis, and Jan van Leeuwen

Yun Q. Shi (Ed.)

Transactions on Data Hiding and Multimedia Security I

 Springer

Volume Editor

Yun Q. Shi
New Jersey Institute of Technology
Department of Electrical and Computer Engineering
323, M.L. King Blvd., Newark, NJ 07102, USA
E-mail: shi@njit.edu

Library of Congress Control Number: 2006935869

CR Subject Classification (1998): K.4.1, K.6.5, H.5.1, D.4.6, E.3, E.4, F.2.2, H.3, I.4

LNCS Sublibrary: SL 4 – Security and Cryptology

ISSN   0302-9743
ISBN   3-540-49071-X Springer Berlin Heidelberg New York
ISBN   978-3-540-49071-5 Springer Berlin Heidelberg New York

Typesetting: Camera-ready by author, data conversion by Scientific Publishing Services, Chennai, India
Printed on acid-free paper   SPIN: 11926214   06/3142   5 4 3 2 1 0

Preface

It is our great pleasure to present in this volume the inaugural issue of the *LNCS Transactions on Data Hiding and Multimedia Security*. Since the mid-1990s, digital data hiding has been proposed as an enabling technology for solving security problems in multimedia distribution. Digital watermarks have now been used in applications including broadcast monitoring, movie fingerprinting, digital rights management, steganography, video indexing and retrieval, and image authentication, to name but a few. In some of these applications, data hiding and cryptographic techniques are combined to complement each other to achieve the goal. This combination resulted in a completely new research field, which now forms one important branch of multimedia security. It is expected that multimedia security will become more and more mature and will play a significant role in future commercial multimedia applications. Besides data hiding, the two related disciplines steganalysis and data forensics, which try, respectively, to detect steganographic transmission and to assert the integrity of media data, are increasingly attracting researchers. They have become another important branch of multimedia security. This new journal, *LNCS Transactions on Data Hiding and Multimedia Security*, aims to be a forum for all researchers in these important and new fields by publishing both original and archival research results.

This first issue contains five papers, divided into three groups. The first group consists of two papers dealing with watermarking. Dittmann et al. introduce a theoretical framework for robust digital audio watermarking algorithms, focusing on the triangle of robustness, transparency and capacity. The authors then compare selected audio watermarking algorithms in the newly developed model. In the second paper, Perez-Freire et al. provide a survey of watermarking security. Whereas watermark robustness has been generally identified with decoding error rate or resistance against intentional removal, watermark security is still a relatively fuzzy concept. This paper clarifies the concepts of watermark security and provides an exhaustive literature overview. It can serve as a starting point for newcomers interested in this important research topic.

The second group contains two papers. Adelsbach et al. discuss efficient implementations of zero-knowledge watermark detectors, which were recently proposed to overcome the drawbacks of symmetric watermarking schemes, i.e., the required disclosure of critical information (such as watermark and key) that jeopardizes the security of embedded watermark once the information is revealed. The authors propose efficient solutions for correlation-based detectors and more generally for watermarking schemes whose detection criteria can be expressed as a polynomial in the quantities required for detection. In the second paper, Koster et al. introduce the concept of personal entertainment domains (PED) in digital rights management (DRM) and outline the architecture of a complete PED-DRM scheme. In PEDs, content is bound to a person rather than to a device, thus providing a better user experience than in current DRM solutions.

The third group contains one paper dealing with steganalysis. Kharrazi et al. report on the use of fusion techniques to improve the detection accuracy of steganalysis. As various powerful staganalysis schemes have been reported in the literature in the past, in practice a steganalyst has to select one or more techniques which he or she applies on a suspected stego image. In the paper, the authors investigate methods that allow one to come to a conclusion if the decisions from these selected steganalytic techniques are contradictory.

We do hope that the inaugural issue of the *LNCS Transactions of Data Hiding and Multimedia Security* is of great interest to this research community and will trigger new research in this exciting field.

Finally, we sincerely thank all of the authors, reviewers and editors who have devoted their time to the success of the journal. Last but not the least special thanks go to Springer and Alfred Hofmann for their continuous support.

September 2006

Yun Q. Shi
Editor-in-Chief
Hyoung-Joong Kim
Vice Editor-in-Chief
Stefan Katzenbeisser
Vice Editor-in-Chief

Table of Contents

Theoretical Framework for a Practical Evaluation and Comparison
of Audio Watermarking Schemes in the Triangle of Robustness,
Transparency and Capacity 1
  Jana Dittmann, David Megías, Andreas Lang,
  Jordi Herrera-Joancomartí

Watermarking Security: A Survey 41
  Luis Pérez-Freire, Pedro Comesaña,
  Juan Ramón Troncoso-Pastoriza, Fernando Pérez-González

Efficient Implementation of Zero-Knowledge Proofs for Watermark
Detection in Multimedia Data 73
  André Adelsbach, Markus Rohe, Ahmad-Reza Sadeghi

Identity-Based DRM: Personal Entertainment Domain 104
  Paul Koster, Frank Kamperman, Peter Lenoir, Koen Vrielink

Improving Steganalysis by Fusion Techniques: A Case Study with
Image Steganography 123
  Mehdi Kharrazi, Husrev T. Sencar, Nasir Memon

Author Index 139

Theoretical Framework for a Practical Evaluation and Comparison of Audio Watermarking Schemes in the Triangle of Robustness, Transparency and Capacity

Jana Dittmann[1], David Megías[2], Andreas Lang[1], and Jordi Herrera-Joancomartí[2]

[1] Otto-von-Guericke University of Magdeburg, Germany
[2] Universitat Oberta de Catalunya, Spain

Abstract. Digital watermarking is a growing research area to mark digital content (image, audio, video, etc.) by embedding information into the content itself. This technique opens or provides additional and useful features for many application fields (like DRM, annotation, integrity proof and many more). The role of watermarking algorithm evaluation (in a broader sense benchmarking) is to provide a fair and automated analysis of a specific approach if it can fulfill certain application requirements and to perform a comparison with different or similar approaches. Today most algorithm designers use their own methodology and therefore the results are hardly comparable. Derived from the variety of actually presented evaluation procedures in this paper, firstly we introduce a theoretical framework for digital robust watermarking algorithms where we focus on the triangle of robustness, transparency and capacity. The main properties and measuring methods are described. Secondly, a practical environment shows the predefined definition and introduces the practical relevance needed for robust audio watermarking benchmarking. Our goal is to provide a more partial precise methodology to test and compare watermarking algorithms. The hope is that watermarking algorithm designers will use our introduced methodology for testing their algorithms to allow a comparison with existing algorithms more easily. Our work should be seen as a scalable and improvable attempt for a formalization of a benchmarking methodology in the triangle of transparency, capacity and robustness.

1 Introduction

Digital watermarking has been proposed for a variety of applications, including content protection, authentication, integrity, verification, digital rights management and annotation or illustration and many more. A variety of watermarking techniques have been introduced with different promises regarding performance, such as transparency, robustness, capacity, complexity and security. Depending on the watermarking application it is currently not easy to objectively evaluate these performance claims. Watermark evaluation methodologies and tools

Y.Q. Shi (Ed.): Transactions on DHMS I, LNCS 4300, pp. 1–40, 2006.

are therefore important to allow an objective comparison of performance claims and facilitate the development of improved watermarking techniques. The performance of watermarking techniques may also be compared with the specific requirements of applications.

The evaluation process can therefore be very complex and the actual research investigates into evaluation approaches with special attacks for images (see, for example, available tools include Stirmark [35], Optimark [30], Checkmark [5]) or for a specific applications like DRM, see, for example, [2] or so-called profiles, see, for example, [21,32]. In profile based testing we find basic profiles, extended profiles and application profiles. For example a basic profile is the transparency [21], an extended profile is lossy compression [21] and an application profile is the biometric watermarking profile [37,22]. For the later beside the evaluation of basic watermark performance parameters, the impact of the introduced signal distortions to the overall biometric error rates for user authentication needs to be evaluated.

In general, a distinction between two types of attackers [24] exists. The first type of attackers uses a single specific or a combination of signal modifications to destroy the watermark or to confuse the detection/retrieval function explicitly. These attackers are malicious and can be classified as powerful. The other type of attackers use the audio signal in a normal environment and they produce single or combined signal modifications implicitly without the goal to destroy the watermark (for example lossy compression). These attackers are non-malicious and they are not interested in attacking the digital audio watermark explicitly. In this paper, we do not distinguish between these types of attackers. A classification of general watermarking attacks to evaluate the robustness is introduced for example in [19]. Therein attacks are classified into removal, geometrical, security and protocol attacks. [38] extends the definition by including estimation attacks or [16,31,3,4] introduce attacks to gain knowledge about the secrets of the system (embedding and/or detection/retrieval) to also evaluate the security of watermarking algorithms. Besides the focus on the robustness and security evaluation for example in [18] the transparency of different steganographic and watermarking algorithms is analyzed.

The goal of our work is to design a theoretical framework to describe and formalize three evaluation properties, namely, robustness, transparency and capacity. With this formalization, watermarking algorithms can be evaluated and their performance can be compared more precisely. Specific measures to evaluate fragility for integrity verification are beyond the scope of our discussion and open for future work. The interested reader find first formalizations for content fragility in [9].

From the software evaluation strategies [1], two general different approaches are known: glass (white) and black box tests. In our case, the watermarking algorithm can be seen as a box, where the cover signal and additional parameters are the input and the marked signal is the output of the box. The two existing types of boxes can be seen as follows. In case of a black box, the evaluation function does not know anything about the watermarking algorithm itself.

Therefore, it is unknown for example in which domain the watermark is embedded and what the meaning of the parameters is. The opposite of it is the glass box, where testing involves the knowledge of the watermarking algorithm internals. Hence for example, the working domain and the detailed embedding technique are known. For the evaluation function, it can be very helpful to know the internals about the watermarking algorithm, because the identification of the parameters for a special application field can easily be optimized. Furthermore, if a new watermarking algorithm is introduced the evaluation can make use of the previous knowledge from other algorithms to reduce the costs (time and resources) needed to evaluate it completely. In case of black box testing where only the functional properties are known, the whole evaluation function starts at the beginning with, for example a brute force strategy to optimize the watermarking algorithm parameters. Also a third class of boxes exists, the gray box [1]. In that case, algorithm testing design is educated by information about the watermarking algorithm, like the type of parameters for the program behavior. If, for example, the watermarking embedding function needs a frequency range as a parameter, then its is suggested, that the embedding function works in a specific frequency domain and the evaluation could be tuned for it.

In our work, we set our focus for the practical framework only on black box evaluation, even if the type and usage of the parameters is known. That means that we use brute force mechanisms to evaluate the properties of different embedding algorithms with (if possible) different parameter settings.

The paper is structured as follows. Section 2 introduces the theoretical framework and discusses the properties capacity, transparency and robustness in detail for the embedding, attacking and detection/retrieval evaluation functions. Based on the theoretical framework, our practical evaluation is performed and introduced in section 3. The goal is to show the practicability and applicability of the theoretical framework with five selected audio watermarking algorithms. Section 4 shows and discusses the test results and provides the parameter based comparison within the triangle of robustness, transparency and capacity. The paper closes in section 5 with the conclusions and some suggestions for future work.

2 Theoretical Framework

In this section, the theoretical framework to describe watermarking algorithms and its properties is presented. Furthermore, the formalization of measured test results to provide comparability is introduced. Therefore, we begin with basic definitions, followed by the formalization of selected properties for the evaluation of embedding, detection/retrieval and attacking function. From our formalization, evaluation measures are derived and the interested reader can easily enhance our framework and its introduced methodology.

2.1 Basic Definitions

In this subsection the basic definitions of the theoretical framework to compare different watermarking schemes are provided. Therein, we introduce the watermarking scheme, the cover and the marked object, the embedding message and the overall watermarking properties.

A *watermarking scheme* Ω can be defined as the 7-tuple given by

$$\Omega = (E, D, R, M, \mathcal{P}_E, \mathcal{P}_D, \mathcal{P}_R), \tag{1}$$

where E is the embedding function, D is the detection function, R is the retrieval function, M is the domain of the hidden message and $\mathcal{P}_E$, $\mathcal{P}_D$, $\mathcal{P}_R$ are, respectively, the domains for the parameters settings used for embedding, detection and retrieval.

Although more precise definitions are provided below for the different functions involved, it is worth pointing out that the detection and retrieval functions are often dependent. On the one hand, some schemes only provide a method to detect whether the watermark is present in an object or not. These schemes define detection functions D but no retrieval mechanisms. On the other hand, different schemes make it possible to recover an identified version of the embedded message and a retrieval R function is defined. In such a case, a detection function D may be defined in terms of the retrieval function. For example, the retrieved message should be identical to the embedded one (at least above some threshold) to report detection. An example of this kind of detection function defined in terms of retrieval is the spread spectrum scheme in [6].

Three important properties of watermarking schemes are usually applied to assess performance, namely *robustness*, *capacity* and *transparency* [12]. Often, an improvement in one of these properties implies a decline in some of the other ones and, thus, some trade-off solution must be attained. For example, if robustness is increased by optimizing the watermark embedding parameters, then the capacity and/or transparency is often decreased. If the capacity can be increased, then in most cases the robustness or transparency decreases. The following Figure 1 introduces the triangle between the three properties on two examples [8]. The embedding parameters for the watermarking scheme Ω_A are tuned to provide high robustness. The price for the robustness of Ω_A is a bad transparency and a low embedding capacity. Therefore Ω_A is located close to the robustness corner of the triangle. Watermark Ω_B is tuned for a high transparency. The result is a low robustness and a low capacity. Therefore Ω_B is located close to the transparency corner of the triangle.

If other properties of the watermark are needed, then the algorithm parameters (if possible) can be modified to locate the watermark on any point inside the triangle in Figure 1. The requirements of the properties depend on the application used. Remark: unfortunately, two different algorithms, one with 50% transparency, 50% capacity and 50% robustness and the other with 100% transparency, 100% capacity and 100% robustness, would produce the same position middled of the triangle.

Instance of a Watermarking Scheme. The Equation (1) defines a general watermarking scheme where several parameters can adopt different values. In particular, there are embedding parameters $\boldsymbol{p}_E \in \mathcal{P}_E$, detection parameters $\boldsymbol{p}_D \in \mathcal{P}_D$ and retrieval parameters $\boldsymbol{p}_R \in \mathcal{P}_R$. Hence, each watermarking scheme Ω may

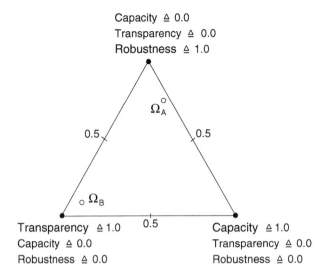

Capacity ≙ 0.0
Transparency ≙ 0.0
Robustness ≙ 1.0

Ω_A°

0.5   0.5

$\circ\,\Omega_B$

Transparency ≙ 1.0   0.5   Capacity ≙ 1.0
Capacity ≙ 0.0   Transparency ≙ 0.0
Robustness ≙ 0.0   Robustness ≙ 0.0

Fig. 1. Illustration of the trade-off between robustness, transparency and capacity

have different instances according to the values that these parameters may adopt. We define an instance Ω^* of the watermarking scheme Ω for a particular value of the parameter vectors:

$$\Omega^* = (E, D, R, M, \boldsymbol{\alpha}, \boldsymbol{\beta}, \boldsymbol{\gamma}), \tag{2}$$

for $\boldsymbol{\alpha} \in \mathcal{P}_E$, $\boldsymbol{\beta} \in \mathcal{P}_D$ and $\boldsymbol{\gamma} \in \mathcal{P}_R$.

Cover and Marked Object. The cover object S is the original content to be marked. Here, the general term "object" is used to refer to audio signals, digital images, video and any other type of object which can be marked. Once the message is embedded into the object S, a marked object $\hat{S}$ is obtained.

Watermark and Message. Depending on the watermarking algorithm, the watermark message m is given by the application or the user. In addition, it must be taken into account that the message m and the actual embedded bits may differ. For example, redundancy may be introduced for error detection or correction [10]. Hence, we introduce the notation w to denote the *watermark* (or *mark*) which refers to the true embedded bit stream. w is obtained as the result of some coding function of the message m. In any case, the embedding capacity of a watermarking scheme is measured according to the entropy of the original message m and not the embedded mark w:

$$w = \mathrm{cod}(m, \boldsymbol{p}_{\mathrm{cod}}), \tag{3}$$

where cod is some coding function and $\boldsymbol{p}_{\mathrm{cod}} \in \mathcal{P}_{\mathrm{cod}}$, with $\mathcal{P}_{\mathrm{cod}} \subseteq \mathcal{P}_E$, are the coding parameters. These parameters may include secret or public keys for security reasons.

Classification According to the Length of the Transmitted Message.
The length of the embedded message $|m|$ determines two different classes of
watermarking schemes:

- $|m| = 0$: The message m is *conceptually* zero-bit long and the system is
  designed in order to detect **only** the presence or the absence of the watermark
  w in the marked object $\hat{S}$. This kind of schemes are usually referred to as *zero-
  bit* or *presence watermarking schemes*. Sometimes, this type of watermarking
  scheme is called 1-bit watermark, because a 1 denotes the presence and a 0
  the absence of a watermark.
- $|m| = n > 0$: The message m is a n-bit long stream or $M = \{0,1\}^n$ and will
  be modulated in w. This kind of schemes are usually referred to as *multiple
  bit watermarking* – or *non zero-bit watermarking schemes*.

2.2   Embedding Function

Given the *cover object* (such as an original unmarked audio signal) S, the watermark or mark w and a vector of embedding parameters $\boldsymbol{p}_E$, the marked object
$\hat{S}$ is obtained by means of an embedding function E as follows:

$$\hat{S} = E(S, w, \boldsymbol{p}_E) = E\left(S, \mathrm{cod}(m, \boldsymbol{p}_{\mathrm{cod}}), \boldsymbol{p}_E\right), \tag{4}$$

where specific values must be provided for the coding and the embedding pa-
rameters $\boldsymbol{p}_{\mathrm{cod}}$ and $\boldsymbol{p}_E \in \mathcal{P}_E$ and $\mathcal{P}_E$ denotes the domain for the embedding
parameters.

The embedding process can usually be tuned with different parameters. Some
examples of which kind of parameters can be used are provided in Section 3.
In addition, it must be taken into account that several watermarking schemes
require public or private (encryption) keys defined by the Kerckhoffs principle
to introduce security. Those keys k belong to a key space $\mathcal{K}$ ($k \in \mathcal{K}$) and, if
present, are also a component of the vector $\boldsymbol{p}_E$ of embedding parameters. If
a watermarking scheme embeds m multiple times and can be controlled by a
parameter p_{max}, then it is part of $\boldsymbol{p}_E$.

Embedding Capacity. The embedding capacity cap_E of a watermarking scheme is defined as the amount of information that is embedded into the cover
object to obtain the marked object. A simple definition for a capacity measure
cap_E^* would be related to the size of the embedded message, *i.e.* $\mathrm{cap}_E^*(\Omega, \hat{S}) =
\mathrm{size}(m) = |m|$. In addition, capacity is often given relative to the size of the
cover object:

$$\mathrm{cap}_{E\,\mathrm{rel}}(\Omega^*, \hat{S}) = \frac{\mathrm{cap}_E^*}{\mathrm{size}(\hat{S})}. \tag{5}$$

Note that such measure only takes into account the information embedded,
but not the information that is retrieved. Note, also, that this measure does not
consider the possibility of *repeated coding*, in which the mark is replicated as
many times as needed prior to its insertion. All these issues are related to the
retrieval capacity which is defined in subsection 2.3.

Embedding Transparency. *Transparency (or Imperceptibility) function.* Given a reference object S_{ref} and a test object S_{test} the transparency function T provides a measure of the perceptible distortion between S_{ref} and S_{test}[1]. Without loss of generality, such a function may take values in the closed interval $[0, 1]$ where 0 provides the worst case (the signals S_{ref} and S_{test} are so different that S_{test} cannot be recognized as a version of S_{ref}) and 1 is the best case (an observer does not perceive any significant difference between S_{ref} and S_{test}):

$$T(S_{ref}, S_{test}) \rightarrow [0, 1]. \tag{6}$$

In case of signal to noise ratio (SNR) measures, the transparency function can be chosen as follows:

$$\overline{\text{SNR}}(S_{ref}, S_{test}) = \max(0, 10 \log_{10} \text{SNR}(S_{ref}, S_{test})) \tag{7}$$

$$T_{\text{SNR}}(S_{ref}, S_{test}) = 1 - \exp(-k \cdot \overline{\text{SNR}}(S_{ref}, S_{test})) \tag{8}$$

where k is some positive constant which can be chosen to provide an appropriate scale. Note that for $\text{SNR}(S_{ref}, S_{test}) \in (-\infty, 0]$ dB, $T_{\text{SNR}}(S_{ref}, S_{test}) = 0$. If we choose $k = 0.075$, then SNR = 10 dB implies $T_{\text{SNR}} = 0.52$ and SNR = 30 dB implies $T_{\text{SNR}} = 0.89$.

In this paper, however, we have used ODG measures instead of SNR and another transparency function is introduced in Section 3.

We can define a relative transparency for a watermarking scheme Ω^* and a particular object S as follows:

$$\text{tra}_{E\,rel}(\Omega^*, S) = T(S, \hat{S}), \tag{9}$$

where $\hat{S}$ is obtained as per the embedding function Equation (4).

However, this definition of transparency is related to a particular object S. It is usually better to provide some absolute value of transparency which is not related to a particular object S. A definition of "absolute" transparency is related to **a family $\mathcal{S}$ of objects** to be marked and we could apply any of the following definitions:

– Average transparency:

$$\text{tra}_{E\,ave}(\Omega^*) = \frac{1}{|\mathcal{S}|} \sum_{S \in \mathcal{S}} \text{tra}_{E\,rel}(\Omega^*, S). \tag{10}$$

– Maximum transparency:

$$\text{tra}_{E\,max}(\Omega^*) = \max_{S \in \mathcal{S}} \{\text{tra}_{E\,rel}(\Omega^*, S)\}. \tag{11}$$

– Minimum transparency:

$$\text{tra}_{E\,min}(\Omega^*) = \min_{S \in \mathcal{S}} \{\text{tra}_{E\,rel}(\Omega^*, S)\}. \tag{12}$$

---

[1] Note that signal to noise ratio (SNR) for audio or peak signal to noise ratio (PSNR) for images is widely used as transparency measure.

2.3 Detection and Retrieval Function

This subsection is devoted to the question related to watermark or message detection and retrieval.

Detection Function. Given a test object $\tilde{S}$ (which is suspected to be a possibly attacked or modified version of the marked object $\hat{S}$), a vector of embedding parameters $\boldsymbol{p}_E$, a vector $\boldsymbol{p}_D \in \mathcal{P}_D$ of detection parameters, the domain $\mathcal{P}_D$ of all possible values of the detection parameters and, possibly, the cover object S and/or the embedded message m, a detection function D can be defined in the following manner:

$$D(\tilde{S}, \boldsymbol{p}_E, \boldsymbol{p}_D, [S, m]) \rightarrow \{0, 1\}, \tag{13}$$

where D returns 1 if m is detected in $\tilde{S}$ and 0 otherwise. Note that such a function can be used in either zero-bit or non zero-bit watermarking schemes. Of course, in zero-bit watermarking schemes, the message m is not used. Furthermore, if the watermarking scheme requires a public or private key for the detection process, then the key k belonging to a key space $\mathcal{K}$ ($k \in \mathcal{K}$) is a component of the vector $\boldsymbol{p}_E$, which is a parameter vector introduced in Equation (13).

Retrieval Function. The definition of a retrieval function is only appropriate in non zero-bit watermarking schemes. Given a test object $\tilde{S}$ (which suspected to be a possibly attacked or modified version of the marked object), a vector of embedding parameters $\boldsymbol{p}_E$, a vector $\boldsymbol{p}_R \in \mathcal{P}_R$ of retrieval parameters, the domain $\mathcal{P}_R$ of all possible values of the retrieval parameters and, possibly, the cover object S and/or the original message m, a retrieval function R can be defined in the following manner:

$$m' = R(\tilde{S}, \boldsymbol{p}_E, \boldsymbol{p}_R, [S, m]), \tag{14}$$

where $m' \in M$ is an estimate of the embedded message referred to as the "identified message".

In case of repeated coding, the message m might have been embedded several times within the marked object. In this situation, some retrieval functions return all the different repetitions of the embedded message, whereas others use voting schemes and return just a single copy of the identified message. In the former case, the retrieved or identified message m' may consist of a longer bit stream compared to the inserted message m. As part of $\boldsymbol{p}_R$, the maximum number of multiple embedded m is known and denoted as $p_{\max}$. Furthermore, if the watermarking scheme requires a public or private key for the retrieval process, then the key k belonging to a key space $\mathcal{K}$ ($k \in \mathcal{K}$) is a component of the vector $\boldsymbol{p}_E$, which is a parameter vector introduced in Equation (14).

Note, also, that a detection function can be easily constructed from a retrieval function (but not conversely). Because of this, many multiple-bit watermarking schemes define retrieval functions instead of detection ones. Therefore, the following Table 1 introduces the dependencies between the retrieval and detection function and the zero-bit and n-bit watermark by introducing the watermark w and message m.

Table 1. Verification cases

	Detection	Retrieval
Zero-bit watermarking	w in $\tilde{S}$? (yes/no)	not available
n-bit watermarking	w in $\tilde{S}$? (yes/no)	m'

Classification According to the Information Needed by the Detection or Retrieval Function. The schemes, which require the cover object S in the detection function, are referred to as *informed* or *non-blind*. Some schemes require the original message m and/or p_E for detection or retrieval. These schemes are referred to as *semi-blind*. Finally, the schemes which do not require the original cover object S nor the original message m are referred to as *blind*.

Retrieval Capacity. Now we can define capacity with respect to the retrieved message m'. First of all, zero-bit watermarking schemes do not transmit any message, since the watermark w is just detected but a message m is not retrieved. In such a case, the retrieval capacity of these schemes is *zero*.

For non zero-bit watermarking schemes we should consider capacity *after* data extraction. Thus, given the retrieval function of Equation (14), we can define the following capacity $\mathrm{cap}^*_{R\mathrm{rel}}$ function:

$$\mathrm{cap}^*_{R\mathrm{rel}}(\Omega^*, \tilde{S}) = |m| - \sum_{i=1}^{|m|} m_i \oplus m'_i, \tag{15}$$

where $m = m_1 m_2 \ldots m_{|m|}$, $m' = m'_1 m'_2 \ldots m'_{|m|}$ and $\oplus$ depicts the exclusive or operation. This equation counts the number of correctly transmitted bits (those which are equal on both sides of the communication channel) and it is assumed that m and m' have exactly the same length (otherwise m or m' should be padded or cut in some manner).

In case of repeated coding, the retrieved message will be several times longer than the embedded message: $m' = m'_{11} m'_{12} \ldots m'_{1|m|} m'_{21} m'_{22} \ldots m'_{2|m|} \ldots m'_{p_{\max}|m|}$. In such a situation, the retrieval capacity should consider all the repetitions as follows[2]:

$$\mathrm{cap}^*_{R\mathrm{rel}}(\Omega^*, \tilde{S}) = \sum_{j=1}^{p_{\max}} \left[|m| - \sum_{i=1}^{|m|} m_i \oplus m'_{ji} \right], \tag{16}$$

where $p_{\max}$ is the counted number of maximal retrieved m'. In the sequel, no repeated coding is assumed for notational simplicity, but all the formulae can be easily extended to that case. If the watermark is not embedded multiple times, then $p_{\max} = 1$, which provides Equation (15).

---

[2] It is not required that the number of message repetitions is an integer. The last repetition could be trimmed in the last few bits. For simplicity, the notation considers an integer number of repetitions.

There are two relevant comments about this definition of relative capacity. The first is that usually this kind of measure is given in terms of the size of the cover object S:

$$\text{cap}_{R\text{rel}}(\Omega^*, \tilde{S}) = \frac{\text{cap}^*_{R\text{rel}}(\Omega^*, \tilde{S})}{\text{size}(\tilde{S})} \qquad (17)$$

and it is assumed that the sizes of S, and $\tilde{S}$ are, at least, similar. This second definition provides measures such as bits per pixel (in image watermarking), bits per second (in audio watermarking) or in bits of transmitted information per bit of the marked object. If the latter is used, a value in the interval $[0, 1]$ is obtained, where 1 means that all the transmitted bits are used for the message, which is the best case as capacity is concerned. The second comment is that $\text{cap}_{R\text{rel}}$ is relative to a given pair $\tilde{S}$ and S. An absolute measure is provided below.

Another capacity measure can be defined in terms of the ratio of correctly recovered bits normalized by $p_{\max}$. If $p_{\max}$ is unknown, the measure of $\text{cap}^\dagger_{R\text{rel}}$ can also be used, but would result in greater (not normalized) values:

$$\text{cap}^\dagger_{R\text{rel}}(\Omega^*, \tilde{S}) = \frac{\text{cap}^*_{R\text{rel}}(\Omega^*, \tilde{S})}{|m|\, p_{\max}}. \qquad (18)$$

Detection Success Function. To measure the overall success of a detection or retrieval function, we introduce a *detection success* function (see Equation (13)). Therefore, the zero-bit a n-bit watermarking scheme are introduced as follows.

For zero-bit watermarking schemes, $\det_D$ returns 0 if the watermark could not be successful detected and 1 if the detection function is able to detect the watermark:

$$\det_D(\Omega^*, \tilde{S}) = \begin{cases} 0, \text{no successful detection (negative)}, \\ 1, \text{positive successful detection (positive)}. \end{cases} \qquad (19)$$

To measure the successfully embedding rate over a test set, the average of $\det_D$ can be computed as follows:

$$\det_{D\text{ave}}(\Omega^*) = \frac{1}{|\mathcal{S}|} \sum_{S \in \mathcal{S}} \det_D \qquad (20)$$

For n-bit watermarking schemes, it is important to know if the watermark was successfully detected at least once (in case of multiple embedding). If, for example, a watermark scheme embeds the message m multiple times ($p_{\max}$), and the retrieval function $\text{cap}^*_{R\text{rel}}$ returns that 10% are positive retrievable, then it is unknown which m_i are affected. Therefore, it is useful to define a successful detection, if at least one embedded message could be retrieved positively, which is introduced in the following equation.

$$\det_R(\Omega^*, \tilde{S}) = \begin{cases} 1, \exists j \in \{1, \ldots, p_{\max}\} : \sum_{i=1}^{|m|} m'_{ji} \oplus m_i = 0, \\ 0, \text{otherwise}. \end{cases} \qquad (21)$$

Note that this is not the only possible definition of the detection function in case of repeated coding. For example, another definition could be the following:

$$\det{}_{R\tau}(\Omega^*, \tilde{S}) = \begin{cases} 1, \text{if } \mathrm{cap}^\dagger_{R\mathrm{rel}}(\Omega^*, \tilde{S}) \geq \tau, \\ 0, \text{otherwise}. \end{cases} \tag{22}$$

i.e. detection is reported if the ratio of correctly recovered bits is above some threshold τ (which will be equal to or close to 1).

To measure the successfully embedding rate over a test set, the average of $\det_R$ can be computed as follows:

$$\det{}_{R\mathrm{ave}}(\Omega^*) = \frac{1}{|\mathcal{S}|} \sum_{S \in \mathcal{S}} \det{}_R \tag{23}$$

and the average of $\det_{R\tau}$ as follows:

$$\det{}_{R\tau\mathrm{ave}}(\Omega^*) = \frac{1}{|\mathcal{S}|} \sum_{S \in \mathcal{S}} \det{}_{R\tau} \tag{24}$$

2.4   Attacking Functions

An attacking function or attack A distorts a marked object $\hat{S}$ providing a modified version $\tilde{S}$ (test object) aiming to destroy or weaken the embedded information. $\tilde{S}$ is often referred to as the attacked object:

$$\tilde{S} = A(\hat{S}, \boldsymbol{p}_A), \tag{25}$$

where $\boldsymbol{p}_A \in \mathcal{P}_A$ is a set of attacking parameters.

Usually, a family of attacking functions $A_{i,j} \in \mathcal{A}$ exists which may be applied to some object, where i identifies an attack and j is a related parameter combination ($\boldsymbol{p}_{A_{i,j}}$). It is assumed that attacks are "simple". If composite attacks $A_{11} \circ A_{12} \circ \cdots \circ A_{1j} \circ A_{21} \circ \cdots \circ A_{2j} \circ \cdots \circ A_{i_{\max}j_{\max}}(\hat{S})$ are possible, these should be incorporated explicitly into the attack family $\mathcal{A}$. Note that different attack domains $\mathcal{A}$ can be defined according to different scenarios. The concatenation of such single attacks is often referred as profile attacks [20,24,23,21,39].

Robustness. A watermarking scheme Ω is defined to be *robust* if the detection function D for zero-bit watermarking schemes or if the retrieval function R for n-bit watermarking schemes is able to recover the mark even when the attacks contained in a family $\mathcal{A}$ are applied to the marked object. Ω is defined as fragile if the detection function D or retrieval function R is not able to recover the mark *i.e.* to detect after a malicious attack signal change. In our discussion, we conclude on the robustness not on the fragility for detection of content changes. Here specific enhancements like the definition of malicious and non-malicious changes (attacks) become important and are out of the scope of the paper. However, the definition of robustness only classifieswatermarking schemes in two categories:

robust or not robust (fragile) and does not limit the distortion introduced in the marked object by the attacking functions. For example, the attacking function $A_{i,j}(\hat{S}) = \varnothing$, where $\varnothing$ means that the object is deleted, always erases the mark since it deletes the signal itself. However, the attack might certainly produce very bad transparency results: $T(\tilde{S}, \varnothing) \approx 0$. Thus, although the attack is successful in terms of erasing an embedded mark, it would be considered useless for most typical watermarking applications as the overall object quality decreases. If an attack which destroys the embedded mark and, at the same time, produces little distortion exists, this means that the watermarking scheme is not robust enough and should be enhanced. For this reason, we establish a relationship between robustness and attacking transparency by means of a quantitative *robustness measure*, in the following definition.

Robustness measure. The robustness measure rob_{rel} of a watermarking scheme is a value in the closed interval $[0, 1]$, where 0 is the worst possible value (the scheme is not robust for the signal S) and 1 is the best possible value (the method is robust for the signal S). There is a difference, depending on whether the bit error rate (BER) or byte error rate is used to measure the robustness. If the robustness is measured based on the byte error rate rob^{byte}, then a given watermarking scheme is classified as robust if the bytes of the embedded massage (characters) are correctly retrieved. Another robustness measure function based on the bit error rate rob^{bit} returns the percentage robustness of the watermarking scheme measured over the whole attacking and test set. For zero-bit watermarking schemes no retrieval function exists and no classification based on bit or byte error rates is possible. To simplify matters, the robustness measure for zero-bit watermarking schemes is always classified to rob^{byte}. The following example motivates the distinction between the robustness measure based on bit and byte error rate. If the message $m = $ "123", with 3 bytes and $3 \times 8 = 24$ bits, is embedded and, after attacking, the last 6 bits are destroyed and incorrectly retrieved, then the byte error rate returns, that 2 bytes are correct and one is false, which has a value of $\frac{1}{3} = 0.3\bar{3}$. The bit error rate returns, that 18 bits are correct and 6 bits are false, which has a value of $\frac{6}{24} = 0.25$. If the 1st, 2nd, 8th, 9th, 16th and 17th bits are destroyed, then the byte error rate returns that all bytes (characters) are false and the result has a value of $\frac{3}{3} = 1.0$ which means that 100% are destroyed. In contrast, the bit error rate returns, that 18 bits are correct retrieved and 6 bits are wrong, which has a value of $\frac{6}{24} = 0.25$. Although the bit error rate does not change, differences are apparent in the byte error rater. Therefore, the following equations introduce the robustness for n-bit watermarking schemes divided into rob^{byte} and rob^{bit} and for zero-bit watermarking schemes only for rob^{byte}. The two robustness measures rob^{byte} and rob^{bit} returns completely different robustness values. We introduce them to show that different approaches are possible and depending on test goals, choices are to be made to select the measure function. We note, that different measure methods are available to measure the robustness, *i.e.* based on det_R in relation to attacking transparency.

The following function relates robustness based on the byte error rate to transparency for a zero-bit and n-bit watermarking scheme as follows, given $\tilde{S} = A_{i,j}(\hat{S})$:

$$\text{rob}_{\text{rel}}^{\text{byte}}(\Omega^*, \hat{S}) = 1 - \max_{A_{i,j} \in \mathcal{A}} \left\{ T\left(\hat{S}, \tilde{S}\right) : \det{}_D\left(\tilde{S}, \boldsymbol{p}_E^{\text{opt}}, \boldsymbol{p}_D^{\text{opt}}, \boldsymbol{p}_{\text{cod}}, [S, m]\right) = 0 \right\}, \quad (26)$$

and for a n-bit watermarking scheme:

$$\text{rob}_{\text{rel}}^{\text{byte}}(\Omega^*, \hat{S}) = 1 - \max_{A_{i,j} \in \mathcal{A}} \left\{ T\left(\hat{S}, \tilde{S}\right) : \det{}_R\left(\tilde{S}, \boldsymbol{p}_E^{\text{opt}}, \boldsymbol{p}_D^{\text{opt}}, \boldsymbol{p}_{\text{cod}}, [S, m]\right) = 0 \right\}, \quad (27)$$

that is, given a marked object $\hat{S}$ and all the attacks which destroy the mark, even for optimal embedding and detection parameters $(p_E^{\text{opt}}, p_D^{\text{opt}})$, the one which produces less distortion in the marked object $\hat{S}$ determines how robust the scheme is. If none of the attacks in the family $\mathcal{A}$ erases the embedded mark, then this measure is (by definition) equal to 1 (the best possible value).

The functions provided in Equation (26), Equation (27) and Equation (31) measure robustness in a worst case sense. When the security of a system is to be assessed, it is usually considered that a given system is as weak as the weakest of its components. Similarly, Equation (27) establishes that the worst possible attack (in the sense that the mark is erased but the attacked signal preserves good quality) in a given family determines how robust the watermarking scheme Ω is. If the best (maximum) transparency amongst all the attacks which destroy the mark is 0.23, then the robustness of the method as given by Equation (27) is 0.77.

However, the functions of Equation (26) and Equation (27) are *relative* to a given object $\tilde{S}$ (hence the use of the subindex "rel") but we usually want to define the robustness of a watermarking scheme as an inherent property not related to any particular object, but to a family or collection of objects. This may be referred to as the absolute robustness ($\text{rob}_{\text{rel}}^{\text{byte}}$) which can be defined in several ways. Given a family $\mathcal{S}$ of cover objects, and their corresponding marked objects $\hat{S}$ obtained by means of the embedding equation Equation (4), the absolute robustness based on bit and byte error rate can be defined according to different criteria, for example:

– Average robustness based on byte error rate:

$$\text{rob}_{\text{ave}}^{\text{byte}}(\Omega^*) = \frac{1}{|\mathcal{S}|} \sum_{S \in \mathcal{S}} \text{rob}_{\text{rel}}^{\text{byte}}(\Omega^*, \hat{S}). \quad (28)$$

– Minimum robustness (worst case approach) based on byte error rate:

$$\text{rob}_{\text{min}}^{\text{byte}}(\Omega^*) = \min_{S \in \mathcal{S}} \text{rob}_{\text{rel}}^{\text{byte}}(\Omega^*, \hat{S}). \quad (29)$$

– Probabilistic approach based on byte error rate:

$$\text{rob}_{\text{prob}}^{\text{byte}}(\Omega^*, r) = 1 - \underset{S \in \mathcal{S}}{p}\left(\text{rob}_{\text{rel}}^{\text{byte}}(\Omega^*, \hat{S}) < r\right), \quad (30)$$

where p stands for "probability" and r is some given threshold. For example, if $r = 0.75$ and $\mathrm{rob}_{\mathrm{prob}} = 0.9$, this means that 90% of the objects in $\mathcal{S}$ provide a relative robustness greater than or equal to 0.75 for the scheme Ω.

Although a maximum robustness measure could thus be defined, it does not seem to have any applicability, since worst or average cases are often reported as robustness is concerned.

Another robustness measure based on the bit error rate related to the transparency for n-bit watermarking schemes can be defined as:

$$\mathrm{rob}^{\mathrm{bit}}_{\mathrm{ave}}(\Omega^*) = \frac{1}{|\mathcal{S}||\mathcal{A}|} \sum_{S \in \mathcal{S}} \sum_{A_{i,j} \in \mathcal{A}} \begin{cases} 0, \left(\mathrm{cap}^{\dagger}_{R\mathrm{rel}} < \tau\right) \wedge (\mathrm{tra}_{A\mathrm{rel}} > \nu) \\ 1, \mathrm{otherwise} \end{cases}, \quad (31)$$

Attacking Transparency. We can define a relative transparency for the attacking process for a watermarking scheme Ω^* and a particular object S as follows. Two different measures can be provided. The first is the transparency of the attacked object with respect to the marked object (which is the most obvious one):

$$\mathrm{tra}_{A\mathrm{rel}}(\Omega^*, \hat{S}, \tilde{S}) = T(\hat{S}, \tilde{S}), \quad (32)$$

where $\hat{S}$ is obtained as per the embedding function Equation (4) and $\tilde{S} = A_{i,j}(\hat{S})$, $p_{A_{i,j}}$ for some attack.

A second measure could be provided to define the transparency of the attacked signal with respect to the original signal and based $p_{A_{i,j}}$ parameter:

$$\mathrm{tra}^*_{A\mathrm{rel}}(\Omega^*, S, \tilde{S}) = T(S, \tilde{S}). \quad (33)$$

The usefulness of this measure might not be obvious, but it must be taken into account that a given attack could result in an attacked signal which is closer to the original object S than to the marked object $\hat{S}$. In such a case, the attack could provide an object which is even better than the marked one as far as transparency is concerned and the mark could be erased. Hence, this measure should also be considered in some situations.

It is usually better to provide some absolute value of transparency which is not related to a particular object S. We could thus apply any of the following definitions:

- Average transparency:

$$\mathrm{tra}_{A\mathrm{ave}}(\Omega^*) = \frac{1}{|\mathcal{S}||\mathcal{A}|} \sum_{S \in \mathcal{S}} \sum_{A_{i,j} \in \mathcal{A}} \mathrm{tra}_{A\mathrm{rel}}(\Omega^*, \hat{S}, \tilde{S}). \quad (34)$$

- Maximum transparency:

$$\mathrm{tra}_{A\mathrm{max}}(\Omega^*) = \max_{S \in \mathcal{S}} \left\{ \max_{A_{i,j} \in \mathcal{A}} \left\{ \mathrm{tra}_{A\mathrm{rel}}(\Omega^*, \hat{S}, \tilde{S}) \right\} \right\}. \quad (35)$$

– Minimum transparency:

$$\text{tra}_{A\min}(\Omega^*) = \min_{S \in \mathcal{S}} \left\{ \min_{A_{i,j} \in \mathcal{A}} \left\{ \text{tra}_{A\text{rel}}(\Omega^*, \hat{S}, \tilde{S}) \right\} \right\}. \tag{36}$$

Note that similar definitions can be provided with respect to $\text{tra}^*_{A\text{rel}}(\Omega^*, S, \tilde{S})$.

Attacking Capacity. Finally, the capacity of a watermarking scheme can now be related to a family of attacks $\mathcal{A}$ and a family of objects $\mathcal{S}$ as follows:

– Average capacity:

$$\text{cap}_{A\text{ave}}(\Omega^*) = \frac{1}{|\mathcal{S}||\mathcal{A}|} \sum_{S \in \mathcal{S}} \sum_{A_{i,j} \in \mathcal{A}} \text{cap}_{R\text{rel}}(\Omega^*, \tilde{S}). \tag{37}$$

– Maximum capacity:

$$\text{cap}_{A\max}(\Omega^*) = \max_{S \in \mathcal{S}} \left\{ \max_{A_{i,j} \in \mathcal{A}} \left\{ \text{cap}_{R\text{rel}}(\Omega^*, \tilde{S}) \right\} \right\}. \tag{38}$$

– Minimum capacity:

$$\text{cap}_{A\min}(\Omega^*) = \min_{S \in \mathcal{S}} \left\{ \min_{A_{i,j} \in \mathcal{A}} \left\{ \text{cap}_{R\text{rel}}(\Omega^*, \tilde{S}) \right\} \right\}. \tag{39}$$

Therefore, based on the retrieved capacity $\text{cap}_{R\text{rel}}$ from R, the attacking capacities $\text{cap}_{A\text{ave}}, \text{cap}_{A\max}$ and $\text{cap}_{A\min}$ are introduced as shown above. It is also possible to describe other measurable attacking capacities based on the other two defined retrieving capacities $\text{cap}^*_{R\text{rel}}$ or $\text{cap}^\dagger_{R\text{rel}}$.

Relationship Between Capacity and Robustness. Taking the definitions into account provided above, it may seem that capacity and robustness are not related, because the formulae provided do not involve both of them in a particular equation. However, it must be taken into account that robustness is related to the detection function $\det_D$ or $\det_R$. Following that successful detection after attacking $\det_A$ for a specific attack or $\det_{A\text{ave}}$ for an average value over a set of attacks with $\boldsymbol{p}_A$ can be described for zero-bit watermarking schemes as:

$$\det_A = \frac{1}{|\mathcal{S}|} \sum_{S \in \mathcal{S}} \det_D, \text{ for a specific attack } A_{i,j} \tag{40}$$

and for n-bit watermarking schemes as:

$$\det_A = \frac{1}{|\mathcal{S}|} \sum_{S \in \mathcal{S}} \det_R, \text{ for a specific attack } A_{i,j} \tag{41}$$

The average detection success for zero-bit watermarking schemes is:

$$\det_{A\text{ave}} = \frac{1}{|\mathcal{S}||\mathcal{A}|} \sum_{S \in \mathcal{S}} \sum_{A_{i,j} \in \mathcal{A}} \det_D \tag{42}$$

and for n-bit watermarking schemes as:

$$\det{}_{A\text{ave}} = \frac{1}{|\mathcal{S}||\mathcal{A}|} \sum_{S \in \mathcal{S}} \sum_{A_{i,j} \in \mathcal{A}} \det{}_R \tag{43}$$

With $\det_{A\text{ave}}$ the normalized successful detection after attacking can be measured and the result is in the range $[0, 1]$. If the function $\det_{R_\tau}$ is used to measure the successful detection, then the detection success after attacking would be $\det_{A_\tau}$ for a specific attack or $\det_{A_\tau\text{ave}}$ as an average value over a given test set and attacking set.

2.5 Evaluation Methodology for the Triangle

From the introduced parameters and measures in the previous subsections we can now derive an evaluation methodology to analyze one given algorithm (intra–algorithm evaluation or analysis) and to compare different algorithms (inter–algorithm evaluation or analysis) in the triangle created by the embedding, detection/retrieval and attacking function. Our evaluation methodology uses all the defined parameters and measures are summarized in Table 2. The idea is to describe firstly the general parameters for each watermarking algorithm and secondly the achieved results from the embedding, detection/retrieval and attacking functions for each algorithm itself as well as in comparison to other. If the algorithm itself is analyzed, it might be of interest to consider different parameter settings of embedding, detection and retrieval parameters and its influence to transparency, robustness and capacity as well as the specific behavior to a specific attack parameter setting on a selected test set. Furthermore in the case of a comparison of different algorithms it might be of interest to determine the best algorithm in the triangle where the different measures allow to specify a certain objective to achieve (*i.e.*the overall transparency as average function or minimal transparency as lower bound).

Our methodology therefore requires firstly the definition of all possible parameters needed by the embedding, detection/retrieval and attacking functions to setup Ω for a specific algorithm. These parameters are needed to compare different parameter settings or different test set classifications for one algorithm (intra–algorithm analysis) as well as compare different parameter settings and test set settings S and m between different algorithms (inter–algorithm analysis) of all functions E, D, R and A.

Secondly our methodology evaluates the algorithm with different input and output parameters, summarized in the first row by measuring the embedding, detection/retrieval and attacking performance with the measures summarized in the rows of the second, third and fourth columns. With this methodology an (one) algorithm can be tested with different parameter settings and placed in one triangle to compare the different performance results from these different parameter setting (intra–algorithm analysis). In our tests, for example, we compare the influence of different attack parameter settings to one specific embedding and detection/retrieval setting to one algorithm. Furthermore, if we compare

Table 2. Summarizing of evaluation methodology

	embedding	detection/retrieval	attacking
$\Omega_i(E, D, R, M, \mathcal{P}_E, \mathcal{P}_D, \mathcal{P}_R)$	$\boldsymbol{p}_E \in \mathcal{P}_E,$	$\boldsymbol{p}_D \in \mathcal{P}_D, \boldsymbol{p}_R \in \mathcal{P}_R,$	$\boldsymbol{p}_A \in \mathcal{P}_A$
m, m'	cap_E^*, $\mathrm{cap}_{E\mathrm{rel}}$	$\mathrm{cap}_{R\mathrm{rel}}^*$, $\mathrm{cap}_{R\mathrm{rel}}$, $\mathrm{cap}_{R\mathrm{rel}}^\dagger$, $\det_R$, $\det_{R\tau}$, $\det_{R\mathrm{ave}}$	$\mathrm{cap}_{A\mathrm{rel}}$, $\mathrm{cap}_{A\mathrm{ave}}$, $\mathrm{cap}_{A\min}$, $\mathrm{cap}_{A\mathrm{ave}}^\dagger$, $\mathrm{cap}_{A\mathrm{ave}}^*$, $\mathrm{cap}_{A\max}$, $\det_A$, $\det_{A\mathrm{ave}}$, $\det_{A\tau}$, $\det_{A\tau\mathrm{ave}}$, $\det_{A\tau\max}$, $\det_{A\tau\min}$
w		$\det_D$, $\det_{D\mathrm{ave}}$	$\det_A$, $\det_{A\mathrm{ave}}$
$S, \hat{S}$	$\mathrm{tra}_{E\mathrm{rel}}$, $\mathrm{tra}_{E\mathrm{ave}}$, $\mathrm{tra}_{E\min}$, $\mathrm{tra}_{E\max}$		
$\hat{S}, \tilde{S}$			$\mathrm{tra}_{A\mathrm{rel}}$, $\mathrm{tra}_{A\mathrm{ave}}$, $\mathrm{tra}_{A\min}$, $\mathrm{tra}_{A\max}$
$S, \tilde{S}$			$\mathrm{tra}_{A\mathrm{rel}}^*$, $\mathrm{tra}_{A\mathrm{ave}}^*$, $\mathrm{tra}_{A\min}^*$, $\mathrm{tra}_{A\max}^*$
$m', \tilde{S}$			$\mathrm{rob}_{\mathrm{rel}}^{byte}$, $\mathrm{rob}_{\mathrm{ave}}^{byte}$, $\mathrm{rob}_{\min}^{byte}$, $\mathrm{rob}_{\mathrm{prob}}^{byte}$, $\mathrm{rob}_{\mathrm{ave}}^{cod}$

different algorithms we can place the algorithms in the same or in a different triangle depending on the test results in order to show the performance differences (inter–algorithm analysis).

In particular the evaluation of capacity for embedding or retrieval depends on m and m'. For embedding, cap_E^* defines the absolute length of m and $\mathrm{cap}_{E\mathrm{rel}}^*$ the relative length of m normalized to the length of the audio signal. For retrieval, $\mathrm{cap}_{R\mathrm{rel}}^*$ defines the absolute lengths of retrieved m'. Therefore, it is used to measure for example the bit error rate (BER) or byte error rate over the whole audio signal. A repeated embedding of m can be identified as well in the $\mathrm{cap}_{R\mathrm{rel}}^\dagger$. The retrieved capacity can be normalized to the length of the audio signal (or frames of it) with $\mathrm{cap}_{R\mathrm{rel}}$ or to the length of m with $\mathrm{cap}_{R\mathrm{rel}}^\dagger$. For attacking, the capacity $\text{cap}_{A\text{ave}}$ defines the normalized average capacity after one or more attacks to an audio test set. Furthermore, $\text{cap}_{A\text{min}}$ and $\text{cap}_{A\text{max}}$ defines the minimum and maximum received capacity after one or more attacks on a given audio test set. The function $\det_D$ for a zero-bit watermarking scheme and $\det_R$ for n-bit watermarking scheme determine, if a given m can be embedded into an audio signal or not. Therefore, the average values of them $\det_{D\text{ave}}$ and $\det_{R\text{ave}}$ shows the average success of the embedding function by using directly after embedding the detection or retrieval function as verification.

The transparency of the embedding function (between $S, \hat{S}$) can be measured with $\text{tra}_{E\text{rel}}$ for a specific watermarking algorithm and a specific audio signal with a given parameter set. Furthermore, $\text{tra}_{E\text{ave}}$, $\text{tra}_{E\text{min}}$ and $\text{tra}_{E\text{max}}$ defines the average, minimal and maximal transparency of a watermarking algorithm applied to a test set. The attacking transparency between the marked and attacked signal $(\hat{S}, \tilde{S})$ is similar measured to the embedding transparency. Therefore, relative ($\text{tra}_{A\text{rel}}$), average ($\text{tra}_{A\text{ave}}$), minimal ($\text{tra}_{A\text{min}}$) and maximal ($\text{tra}_{A\text{max}}$) transparency can be measured and compared. If the attacking transparency is measured between the attacked and original signal $(S, \tilde{S})$, then the same types of transparencies are defined: relative ($\text{tra}^*_{A\text{rel}}$), average ($\text{tra}^*_{A\text{ave}}$), minimal ($\text{tra}^*_{A\text{min}}$) and maximal ($\text{tra}^*_{A\text{max}}$). The functions $\det_D$ and $\det_R$ measure the positive detection of m'. Therefore, the result is 0 (zero), if $m \neq m'$ and 1, if $m = m'$ at least once for a given audio signal. The average result over a test set is measured with $\det_A$, which is in range $[0, 1]$.

The robustness of a watermarking algorithm based on the bit or byte error rate can be measured with the average over the whole test set $\left(\text{rob}^{\text{byte}}_{\text{ave}}, \text{rob}^{\text{bit}}_{\text{ave}}\right)$, the minimum $\left(\text{rob}^{\text{byte}}_{\text{min}}\right)$ which includes the best attacking transparency and the best detection/retrieving results and a probabilistic result $\left(\text{rob}^{\text{byte}}_{\text{prob}}\right)$. Therefore, m' is retrieved with function R of Ω^* and m must be known to measure $\text{cap}^{\dagger}_{R\text{rel}}$. For $\text{rob}^{\text{bit}}_{\text{ave}}$, the thresholds τ and ν define with the function $\det_{R\tau}$, if Ω^* is robust or not against $A_{i,j}$ by using a detection of m' depending on τ. Furthermore, the results of $\det_{A\tau}$ for a specific or $\det_{A\tau\text{ave}}$ for all attacks depict the average of successful detection. If no threshold is needed, because the application scenario requires the complete message, then $\det_A$ and its average values are measurable. This result is a *byte error rate* because it is successfully only if at least once w can be detected for zero-bit or $m' = m$ retrieved for n-bit watermarking schemes.

The introduced methodology allows intra and inter–algorithm evaluation or analysis as well as the separate selection of embedding, detection/retrieval parameters for Ω^*, the attacking functions and its parameters, the test set S and the overall attack set $\mathcal{A}$.

3   Practical Evaluation

In this section, we set up a practical evaluation based on the described theoretical framework in order to show how to perform a practical evaluation (comparison)

Table 3. Practical used evaluation

	embedding	detection/retrieval	attacking
$\Omega_i(E,D,R,M,\mathcal{P}_E,\mathcal{P}_D,\mathcal{P}_R)$	$\boldsymbol{p}_E \in \mathcal{P}_E,$	$\boldsymbol{p}_D \in \mathcal{P}_D, \boldsymbol{p}_R \in \mathcal{P}_R,$	$\boldsymbol{p}_A \in \mathcal{P}_A$
m, m'	cap_E^*	$\det_{R\mathrm{ave}},\quad \det_{R\tau},$ $\mathrm{cap}_{R\mathrm{rel}}^*$	$\mathrm{cap}_{A\mathrm{ave}},$ $\mathrm{cap}_{A\mathrm{min}},$ $\mathrm{cap}_{A\mathrm{max}},$ $\mathrm{cap}_{A\mathrm{ave}}^{\dagger},$ $\mathrm{cap}_{A\mathrm{ave}}^{\dagger},$ $\mathrm{cap}_{A\mathrm{ave}}^{\dagger},$ $\det_{A\mathrm{ave}},$ $\det_{A\tau\mathrm{ave}},$
w		$\det_{D\mathrm{ave}}$	$\det_{A\mathrm{ave}}$
$S, \hat{S}$	$\mathrm{tra}_{E\mathrm{ave}},$ $\mathrm{tra}_{E\mathrm{min}},$ $\mathrm{tra}_{E\mathrm{max}}$		
$\tilde{S}, \hat{\tilde{S}}$			$\mathrm{tra}_{A\mathrm{ave}},$ $\mathrm{tra}_{A\mathrm{min}},$ $\mathrm{tra}_{A\mathrm{max}}$
$m', \tilde{S}$			$\mathrm{rob}_{\mathrm{ave}}^{\mathrm{byte}}$

of audio watermarking algorithms. In the subsection 3.1 the five example audio watermarking algorithms and their parameters ($\boldsymbol{p}_E$ and $\boldsymbol{p}_D, \boldsymbol{p}_R$) are introduced. The audio test set and the test scenario (practical evaluation framework) used in subsection 3.2 is shown with attacks $A_{i,j}$ and $\boldsymbol{p}_{A i,j}$. Our test goals are introduced in subsection 3.3.

From the methodology introduced in section 2.5 we select a subset of measures to perform a proof of concept evaluation (practical usage) of the theoretical framework. Therefore, the following Table 3 shows the prototypical implemented functions.

The methodology allows us to provide an intra–algorithm evaluation and analysis by using different parameter settings for the attacks as well as an inter–algorithm analysis to provide comparability between selected watermarking algorithms.

3.1   Evaluated Watermarking Algorithms: Basic Definitions

For our exemplary evaluation we use five different audio watermarking algorithms ($\Omega_1, \ldots, \Omega_5$). The following description contains the general parameter description and some more internals by describing the working domain of the functions E, D and R as additional information for a classification of the test results. In our later test setup the watermarking algorithms are seen as black boxes.

Ω_1: This watermarking algorithm is a n-bit watermarking algorithm. It embeds m once, works in the wavelet domain and embeds the watermark on selected zero tree nodes [33]. It does not use a secret key and can therefore categorized, from the application point of view, as an annotation watermarking scheme. An additional file is created, where the marking positions are stored to retrieve the watermark information in detection/retrieval function (non blind) [13]. By using Ω_1, the following parameters are defined for this algorithm:

- p_1: specifies the internal embedding method and at present only ZT (zerotree) is possible.
- p_2: specifies the internal coding method and at present, only binary (BIN) is possible. As $\boldsymbol{p}_{\mathrm{cod}} \in \boldsymbol{p}_E$ the coding method used for $\boldsymbol{p}_{\mathrm{cod}}$ is seen as $\boldsymbol{p}_E$.

Embedding Function: As input audio signal S, this watermarking scheme reads only uncompressed PCM audio files in WAVE format. The output signal $\hat{S}$ is only writable in uncompressed PCM WAVE file format. The parameters needed for E are $\boldsymbol{p}_E = (p_1, p_2)$.

Detection/Retrieval Function: As input audio signal $\hat{S}$ or $\tilde{S}$ only uncompressed PCM audio files in WAVE format are supported. Furthermore, there is no distinction between D and R. Therefore, only the retrieval function R can be used. The parameters needed for R are $\boldsymbol{p}_R = (p_1, p_2)$, $D = \varnothing$.

The introduced parameters are subsequently assigned to $\boldsymbol{p}_E$, $\boldsymbol{p}_D$ and $\boldsymbol{p}_R$. Therefore, this watermarking scheme can be described as follows:

$$\Omega_1 = (E, \varnothing, R, m, \{p_1 = BIN, p_2 = ZT\}, \varnothing, \{p_1 = BIN, p_2 = ZT\})$$

Other parameter combinations are currently not available. The working domain of this algorithm is wavelet and can exemplary be described as:

$$\Omega_1 = (E_{wavlet}, \varnothing, R_{wavelet}, m, \{p_1 = BIN, p_2 = ZT\},$$
$$\varnothing, \{p_1 = BIN, p_2 = ZT\})$$

$\boldsymbol{\Omega_2}$: This n-bit stream watermarking algorithm works in the frequency domain and embeds the watermark in the frequency coefficients by using a spread spectrum technique [17]. It does not use a secret key and can therefore also be categorized as annotation watermarking scheme. This algorithm has only the message m as input parameter:

- m: specifies the watermarking message, which will be embedded. It can be a string with characters [a-zA-Z0-9].

Embedding Function: As input audio signal S, the well known uncompressed PCM audio WAVE format is supported (more formats information are not available currently). The output signal $\hat{S}$ can also be written in uncompressed PCM WAVE file format. There are no parameters for E defined; $(\boldsymbol{p}_E = (\varnothing))$.

Detection/Retrieval Function: As input audio signals $\hat{S}$ or $\tilde{S}$ it is uncompressed PCM audio files in WAVE format are supported (more formats are not known yet). Furthermore, there is also no distinguish between D and R. Therefore, only the retrieval function R can be used. The parameters required for R are $\boldsymbol{p}_R = (\varnothing)$.

Therefore, Ω_2 has no parameters for $\boldsymbol{p}_E$, $\boldsymbol{p}_D$ and $\boldsymbol{p}_R$, which can be changed for the embedding and detecting/retrieval function. For an intra–algorithm analysis, only the test set, attack set and/or attacking parameters can be changed.

This watermarking algorithms can be described as follows:

$$\Omega_2 = (E, \varnothing, R, m, \varnothing, \varnothing, \varnothing)$$

The working domain of this algorithm is the frequency domain and can be described with:

$$\Omega_2 = (E_{freq}, \varnothing, R_{freq}, m, \varnothing, \varnothing, \varnothing)$$

$\boldsymbol{\Omega_3}$: This n-bit stream watermarking algorithm works in the frequency domain and embeds w ($w = cod(m, \boldsymbol{p}_{cod})$) in a selected frequency band by using a spread spectrum technique multiple times. Therefore a scaled sequence of random values is added to the frequency coefficients of the audio signal. This algorithm has the following parameters:

- k: defines the secret key and is an integer value
- p_1: is the scaling factor used to define the embedding strength
- p_2: defines the lower frequency bound in range $[0, \frac{samplerate}{2}]$
- p_3: defines the upper frequency bound in range $[0, \frac{samplerate}{2}]$ and $p_2 \leq p_3$
- p_4: defines the frame size used for the windowing function typical power of 2
- p_5: defines a threshold needed to retrieve m' in range $[0, 1]$.

Embedding Function: As input audio signal S, this watermarking scheme is able to read and write all file formats provided by the *libsndfile* library [26]. The parameters needed for E are $\boldsymbol{p}_E = (k, p_1, p_2, p_3, p_4)$.

Detection/Retrieval Function: Supported input audio signals $\tilde{S}$ or $\tilde{\tilde{S}}$ are all file formats provided by the *libsndfile* library. The implementation of Ω_3 does not distinguish between D and R. Therefore, only the retrieval function R can be used. The parameters needed for R are $\boldsymbol{p}_R = (k, p_2, p_3, p_4, p_5)$.

The maximum frequency of the frequency bound depends on the sampling rate and is defines as $f_{tot} = \frac{sampling\ rate}{2}$ [15]. Ω_3 can be described as follows:

$$\Omega_3 = (E, \varnothing, R, m, \{k, p_1 \in [0, \infty], p_2 \in [0, f_{tot}], p_3 \in [0, f_{tot}],$$
$$p_4 = 2^x, x \in N\}, \varnothing, \{p_2 \in [0, f_{tot}], p_3 \in [0, f_{tot}], t \in [0, 1], p_4, p_5\})$$

The constrain $p_2 \leq p_3$ needs to be satisfied. The working domain of this algorithm is also the frequency domain and can be described as:

$$\Omega_3 = (E_{freq}, \varnothing, R_{freq}, m, p_1 \in [0, \infty], \{p_2 \in [0, f_{tot}], p_3 \in [0, f_{tot}],$$
$$p_4 = 2^x, x \in N\}, \varnothing, \{p_2 \in [0, f_{tot}], p_3 \in [0, f_{tot}], t \in [0, 1], p_4, p_5\})$$

$\boldsymbol{\Omega_4}$: This watermarking algorithm is classified as a zero-bit watermark. It works in the wavelet domain and embeds the watermark in selected coefficients [11]. To embed the watermark into the audio signal a three level DWT domain and a Daubechies 8-tap filter is used [11]. The following parameters can be defined:

- k: defines the secret key as integer value
- p_1: defines a threshold, which selects the coefficients for embedding. The default value is $p_1 = 40$
- p_2: defines a scale factor and which describes the embedding strength. The default value is $p_2 = 0.2$.

Embedding Function: As input audio signal S, this watermarking scheme reads and writes all file formats provided by the *libsndfile* library [26]. The parameters needed for E are $\boldsymbol{p}_E = (k, p_1, p_2)$.

Detection/Retrieval Function: Supported input audio signals $\hat{S}$ or $\tilde{S}$ are all file formats provided by the *libsndfile* library. Only the detection is possible and the parameters for D are $\boldsymbol{p}_D = (k, p_1, p_2)$.

Therefore, Ω_4 is a zero-bit watermarking scheme, only D can be used for detection.

This watermarking algorithms can be described as follows:

$$\Omega_4 = (E, D, \varnothing, \varnothing, \boldsymbol{p}_E(k, t, s), \boldsymbol{p}_D(k, t, s), \varnothing)$$

The working domain of this algorithm is the wavelet domain and can be described as:

$$\Omega_4 = (E_{wavelet}, D_{wavelet}, \varnothing, \varnothing, \boldsymbol{p}_E(k, t, s), \boldsymbol{p}_D(k, t, s), \varnothing)$$

$\boldsymbol{\Omega_5}$: This watermarking algorithm [27,28] works in frequency domain and embeds the watermark w at different frequencies which are chosen by comparing the original audio signal S with a modified version S' which is obtained using an MP3 compressor and decompressor multiple times. The watermark w is built using a Dual Hamming code $DH(31,5)$ for error correction from the message m ($w = cod(m, 31, 5) = DH(m, 31, 5)$) and repeated coding is used. Both detection and retrieval functions are implemented. The retrieval function recovers all the repetitions of the message m and the detection one uses a voting scheme to determine a single value for each message bit. Then, the identified value is compared to the original and detection is reported if 90% or more bits are correctly recovered. In addition, a secret key k is used to generate a pseudo-random sequence which is added to the watermark prior to embedding in order to generate a non-repetitive binary sequence in the embedding process. This step is intended to avoid some types of attacks which may exploit the cyclic repetition of the same bits at different frequencies. In summary:

- m is a n-bit stream which defines the transmitted message.
- w is the message m encoded using the $w = cod(m, DH(31,5))$.
- k: secret key, as 64 bit long value, therefore $k \in [0, 2^{64} - 1]$

Embedding function: The following embedding parameters $\boldsymbol{p}_E$ are used:
- p_1: bit rate of the MP3 compressor/decompressor.
- $p_2 \in [0, 100]$: percentage of the maximum magnitude to choose the relevant frequencies.

- $p_3 \in [0,1]$: maximum relative error between the magnitudes of the original and modified (compressed-decompressed) signals to choose a frequency.
- $p_4 \in [0,\infty)$: magnitude modification parameter (in dB).

Retrieval function: The following embedding parameters $\boldsymbol{p}_D$ are used:
- $q \in [0,100]$: percentage (tolerance) to recover the embedded bits.

Detection function: the embedded message is identified and a voting scheme is applied to obtain a single copy of each bit. If 90% or more bits are identical, detection is returned. Thus, detection is built in terms of retrieval.

This watermarking algorithms can be described as follows:

$$\Omega_5 = (E, \varnothing, R, m, (p_1 = 128, p_2 = 5, p_3 = 0.02, p_4 = 0.2), \varnothing, q = 2)$$

The working domain of this algorithm is the wavelet domain and can be described as:

$$\Omega_5 = (E_{freq}, \varnothing, R_{freq}, m, (p_1 = 128, p_2 = 5, p_3 = 0.02, p_4 = 0.2), \varnothing, q = 2)$$

The different parameters for values for $\Omega_1, \ldots, \Omega_5$ have been chosen according to the tuning guidelines provided in [29] and are summarized in the following Tables 4 and 5.

Table 4. Used embedding parameters $\boldsymbol{p}_E$

Algorithm	embedding parameters
Ω_1^*	$\boldsymbol{p}_E = (p_1 = BIN, p_2 = ZT)$
Ω_2^*	$\boldsymbol{p}_E = (\varnothing)$
Ω_3^*	$\boldsymbol{p}_E = (k = 1234, p_2 = \{500, 2000\}, p_3 = \{5000, 10000\}, p_1 = \{1.5, 3\}, p_4)$
Ω_4^*	$\boldsymbol{p}_E = (k = 1234, p_1 = 0.05, p_2 = 40)$
Ω_5^*	$\boldsymbol{p}_E = [k, p_1 = 128 \text{ kbps}, p_2 = 5, p_3 = 0.02, p_4 = 0.2 \text{ dB}]^{\mathrm{T}}$

where the superscript "T" denotes the transposition operation and the key used for Ω_5^* is $k = $ A71CD57159DA9E2D$_{(16)}$. The footnote $_{(16)}$ indicates the key space.

Table 5. Used detection/retrieval parameters $\boldsymbol{p}_D$ and $\boldsymbol{p}_R$

Algorithm	detection/retrieval parameters
Ω_1^*	$\boldsymbol{p}_R = (p_1 = BIN, p_2 = ZT)$
Ω_2^*	$\boldsymbol{p}_R = (\varnothing)$
Ω_3^*	$\boldsymbol{p}_R = (k = 1234, p_2 = \{500, 2000\}, p_3 = \{5000, 10000\}, p_5 = 0.6, p_4)$
Ω_4^*	$\boldsymbol{p}_D = (k = 1234, p_1 = 0.05, p_2 = 40)$
Ω_5^*	$\boldsymbol{p}_R = \boldsymbol{p}_D = (k = $ A71CD57159DA9E2D$_{(16)}, q = 2)$

To show a practical test setup, we choose the following methodology.

If the watermarking algorithm is a zero-bit-watermark, then the *result* of $\det_D$ can be a 1 (*yes*) if the watermark is present in $\tilde{S}$ or 0 (*no*) if it is not detectable in $\tilde{S}$ depending on $\boldsymbol{p}_D$. Otherwise, if the watermarking algorithms is a n-bit-watermark, the $w = cod(m, \boldsymbol{p}_{\mathrm{cod}})$ is computed for E and R retrieves m' from $\tilde{S}$ with its parameters $\boldsymbol{p}_R$. For both types of algorithms, the robustness ($\mathrm{rob}_{\mathrm{rel}}$) and the transparency ($\mathrm{tra}_{A\mathrm{ave}}$) of $A_{i,j}$ are measured. The Table 6 shows the used watermarking algorithms and its type of classification and if the watermarking algorithms are categorized as a secure scheme (key needed) or not.

Table 6. Types of evaluated watermarking algorithms

watermarking algorithm	type of classification	key required
Ω_1	n-bit watermark	no
Ω_2	n-bit watermark	no
Ω_3	n-bit watermark	yes
Ω_4	zero-bit watermark	yes
Ω_5	n-bit watermark	yes

3.2 Test Scenario – The Practical Framework

In this subsection the used audio test set is introduced and the audio signals and its characteristics are being described. Furthermore, the test set as well as the attacking functions are introduced and summarized.

All five watermarking algorithms use the same audio test set S_{SQAM} which contains 16 different uncompressed audio files for $S \in S_{SQAM}$. The audio signals are the well known SQAM files [34]. All audio signals are in CD quality and they have a sampling rate of $44.1kHz$ with two audio channels (stereo) and $16bit$ sample resolution. The minimal length of an audio signal is $16.3s$, the maximum length $34.9s$ and the average length of all audio signals $21.26s$. Furthermore, the audio files are categorized in three types of content, which is shown in Table 7. Therefore, the first category *single instrument* contains 7 audio files, where a single music instrument is audible, the second category *speech* contains spoken text with female and male voices in the languages English, German and French. The last category *singing* contains female, male and a mixture of both singing voices.

Table 7. Audio files and its classification used for the test scenario

single instruments	speech	singing
harp40_1.wav	spfe49_1.wav	bass47_1.wav
horn23_2.wav	spff51_1.wav	sopr44_1.wav
trpt21_2.wav	spfg53_1.wav	quar48_1.wav
vioo10_2.wav	spme50_1.wav	
gspi35_1.wav	spmf52_1.wav	
gspi35_2.wav	spmg54_1.wav	
frer07_1.wav		

Our test scenario is as follows. All audio signals S are used as cover medium. The embedding function E and its selected parameters $\boldsymbol{p}_E$ embeds the watermark w into S. If it is a n-bin watermark, then $w = \text{cod}(m, \boldsymbol{p}_{\text{cod}})$ is computed in advance. The average, maximal and minimal transparency of E is measured ($\text{tra}_{E\text{ave}}$, $\text{tra}_{E\text{max}}$ and $\text{tra}_{E\text{min}}$) by computing the Objective Difference Grade (ODG) [14] with the implementation of [25]. Furthermore, the detection/retrieval function tries to detect w or to retrieve m' after applying the embedding function in order to measure the detection success $\det_D$ or $\det_R$ and the retrieval capacity. After a successful embedding, the marked audio signal $\hat{S}$ is attacked by single attacks $A_{i,j}$ and its default attack parameters $\boldsymbol{p}_{A_{i,j}}$ provided by StirMark for Audio (SMBA) [36]. The average, maximal and minimal attacking transparency ($\text{tra}_{A\text{ave}}$, $\text{tra}_{A\text{max}}$ and $\text{tra}_{E\text{min}}$) of $A_{i,j}$ with $\boldsymbol{p}_{A i,j}$ is measured. Then, the watermark detector D tries to detect w and depending on the watermark algorithm, the retrieval function R retrieves m' from $\tilde{S}$. For that, the parameters $\boldsymbol{p}_D$ are used for D and $\boldsymbol{p}_R$ for R. The following Figure 2 shows the test scenario and introduces the simple measuring points.

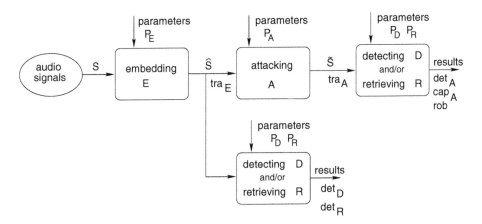

Fig. 2. Test Environment

The detection/retrieval function measures $\det_D$ and $\det_R$ and its derived average values $\det_{D\text{ave}}$ and $\det_{R\text{ave}}$ after embedding. If this value is ≈ 0.00, which indicates, that the embedding fails for all given audio files, then the attacking and the measurement of its derived values ($\text{rob}_{\text{ave}}^{\text{byte}}$, cap_A, $\det_{A\text{ave}}$ and $\det_{A\tau\text{ave}}$) also does not provide usable test results. A possible reason is, that the cover signal S does not provide enough marking positions for w, which means, that m cannot be embedded completely. If this happens in our tests, then we firstly deduce hat m does not fits into S. Secondly, we obtain the retrieved capacity and based on this value, the attacking capacity and robustness is measured.

Embedding Function

For the embedding function ($\hat{S} = E(S, \text{cod}(m, \boldsymbol{p}_{cod}), \boldsymbol{p}_E)$) the parameters are introduced in the following. For $\boldsymbol{p}_E$, we use default and/or transparency optimized parameters to provide a comparability with respect to robustness and capacity [21,27]. Thereby, Table 4 shows the used embedding parameters setting. If Ω needs m, then for all tests $m=$"Tests" with $\text{cap}_E^*($"Tests"$) = 40$ bits $\hat{=} 5$ bytes. Thereby, for all test, a fixed embedding capacity (cap_E) is used. If a secret key is needed, then mostly $k = 1234$ is used. The following Table 8 summarizes the embedding and evaluation setting.

Table 8. Used embedding parameters for the measure functions

embedding and evaluation setting	value
m	"Tests"
cap_E^*	40 bits $\hat{=}$ 5 bytes

The value $\tau = 0.7$ ensures, that only attacks with $\text{tra}_{A\text{rel}} > 0.7$ are able to destroy the watermark successful. The other attacks does not achieve the requested quality. The fix set value $\nu = 0.7$ defines, that a retrieved message m' is destroyed, when at least 70% of the retrieved message is false.

Attacking Function
The attacking function A uses all of the single attacks provided by SMBA. Therefore, 42 different single attacks are used on $\hat{S}$. Firstly, the attacks run with their default parameters $(\boldsymbol{p}_{Ai,2})$ from SMBA and secondly, the parameters for the attacks are changed twice to optimize the attacking strength and attacking transparency $(\boldsymbol{p}_{Ai,1}, \boldsymbol{p}_{Ai,3})$ and thirdly, another set of attacking functions $(\boldsymbol{p}_{Ai,4})$ is used. The following Table 9 shows the attacks and their used parameter settings. The first column shows the name of the single attack. The second, third and fourth column show the attacks and its attacking parameters in use. $\boldsymbol{p}_{Ai,1}$ and $\boldsymbol{p}_{Ai,2}$ contain 29 attacks and $\boldsymbol{p}_{Ai,3}$ contains 26 attacks. The fifth column shows the 13 attacks for $\boldsymbol{p}_{Ai,4}$, which only contain the attacks with unchanged parameters for attack tuning, marked with $\varnothing$. An empty cell means, that this attack does not exist in the attacking set.

For our inter–algorithm evaluation, we use all of the attacks $\boldsymbol{p}_{Ai,(1,\dots,4)}$ to provide a large attacking set $\mathcal{A}$. In contrast, the attacking set is split into four attacking sets $\boldsymbol{p}_{Ai,1}$, $\boldsymbol{p}_{Ai,2}$, $\boldsymbol{p}_{Ai,3}$ and $\boldsymbol{p}_{Ai,4}$ with $i = \{1, \dots 42\}$ for our intra–algorithm evaluation and analysis.

The transparency of E and A is measured by computing the ODG value of $\text{tra}_{E\text{rel}}(\Omega^*, S)$ and $\text{tra}_{A\text{rel}}(\Omega^*, \hat{S}, \tilde{S})$, which is needed to identify the transparency success of $A_{i,j}$. The measured ODG values are in the range of $[-4, 0]$ (where -4 is the worst, -3 is bad, -2 is good, -1 is better and 0 the best) and are scaled into a range of $[0, 1]$ by computing: $\left(1 - \frac{|[-4,0]|}{-4}\right) \rightarrow [0, 1]$.

Detection/Retrieval Function
The detection function $D(\tilde{S}, \boldsymbol{p}_E, \boldsymbol{p}_D, \boldsymbol{p}_{cod}, [S, m|) \rightarrow \{0, 1\})$ of the evaluated watermarking algorithms tries to detect w and, if possible, $R(\tilde{S}, \boldsymbol{p}_E, \boldsymbol{p}_R, [S, m])$ tries

Table 9. Used attacking parameters $p_{A_{i,j}}$, $(i = \{1,\ldots,42\}, j = \{1,\ldots,4\})$

attack $A_{i,j}$	$p_{A_{i,1}}$	$p_{A_{i,2}}$	$p_{A_{i,3}}$	$p_{A_{i,4}}$
$A_{1,j}$=AddBrumm	2000,55	2500,55	3000,55	
$A_{2,j}$=AddDynNoise	10	20	30	
$A_{3,j}$=AddFFTNoise	1024,20000	1024,30000	1024,40000	
$A_{4,j}$=AddNoise	700	1000	1300	
$A_{5,j}$=AddSinus	80,3000	120,3000	130,3000	
$A_{6,j}$=Amplify	80	50	120	
$A_{7,j}$=BassBoost	150,4	150,6.123	150,8	
$A_{8,j}$=BitChanger	100,99.9	100,99.9	1000,99.9	
$A_{9,j}$=Compressor	6.123,1.5	6.123,2.1	6.123,3.5	
$A_{10,j}$=CopySample	10000,20,6000	10000,2000,6000	10000,200,6000	
$A_{11,j}$=CutSamples	100,7	1000,7	10000,7	
$A_{12,j}$=DynamicPitchScale	0.6,3,32000,64000	1.4,3,32000,64000	1.1,3,32000,64000	
$A_{13,j}$=DynamicTimeStretch	0.6,3,32000,64000	1.4,3,32000,64000	1.1,3,32000,64000	
$A_{14,j}$=Echo	20	2000	200	
$A_{15,j}$=Exchange				∅
$A_{16,j}$=ExtraStereo	10	20	30	
$A_{17,j}$=FFT_HLPassQuick	1024,150,13000	1024,300,15000	1024,150,15000	
$A_{18,j}$=FFT_Invert				1024
$A_{19,j}$=FFT_RealReverse				1024
$A_{20,j}$=FFT_Stat1				1024
$A_{21,j}$=FlippSample	10000,20,6000	10000,2000,6000	10000,200,6000	
$A_{22,j}$=Invert				∅
$A_{23,j}$=LSBZero				∅
$A_{24,j}$=Noise_Max	23,1365,200	23,1365,300	23,1365,400	
$A_{25,j}$=Normalizer1	2048,28000,1	2048,28000,0		
$A_{26,j}$=Normalizer2	2048,28000,1,2500	2048,28000,0,2500		
$A_{27,j}$=Nothing				∅
$A_{28,j}$=Pitchscale	0.95	1.05	1.01	
$A_{29,j}$=RC_HighPass	70	150	300	
$A_{30,j}$=RC_LowPass	12000	15000	17000	
$A_{31,j}$=ReplaceSamples	20,1.5	150,1.5	525,1.5	
$A_{32,j}$=Resampling	11025	22050		
$A_{33,j}$=Smooth				∅
$A_{34,j}$=Smooth2				∅
$A_{35,j}$=Stat1				∅
$A_{36,j}$=Stat2				∅
$A_{37,j}$=TimeStretch	0.95	1.05	1.01	
$A_{38,j}$=VoiceRemove				∅
$A_{39,j}$=ZeroCross	100	1000	3000	
$A_{40,j}$=ZeroLength1	5	10	50	
$A_{41,j}$=ZeroLength2	5	10	50	
$A_{42,j}$=ZeroRemove				∅

to retrieve m' from $\tilde{S}$. Therefore, we count the number of positive detected w $(det_{D\mathrm{ave}})$ and correctly retrieved m' $(\det_{R\mathrm{ave}})$ and measure the capacity $cap^*_{R\mathrm{rel}}$ and $\det_A$ and $\det_{A\mathrm{ave}}$. If the retrieved capacity after embedding is lower than the embedding capacity for all audio signals, then the given watermarking scheme does not provide enough marking positions for m. In this case, the size of $|m'|$, which is similar to the maximum possible embedding capacity for the given test set, is used for the following measurements.

3.3   Test Goals

The introduced test scenario from Table 3 is used to evaluate and compare the selected watermarking algorithms with inter– and intra–algorithm evaluation and analysis and to show the usage of the predefined theoretical framework. Thereby, the theoretical framework is prototypically implemented to show on a practical example how to measure and compare the transparency of E and A. Furthermore, the detectability of w and/or the retrieveability of m' in $\hat{S}$ and $\tilde{S}$ are measured after embedding and attacking. The relationship between attacking transparency and robustness is used to identify the successful attacks, as well as the relationship between robustness and capacity to show the effect of an attack. Therefore, the following summary shows the test goals together with the measured parameters.

- Embedding function:
  - Embedding transparency: $\text{tra}_{E\,\text{ave}}$, $\text{tra}_{E\,\text{max}}$ and $\text{tra}_{E\,\text{min}}$
  - Embedding capacity: cap_E^*, a given fixed value
- Detection/Retrieval function:
  - Detection/Retrieval success: $\det_{D\,\text{ave}}$ only for Ω_4 and $\det_{R\,\text{ave}}$, $\det_{R\tau\,\text{ave}}$ and $\text{cap}_{R\,\text{rel}}^*$ for Ω_1, Ω_2, Ω_3 and Ω_5
- Attacking function:
  - Attacking transparency: $\text{tra}_{A\,\text{ave}}$, $\text{tra}_{A\,\text{max}}$ and $\text{tra}_{E\,\text{min}}$
  - Robustness: $\text{rob}_{\text{ave}}^{\text{byte}}$, $\det_{A\,\text{ave}}$, $\det_{A\tau\,\text{ave}}$
  - Attacking capacity: $\text{cap}_{A\,\text{ave}}$, $\text{cap}_{A\,\text{max}}$ and $\text{cap}_{E\,\text{min}}$

These properties are measured on the test set S_{SQAM} and in the following section their results are presented.

4   Test Results

In this section we show and discuss the test results. Therefore, we introduce firstly the test results for the embedding, attacking and detection/retrieval function of each watermarking algorithm to compare them each other with inter–algorithm evaluation. Secondly, we show and discuss the test results for an intra–algorithm analysis, where one watermarking algorithm (Ω_1^*) is evaluated with four different attacking parameter sets.

Inter–algorithm evaluation
For all watermarking algorithms, the embedding function E is used 16 times (because of 16 audio files) and if it is able to successfully embed m into all audio files, then the full attacking set $\mathcal{A}$ is used 97 times (because of the different attacks and different attacking parameters $\boldsymbol{p}_A$). Therefore, the detection and/or

retrieving function is also called 1552 times. If the embedding fails, then a minor number of detection/retrieval functions is performed.

Ω_1 : This watermarking scheme is able to embed m into all audio files successfully ($\det_{R\text{ave}} = 1.00$). Thereby, a fixed embedding capacity $\text{cap}_E^* = 40$ (bits) is used for embedding and the retrieval function returned $\text{cap}_{R\text{rel}}^* = 40$ for all audio files. The test results for the embedding, retrieval and attacking function are shown in the following Table 10.

Table 10. Test results for Ω_1^*

embedding E	retrieval R	attacking A
$\text{cap}_E^* = 40$	$\det_{R\text{ave}} = 1.00$, $\text{cap}_{R\text{rel}}^* = 40$	$\text{cap}_{A\text{ave}} = 0.80$, $\text{cap}_{A\text{min}} = 0.00$, $\text{cap}_{A\text{max}} = 1.00$, $\det_{A\text{ave}} = 0.44$
$\text{tra}_{E\text{ave}} = 0.63$, $\text{tra}_{E\text{min}} = 0.02$, $\text{tra}_{E\text{max}} = 0.95$		$\text{tra}_{A\text{ave}} = 0.38$, $\text{tra}_{A\text{min}} = 0.02$, $\text{tra}_{A\text{max}} = 1.00$
		$\text{rob}_{\text{ave}}^{\text{byte}} = 0.37$

The best embedding transparency is measured with $\text{tra}_{E\text{max}} = 0.95$ for the audio test file *spmg54_1.wav* (which is speech) and the worst with $\text{tra}_{E\text{min}} = 0.02$ for audio test file *frer07_1.wav* (which is a single instrument). The average embedding transparency is measured with $\text{tra}_{E\text{ave}} = 0.63$. These measured results shows, that the embedding transparency of Ω_1^* depends on S and therefore, the quality of E depends on the type of audio content. The retrieval after embedding measured with $\det_{R\text{ave}} = 1.00$ shows, that the given message m fits into all audio files. The test results for the attacking function with the following retrieval show, that Ω_1^* is not robust against the attacks $A_{18,4}$ and $A_{22,4)}$ (FFT_Invert and Invert), which provides also a attacking transparency $\text{tra}_{A\text{ave}} = 0.72$. If the detection success after attacking function is measured, then Ω_1^* has a value of $\det_{A\text{ave}} = 0.44$, which means that this watermarking scheme is robust against all performed attacks in about 44% independent of the attacking transparency. In contrast, the average robustness, has a value $\text{rob}_{\text{ave}}^{\text{byte}} = 0.38$.

Ω_2 : This watermarking scheme could not embed m into all audio files successfully. A successful detection of m' after embedding failed. Hence, the retrieved capacity after embedding $\text{cap}_{R\text{rel}}^* = 8$ shows that m did not fit into S. Only first few bits are retrievable which implies a low embedding capacity. Therefore, only the first 8 bits of m ("T") are used by setting $\text{cap}_E^* = 8$ for the following measures of robustness and attacking capacity. Furthermore, Ω_2^* could only embed the watermark into 12 audio files. For *frer07_1.wav*, *gspi35_2.wav*, *gspi35_2.wav* and *horn23_2.wav* (which are all single instruments) the embedding of any bits fails and these files are excluded from the test set. In this case, where $m' \neq m$

is not retrievable for any S of S_{SQAM}, $\det_{R\mathrm{ave}} = 0.00$. This shows, that the given watermarking scheme does not provide enough marking positions. In our exemplary test evaluation, the measured retrieval capacity $\mathrm{cap}^*_{R\mathrm{rel}} = 8$ bits is measured. Therefore, the following measures are based on the lower retrieved capacity of 8 bits needed for the normalization. The following Table 11 shows the test results for the Ω^*_2 watermarking scheme.

Table 11. Test results for Ω^*_2

embedding E	retrieval R	attacking A
$\mathrm{cap}^*_E = 40$	$\det_{R\mathrm{ave}} = 0.00$, $\mathrm{cap}^*_{R\mathrm{rel}} = 8$	$\mathrm{cap}_{A\mathrm{ave}} = 0.19$, $\mathrm{cap}_{A\mathrm{min}} = 0.00$, $\mathrm{cap}_{A\mathrm{max}} = 0.20$, $\det_{A\mathrm{ave}} = 0.00$
$\mathrm{tra}_{E\mathrm{ave}} = 0.66$, $\mathrm{tra}_{E\mathrm{min}} = 0.10$, $\mathrm{tra}_{E\mathrm{max}} = 0.95$		$\mathrm{tra}_{A\mathrm{ave}} = 0.43$, $\mathrm{tra}_{A\mathrm{min}} = 0.02$, $\mathrm{tra}_{A\mathrm{max}} = 1.00$
		$\mathrm{rob}^{\mathrm{byte}}_{\mathrm{ave}} = 0.91$

The best embedding transparency is achieved with $\mathrm{tra}_{E\mathrm{max}} = 0.947$ for the test file *frer07_1.wav* (which is a single instrument) and the worst with $\mathrm{tra}_{E\mathrm{min}} = 0.10$ for test file *gspi35_1.wav* (which is a single instrument). The average embedding transparency is 0.66 over S_{SQAM}. The detection success is measured with $\det_{R\mathrm{ave}} = 0.00$ because of the impossibility to embed of the complete lengths of $|m|$. Therefore, the average attacking capacity is $\mathrm{cap}_{A\mathrm{ave}} = 0.19$ and shows, that this watermarking scheme has a low embedding capacity for the given test set and given embedding parameters. The results for the robustness measure, normalized on the correctly embedded 8 bits shows, that the robustness measured on bit and byte errors of Ω^*_2 is high $\left(\mathrm{rob}^{\mathrm{byte}}_{\mathrm{ave}} = 0.91\right)$ It means, that only the attacks with a worse transparency results are able to destroy the watermark successful. Selected attacks are $A_{12,(1,2,3)}$, $A_{13,(1,2,3)}$, $A_{28,(1,2,3)}$, $A_{37,(1,2,3)}$ and $A_{10,(1,2,3)}$, $A_{41,(1,2,3)}$ and $A_{41,(1,2,3)}$ which have a worse attacking transparency.

Ω_3 : This watermarking scheme was not able to embed m into all audio files successfully. The audio file *frer07_1.wav* (which is single instrument) did not provide marking positions for w in S and a retrieval of $m' = m$ directly after the embedding was not successful. Therefore, the average retrieval success is $\det_{R\mathrm{ave}} = \frac{15}{16} = 0.94$. In the following evaluations, this audio file is neglected. The following Table 12 shows the test results for the Ω^*_3 watermarking scheme, excluding this audio file.

The best embedding transparency is measured with $\mathrm{tra}_{E\mathrm{max}} = 0.37$ for the test file *harp40_1.wav* (which is a single instrument) and the worst with $\mathrm{tra}_{E\mathrm{min}} = 0.02$ for test file *gspi35_1.wav* (which is a single instrument). The average embedding transparency is measured with $\mathrm{tra}_{E\mathrm{ave}} = 0.11$, which is worse. These results show,

Table 12. Test results for Ω_3^*

embedding E	retrieval R	attacking A
$\mathrm{cap}_E^*=40$	$\det_{R\,\mathrm{ave}}=0.94,$ $\mathrm{cap}_{R\,\mathrm{rel}}^*=40$	$\mathrm{cap}_{A\,\mathrm{ave}}=0.35,$ $\mathrm{cap}_{A\,\mathrm{min}}=0.00,$ $\mathrm{cap}_{A\,\mathrm{max}}=1.00,$ $\det_{A\,\mathrm{ave}}=0.31$
$\mathrm{tra}_{E\,\mathrm{ave}}=0.11,$ $\mathrm{tra}_{E\,\mathrm{min}}=0.02,$ $\mathrm{tra}_{E\,\mathrm{max}}=0.37$		$\mathrm{tra}_{A\,\mathrm{ave}}=0.41,$ $\mathrm{tra}_{A\,\mathrm{min}}=0.02,$ $\mathrm{tra}_{A\,\mathrm{max}}=1.00$
		$\mathrm{rob}_{\mathrm{ave}}^{\mathrm{byte}}=0.11$

that the used embedding parameters $\boldsymbol{p}_E$ could be tuned and/or the used audio set S_{SQAM} changed to provide better test results for tra_E. This watermarking scheme embeds m multiple times into S. Therefore, m was embedded successfully 1 times ($p_{\max}=1$) in the following 7 audio files: *gspi35_2.wav, harp40_1.wav, horn23_2.wav, trpt21_2.wav, bass47_1.wav, quar48_1.wav* and *sopr44_1.wav*[3]. In contrast, m was two times successfully embedable $p_{\max}=2$ for the following 7 audio files: *gspi35_1.wav, spfe49_1.wav, spff51_1.wav, spfg53_1.wav, spme50_1.wav, spmf52_1.wav* and *spmg54_1.wav*. For only one audio file (*vioo10_2.wav*) m was successfully embedded three times ($p_{\max}=3$). The robustness of Ω_3^* is measured with a value of $\mathrm{rob}_{\mathrm{ave}}^{\mathrm{byte}}=0.11$, whereby the attacks $A_{35,4}$ and $A_{7,(1,2,3)}$ are successful and with good attacking transparency for an attacker.

$\boldsymbol{\Omega_4}$: This watermarking scheme also failed to embed m into all audio files successfully. For four audio files (*frer07_1.wav, gspi35_1.wav, gspi35_2.wav* and *vioo10_2.wav*) it was not possible to compute the correlation value of the embedded w successful. Therefore, the average detection successful rate is $\det_{D\,\mathrm{ave}}=\frac{12}{16}=0.75$ and these audio files are excluded for the following measures. The following Table 13 shows the test results for the Ω_4^* watermarking scheme. If the correlation is reobtained by 70% ($\tau>0.7$) or more, then the watermark is positive detectable.

Table 13. Test results for Ω_4^*

embedding E	retrieval R	attacking A
	$\det_{D\,\mathrm{ave}}=0.75,$ $\mathrm{cap}_{R\,\mathrm{rel}}^*=\varnothing$	$\det_{A\,\mathrm{ave}}=0.70$
$\mathrm{tra}_{E\,\mathrm{ave}}=0.29,$ $\mathrm{tra}_{E\,\mathrm{min}}=0.02,$ $\mathrm{tra}_{E\,\mathrm{max}}=0.85$		$\mathrm{tra}_{A\,\mathrm{ave}}=0.45,$ $\mathrm{tra}_{A\,\mathrm{min}}=0.02,$ $\mathrm{tra}_{A\,\mathrm{max}}=1.00$
		$\mathrm{rob}_{\mathrm{ave}}^{\mathrm{byte}}=0.60$

---

[3] For its classification of the audio content, please see Table 7.

The best embedding transparency is measured with $\mathrm{tra}_{E\max} = 0.85$ for the test file *spmg54_1.wav* (which is speech) and the worst with $\mathrm{tra}_{E\min} = 0.02$ for test file *gspi35_1.wav* (which is a single instrument). The average embedding transparency with $\mathrm{tra}_{E\mathrm{ave}} = 0.45$ is measured over S_{SQAM}. The robustness is measured with $\mathrm{rob}_{\mathrm{ave}}^{\mathrm{byte}} = 0.60$, whereby the watermark can be destroyed with the attacks $A_{6,i}$ (Amplify), $A_{22,4}$ (Invert) and $A_{18,4}$ (FFT_Invert), which have an average attacking transparency only of $\mathrm{tra}_{A\mathrm{ave}} = 0.84$. The test results for the attacking capacity is not provided by this watermarking algorithm, because no message was embedded (zero-bit watermarking scheme).

$\mathbf{\Omega_5}$: This watermarking scheme was also not able to embed m into all audio files successfully. Only for the audio files *gspi35_1.wav* and *gspi35_2.wav* it was not possible to retrieve m' directly after embedding. Therefore, the average retrieval after embedding is measured with $\det_{R\mathrm{ave}} = \frac{14}{16} = 0.87$. This watermarking scheme embeds m multiple times, but it was not able to measure the number of multiple embedding $p_{\max}$. The following Table 14 shows the test results for the Ω_5^* watermarking scheme.

Table 14. Test results for Ω_5^*

embedding E	retrieval R	attacking A
$\mathrm{cap}_E^*{=}40$	$\det_{R\mathrm{ave}}$ $=0.87,$ $\mathrm{cap}_{R\mathrm{rel}}^*{=}40$	$\mathrm{cap}_{A\mathrm{ave}}{=}0.70,$ $\mathrm{cap}_{A\min}{=}0.29,$ $\mathrm{cap}_{A\max}{=}1.00,$ $\det_{A\mathrm{ave}}{=}0.28$
$\mathrm{tra}_{E\mathrm{ave}}{=}0.49,$ $\mathrm{tra}_{E\min}{=}0.09,$ $\mathrm{tra}_{E\max}{=}0.73$		$\mathrm{tra}_{A\mathrm{ave}}{=}0.36,$ $\mathrm{tra}_{A\min}{=}0.02,$ $\mathrm{tra}_{A\max}{=}1.00$
		$\mathrm{rob}_{\mathrm{ave}}^{\mathrm{byte}}{=}0.08$

The best embedding transparency is measured with $\mathrm{tra}_{E\max} = 0.73$ for the test file *sopr44_1.wav* (which is speech) and the worst with $\mathrm{tra}_{E\min} = 0.09$ for test file *frer_1.wav* (which is a single instrument). The average embedding transparency for Ω_5^* is $\mathrm{tra}_{E\mathrm{ave}} = 0.49$. The robustness is measured with 0.08 and the average attacking capacity with 0.70.

Summarizing of the inter–algorithm evaluation and analysis

The test results for the inter–algorithm evaluation and analysis of the five selected watermarking schemes can be summarized as follows. The average embedding transparency $\mathrm{tra}_{E\mathrm{ave}}$ is one of the main properties for the evaluation of watermarking algorithms. Its quality depending on the embedding function has a major importance regarding the watermark application field. As the results show, the measured average embedding transparency differs due to the watermarking schemes. Depending on the embedding parameters and/or the used audio test set, the embedding transparency can be tuned for a specific application field. In contrast, the results of $\det_D$ and $\det_R$ show that either a given audio signal provides enough marking positions to embed the watermark or not. Therefore, a watermarking scheme, which has a low embedding capacity for an application field, can be identified or it can be seen that not all audio files can be marked. Furthermore, the inter–algorithm analysis results show, that the embedded watermark can be destroyed easily with a specific $A_{i,j}$, but mostly, the attacking transparency is worse. A successful removal or disabling of the embedded watermark without audible distortion less than 0.7 is difficult. For Ω_1^* only the two attacks $A_{18,4}$ and $A_{22,4}$ achieve this requirement. Ω_2^* was robust against the attacks with a good attacking transparency whereby the robustness measure increases, but can only measured for the embedded 8 bits. Ω_3^* and Ω_5^* have similar robustness results in our test environment. For Ω_4^* an attacker could destroy the watermark with the attacks $A_{6,1}$, $A_{18,4}$ or $A_{22,4}$ without audible distortions. Our attacking test set shows, that some attacks with $tra_{A\,rel} < 0.7$ have the power to destroy the watermark successful. Therefore, the attacking set or its parameters need to be tuned. The attacking capacity yielded test results, where the watermark can be destroyed without focus on the attacking transparency and possible embedding capacity. This measured value is only useful for n-bit watermarking schemes, because for zero-bit watermarking no embedding and no attacking capacity is available. In our tests we show, that Ω_1^* has the best and Ω_2^* the worse test results for $cap_{A\,ave}$ as the retired $cap_{R\,rel}^*$ which is already only 8bits as mention on page 4.

In the following Table 15 our three selected properties (embedding transparency, attacking capacity and robustness) of the evaluated watermarking algorithms are shown and exemplary discussed to summarize their performance in the triangle of transparency, capacity and robustness.

Table 15. Summarized test results with a fixed capacity of given cap_E^*=40 bits

watermarking scheme	$tra_{E\,ave}$	$cap_{A\,ave}$	rob_{ave}^{bit}
Ω_1^*	0.63	0.80	0.37
Ω_2^*	0.66	0.19	0.91
Ω_3^*	0.11	0.31	0.11
Ω_4^*	0.29	∅	0.60
Ω_5^*	0.49	0.70	0.08

It is shown that the inter–algorithm evaluation analysis comparing all five watermarking schemes provides different test results, and the evaluated properties of them are different when measured on the same audio test and the same attacks with its attacking parameter setting $\boldsymbol{p}_{Ai,(1,...,4)}$. The embedding transparency differs from 0.11 for Ω_3^* up to 0.66 for Ω_2^*. For the average attacking capacity $cap_{A\,ave}$ the test results show, that Ω_2^* has the lowest (0.19) and Ω_1^* the highest (0.80) retrieved capacity after attacking. For Ω_4^* this value is zero, due to its characteristic as a zero-bit watermarking scheme. The highest robustness is provided by Ω_2^* 0.91, which means, that the watermark can only be destroyed with audible distortions. It is assumed, that the price for the high robustness is the low embedding capacity. The attacking transparency is very important for successful attacking. For Ω_1^* the measure robustness is 0.37. The both algorithms Ω_3^* and Ω_5^* have a similar robustness, which is 0.11 and 0.08.

The test results $\text{tra}_{E\text{ave}}$, $\text{cap}_{A\text{ave}}$ and rob_{ave} are exemplary used to discuss and visualize the position of $\Omega_{1,\ldots,5}$ in the triangle. In this visualization, the position inside the triangle depends on the ratio between the values of the corners and it is not simple to identify the exact position. If for example a watermarking scheme is bad for all thee properties, then it has the same position as a watermarking scheme, which is good for all three properties. Furthermore, if the position of a watermarking algorithm is directly located in one corner of the triangle, then this value must be 1.00 and the other two values must be 0.00. Another example to introduce the problems with the triangle is, that for e.g. a watermarking scheme, for which is measured 0.4 for all three properties has the same position as another watermarking scheme with all three values measure of 0.7. Our solution is to identify the best position depending on the ratio between the tree properties. Therefore, the exact values of transparency, capacity and robustness are charted by drawing the values on the bisecting line of an angle, whereby the value 1.00 is the corner. After charting the three properties of an algorithm, the centroid of the resulting triangle is the relative position of the watermarking scheme. Our idea a is to introduce the effect of the measured values for $\text{tra}_{E\text{ave}}$, $\text{rob}_{\text{ave}}^{\text{bit}}$ and $\text{cap}_{A\text{ave}}$, whereby points of the exact measured position are shown for each $\Omega_{1,\ldots,5}$. We selected the symbol ■ for Ω_1^*, the symbol + for Ω_2^*, the symbol ▲ for Ω_3^*, the symbol × for Ω_4^* and the symbol ♦ for Ω_5^*. These symbols are drawn on the bisecting lines of the angles with the corner having the value of 1.00 and the opposite 0.00. The positions of $\Omega_{1,\ldots,5}$ are marked with the selected symbol and an enclosed circle ●.

Figure 3 shows the approximate "position" of the compared watermarking schemes.

The overall goal was to summarize the results exemplarily and from the figure it should be clear, that only the three selected measures can be visualized and not all results can be shown like the number of audio files where no watermark could be embedded.

Intra–algorithm evaluation

In the following, we introduce test results for an intra–algorithm evaluation and analysis of Ω_1^* where four different attack sets and its attacking parameters $\boldsymbol{p}_{Ai,(1,\ldots,4)}$ are used. The test results only for Ω_1^* with these four attacking sets are exemplary summarized in the following Table 16 and introduced as follows: The test results for the embedding transparency and attacking capacity are inherited from the inter–algorithm evaluation. The robustness is measured with the four attacking sets $\boldsymbol{p}_{Ai,1}$, $\boldsymbol{p}_{Ai,2}$, $\boldsymbol{p}_{Ai,3}$ and $\boldsymbol{p}_{Ai,4}$. Thereby it is measured, that the robustness is $\text{rob}_{\text{ave}}^{\text{bit}} = 1.00$ for the three attacking sets $\boldsymbol{p}_{Ai,1}$, $\boldsymbol{p}_{Ai,2}$ and $\boldsymbol{p}_{Ai,3}$. Thereby, it is identified, that the attacks in these attacking sets, which destroy the watermark successful do not have $\text{tra}_{A\text{rel}} > 0.7$ which is required for a successful attack. The fourth attacking set $\boldsymbol{p}_{Ai,4}$ includes the attacks $A_{18,4}$

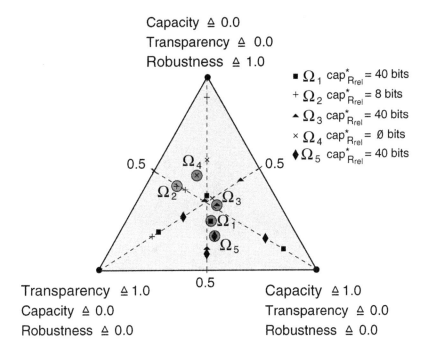

Fig. 3. Test results with attacks in the triangle with a fixed embedding capacity (inter–algorithms evaluation) with the selected measure $\text{tra}_{E\,\text{ave}}$, $\text{cap}_{A\,\text{ave}}$ and $\text{rob}^{\text{bit}}_{\text{ave}}$.

(FFT_Invert) and $A_{22,4}$ (Invert) which destroyed the watermark successfully ($\nu > 0.7$ and $\text{tra}_{A\text{rel}} > 0.7$). Thereby, $p_{Ai,1}$, $p_{Ai,2}$ and $p_{Ai,3}$ have the same measured properties and are located at the same position in the triangle. The robustness of the attacking set $p_{Ai,4}$ differs from the three previous attacking sets and therefore also its position differs in the triangle.

Table 16. Summarized test results for the intra algorithm evaluation of Ω^*_1

watermarking scheme	$\text{tra}_{E\,\text{ave}}$	$\text{cap}_{A\,\text{ave}}$	$\text{rob}^{\text{bit}}_{\text{ave}}$
$p_{Ai,1}$	0.63	0.80	0.87
$p_{Ai,2}$	0.63	0.80	0.93
$p_{Ai,3}$	0.63	0.80	0.99
$p_{Ai,4}$	0.63	0.80	0.06

To visualize the intra–algorithm evaluation and analysis result for Ω^*_1 with four different attacking parameter sets, the following Figure 4 shows the "position" in the triangle of transparency, capacity and robustness. Thereby the same idea (introduced for the inter–algorithm evaluation) to visualize the triangle is used. It is shown, that $p_{Ai,1}$ (■), $p_{Ai,2}$ (+) and $p_{Ai,3}$ (▲) have the same position in the triangle and the fourth $p_{Ai,4}$ (×) differs only a little with regarding to robustness.

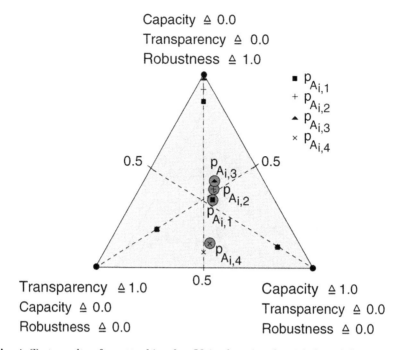

Fig. 4. Test results after attacking for Ω_1^* in the triangle with four different $\boldsymbol{p}_{Ai,(1,\ldots,4)}$ (intra–algorithms evaluation) with the selected measure $\mathrm{tra}_{E\mathrm{ave}}$, $\mathrm{cap}_{A\mathrm{ave}}$ and $\mathrm{rob}_{\mathrm{ave}}^{\mathrm{bit}}$

Therefore it could be shown, that a different attacking sets of $\boldsymbol{p}_{Ai,(1,\ldots,4)}$ effects the measured main properties of a given watermarking scheme. Depending on these sets the properties of the watermarking scheme differ and therefore the appropriate application field might change for the usage of the algorithm. Therefore, the best and worst test results of watermarking schemes depend on the parameter settings used for embedding, attacking and detection/retrieval and the test set used for evaluation.

5   Conclusion and Future Work

In this paper, in the first part we have presented a theoretical framework to provide a description and formalization of the application oriented properties robustness, transparency and capacity of digital watermarking algorithms. Therefore, the embedding, detecting/retrieval and attacking functions with its parameters and the main properties robustness, transparency and capacity are defined. Furthermore, the dependencies between these properties are discussed. To provide evaluation and comparison of watermarking algorithms, measuring methods are derived. Our introduced methodology is easily enhanced by defining derived or new evaluation measures. The idea is to normalize the measures into the triangle within the resolution between 0 and 1.

The second part of the paper has presented a practical usage of the predefined theoretical framework by using selected audio watermarking algorithms for comparing it in the triangle of the main properties with a selected set of defined measures. The evaluation of the algorithms shows that the embedding and detection/ retrieval parameters are different and provide different test results. To allow a comparison we used a fixed test set of 16 audio files and a fixed embedding capacity. The test results for the five watermarking algorithms show that the inter–algorithm evaluation based on a given fixed set of audio files and a given fixed set of attacking parameters provides different results for the watermarking schemes. On the one hand, one watermarking algorithm — a zero-bit watermarking scheme — provides a high robustness, but the transparency of the embedding function is bad. On the other hand, the n-bit watermarking schemes provides good transparency results for the embedding function, but the robustness decreases.

The test results for an intra–algorithm analysis show, that a different attacking parameter setting changes the measured properties of a watermarking scheme. Therefore, the potential attack scenario of a used application field for a watermarking algorithm should be known or estimated before applying the scheme.

We hope that the introduced methodology will be widely used to allow a more precise comparison of watermarking algorithms and their test results. The method has room for enhancement and should be seen as attempt to specify a normalized measure for a more precise inter–algorithm and intra–algorithm evaluation and analysis. Future work is to enhance our theoretical framework with other properties of watermarking algorithms (like fragility for integrity evaluation, security or complexity) and to compare watermarking schemes with different embedding parameter settings. Furthermore, the 2-dimensional geometric triangle should be replaced by another geometric figure (3-dimensional) which provides more and detailed space for the position of a watermarking scheme.

Acknowledgement

The work about the watermarking algorithms and single attacks in this paper has been supported in part by the European Commission through the IST Programme under Contract IST-2002-507932 ECRYPT. The information in this document is provided as is, and no guarantee or warranty is given or implied that the information is fit for any particular purpose. The user thereof uses the information at its sole risk and liability.

Effort for the Audio WET system, which was used for the evaluation, is sponsored by the Air Force Office of Scientific Research, Air Force Materiel Command, USAF, under grant number FA8655-04-1-3010. The U.S. Government is authorized to reproduce and distribute reprints for Governmental purposes notwithstanding any copyright notation thereon. The views and conclusions contained herein are those of the authors and should not be interpreted as necessarily representing the official policies or endorsements, either expressed or implied, of the Air Force Office of Scientific Research or the U.S. Government.

UOC authors are partially supported by the Spanish MCYT and the FEDER funds under grants MULTIMARK TIC2003-08604-C04-04 and PROPRIETAS-WIRELESS SEG2004-04352-C04-04

With respect to the experimental evaluations, this publication has been produced partly with the assistance of the EU-India cross cultural program (project CultureTech, see [7]). The content of this publication is the sole responsibility of the University Magdeburg and their co-authors and can in no way be taken to reflect the views of the European Union.

Furthermore, we thank Jörg Wissen and Raquel Buil who helped us to set up the test environment and to analyze the test results.

References

1. *Evaluation of Natural Language Processing Systems*, FINAL REPORT, EAGLES DOCUMENT EAG-EWG-PR.2, Version of September 1995, section Methods for System Measurement, http://www.issco.unige.ch/ewg95/, May 2006
2. B. Macq, J. Dittmann and E. J. Delp, *Benchmarking of Image Watermarking Algorithms for Digital Rights Management*, Proceedings of the IEEE, Special Issue on: Enabling Security Technology for Digital Rights Management, pp. 971–984, Vol. 92 No. 6, June 2004
3. F. Cayre, C. Fontaine and T. Furon, *Watermarking security, part I: theory*, In: Security, Steganography and Watermarking of Multimedia Contents VII, Ping Wah Wong, Edward J. Delp III, Editors, Proceedings of SPIE Vol. 5681, San Jose, USA, 2005
4. F. Cayre, C. Fontaine and T. Furon, *Watermarking security, part II: practice*, In: Security, Steganography and Watermarking of Multimedia Contents VII, Ping Wah Wong, Edward J. Delp III, Editors, Proceedings of SPIE Vol. 5681, San Jose, USA, 2005
5. Checkmark Benchmarking, *http://watermarking.unige.ch/Checkmark/*, 2006
6. I. J. Cox, J. Kilian, T. Leighton, and T. Shamoon, *Secure spread spectrum watermarking for multimedia*, IEEE Transactions on Image Processing, 6(12):1673–1687, 1997.
7. The Culture Tech Project, Cultural Dimensions in digital Multimedia Security Technology, a project funded under the EU-India Economic Cross Cultural Program, *http://amsl-smb.cs.uni-magdeburg.de/culturetech/*, requested July 2005
8. J. Dittmann, *Digitale Wasserzeichen*, Berlin, Springer, Xpert.press, 2000, ISBN 3-540-66661-3
9. J. Dittmann, M. Steinebach, A. Lang and S. Zmudizinski, *Advanced audio watermarking benchmarking*, Security, Steganography, and Watermarking of Multimedia Contents VI, Edward J. Delp III, Ping W. Wong (Eds.) SPIE Vol. 5306, SPIE and IS&T, pp. 224-235, Electronic Imaging Science and Technology, 19-22 Jan. 2004, San Jose, California, USA, ISBN 0-8194-5209-2, 2004
10. J. Domingo-Ferrer and J. Herrera-Joancomartí. Simple collusion-secure fingerprinting schemes for images. In *Proceedings of the Information Technology: Coding and Computing ITCC'2000*, pages 128–132. IEEE Computer Society, 2000.
11. R. Dugad, K. Ratakonda and N. Ahuja, *A New Wavelet-Based Scheme for Watermarking Images*, IEEE International Conference on Image Processing, Chicago, 1998

12. J. Fridrich, *Applications of data hiding in digital images*, Tutorial for the ISPACS 1998 conference in Melburne, Australia, 1998

13. H. Inoue, A. Miyazaki, A. Yamamoto and T. Katsura, *A Digital Watermarking Technique Based on the Wavelet Transform and Its Robustness on Image Compression and Transformation*, IEICE Trans. Fundamentals, vol. E82-A, no. 1, 1999

14. ITU-R Recommendation BS.1387, *Method for Objective Measurements of Perceived Audio Quality*, *http://www.itu.int/rec/R-REC-bs/en*, Dec. 1998

15. A.J. Jerri, *The Shannon sampling theorem – its various extensions and application: a tutorial review*, Proc. IEEE, 65, 1565-1597, 1977

16. T. Kalker, *Considerations on watermarking security*, In: Proceedings of the IEEE Multimedia Signal Processing MMSP01 workshop, Cannes, France, pp. 201–206, 2001

17. D. Kirovski and H.S. Malvar, *Spread Spectrum Watermarking of Audio Signals*, IEEE Transactions on Signal Processing, Vol.51, (no.4), pp.1020-33, 2003

18. C. Kraetzer, J. Dittmann and A. Lang, *Transparency benchmarking on audio watermarks and steganography*, to appear in SPIE conference, at the Security, Steganography, and Watermarking of Multimedia Contents VIII, IS&T/SPIE Symposium on Electronic Imaging, 15-19th January, 2006, San Jose, USA, 2006

19. M. Kutter, S. Voloshynovskiy and A. Herrigel, *Watermark copy attack*, In Ping Wah Wong and Edward J. Delp eds., IS&T/SPIEs 12th Annual Symposium, Electronic Imaging 2000: Security and Watermarking of Multimedia Content II, Vol. 3971 of SPIE Proceedings, San Jose, California USA, 23-28 January 2000

20. A. Lang and J. Dittmann, *StirMark and profiles: from high end up to preview scenarios*, Virtual Goods 2004, 27-29.05.2004, to appear in http://virtualgoods.tu-ilmenau.de/2004/, Ilmenau, 2004

21. A. Lang and J. Dittmann, *Profiles for Evaluation - the Usage of Audio WET*, to appear in SPIE conference, at the Security, Steganography, and Watermarking of Multimedia Contents VIII, IS&T/SPIE Symposium on Electronic Imaging, 15-19th January, 2006, San Jose, USA, 2006

22. A. Lang and J. Dittmann, *Digital Watermarking of Biometric Speech References: Impact to the EER System Performance*, to appear in SPIE conference, at the Security, Steganography, and Watermarking of Multimedia Contents IX, IS&T/SPIE Symposium on Electronic Imaging, 28th January - 01th February, 2006, San Jose, USA, 2007

23. A. Lang, J. Dittmann, E. T. Lin and E. J. Delp, *Application oriented audio watermark benchmark service*, In: Delp, Edward J. (Hrsg.), Wong, Ping W. (Hrsg.), Security, steganography, and watermarking of multimedia contents VII (Electronic imaging science and technology San Jose, California, USA, 17-20 January 2005), Bellingham, Wash., pp. 275–286, ISBN 0-8194-5654-3, 2005

24. A. Lang, J. Dittmann, R. Spring and C. Vielhauer, *Audio watermark attacks: from single to profile attacks*, In: City University of New York (Veranst.): Multimedia and Security, MM & Sec'05 (Workshop New York, NY, USA August 1-2 2005), New York, NY, ACM, pp. 39–50, ISBN 1-59593-032-9, 2005

25. A. Lerch, zplane.development, *EAQUAL - Evaluation of Audio Quality*, Version: 0.1.3alpha, http://www.mp3-tech.org/programmer/misc.html, 2002

26. libSNDfile library, *http://www.mega-nerd.com/libsndfile/*, May, 2006

27. D. Megías, J. Herrera-Joancomartí, and J. Minguillón, *A robust audio watermarking scheme based on MPEG 1 layer 3 compression*, In Communications and Multimedia Security - CMS 2003, Lecture Notes in Computer Science 2828, pages 226–238, Turin (Italy), October 2003. Springer-Verlag.

28. D. Megías, J. Herrera-Joancomartí, and J. Minguillón. *An audio watermarking scheme robust against stereo attacks*, In Proceedings of the Multimedia and Security Workshop, pages 206–213, Magdeburg (Germany), September 2004. ACM.

29. D. Megías, J. Herrera-Joancomartí, and J. Minguillón. *Robust frequency domain audio watermarking: a tuning analysis*, In International Workshop on Digital Watermarking — IWDW 2004, Lecture Notes in Computer Science 3304, pages 244–258, Seoul (Korea), November 2004. Springer-Verlag.

30. Optimark, *http://poseidon.csd.auth.gr/optimark/*, 2006

31. Luis Pérez-Freire, Pedro Comesaña and Fernando Pérez-González, *Information-Theoretic Analysis of Security in Side-Informed Data Hiding*, Information Hiding, pp. 131–145, 2005

32. F. A. P. Petitcolas, M. Steinebach, F. Raynal, J. Dittmann, C. Fontaine and N. Fates, *Public automated web-based evaluation service for watermarking schemes: StirMark Benchmark*, In: Security and Watermarking of Multimedia Contents III, Ping Wah Wong, Edward J. Delp III, Editors, Proceedings of SPIE Vol. 4314, Bellingham WA, USA, pp. 575–584, ISBN 0-8194-3992-4, 2001.

33. J.M. Shapiro, *Embedded image coding using zerotrees of wavelet coefficients*, IEEE Trans. Signal Processing, vol. 41, no.12, pp. 3445–3462, 1993

34. SQAM — Sound Quality Assessment Material, *http://sound.media.mit.edu/mpeg4/audio/sqam/*, 2006

35. Stirmark Benchmark, *http://www.petitcolas.net/fabien/watermarking/stirmark/*, 2006

36. StirMark Benchmark for Audio, *http://amsl-smb.cs.uni-magdeburg.de/*, 2005

37. C. Vielhauer, T. Scheidat, A. Lang, M. Schott, J. Dittmann, T.K. Basu and P.K. Dutta; *Multimodal Speaker Authentication – Evaluation of Recognition Performance of Watermarked References*; In: Proceedings of MMUA 2006, Toulouse, France, 2006

38. S. Voloshynovskiy et al., *Attacks on Digital Watermarks: Classification, Estimation-Based Attacks, and Benchmarks*, IEEE Communications Magazine, vol. 39(8), pp. 118–126, Aug. 2001

39. Watermark Evaluation Testbed for Audio, *http://audio-wet.cs.uni-magdeburg.de/wet/*, 2006

Watermarking Security: A Survey

Luis Pérez-Freire, Pedro Comesaña, Juan Ramón Troncoso-Pastoriza,
and Fernando Pérez-González

Signal Theory and Communications Department
University of Vigo, Vigo 36310, Spain
{lpfreire, pcomesan, troncoso, fperez}@gts.tsc.uvigo.es

Abstract. Watermarking security has emerged in the last years as as a
new subject in the watermarking area. As it brings new challenges to the
design of watermarking systems, a good understanding of the problem
is fundamental. This paper is intended to clarify the concepts related
to watermarking security, provide an exhaustive literature overview, and
serve as a starting point for newcomers interested in carrying out research
on this topic.

1 Introduction

Watermarking security is an emergent topic. A good indicator of the growing
interest in this subject is the number of special sessions that have been held in
recent conferences [1,2,3,4] and the efforts made in relevant European projects
such as Certimark [5] and Ecrypt [6]. Whereas robustness in watermarking has
been generally identified with probability of decoding error or resistance against
watermark removal, the concept of *watermarking security* is still somewhat fuzzy.
In recent works, it has been agreed that attacks to security have a broader
scope than attacks to robustness, since the former are not only concerned with
a simple impairment of the communication process, but they also consider the
achievement of privileges granted by the secret parameters of the system.

The threats that must be faced by a watermarking scheme depend largely on
the considered application where it is employed. For instance, there are certain
metadata applications [7,8] where the only aim of watermark embedding is to
give an "added value" to the asset in consideration, so they are typically not
susceptible of being attacked; this characteristic is also shared by other applications, as linking contents to a web or database, or controlling electronic devices
(as toys or Personal Video Recorders (PVRs)), where intentional attacks are not
expected. On the other hand, applications such as watermarking of medical images, authentication of legal documents, fingerprinting or data monitoring, must
face extremely hostile environments where the most harmful attacks are not necessarily those aimed at removing the embedded watermarks. In fact, for those
applications somehow related to legal environments, it may be more harmful to
accept a forged content as legal than rejecting a legal one, or to read the watermark instead of erasing it. This kind of considerations gave rise in the last years
to the watermarking security problem. The purpose of this paper is to facilitate

Y.Q. Shi (Ed.): Transactions on DHMS I, LNCS 4300, pp. 41–72, 2006.

future research on this topic by providing a thorough review of the existing literature, showing the most relevant achievements so far, and paying attention to the main open problems and challenges. The interested reader is also referred to the previous survey on watermarking security by Furon [9], which covers the subject from a similar viewpoint.

The paper is organized as follows: Section 2 gives an overview of the most popular forms of digital watermarking emphasizing the role of the secret key, which will be seen to be determinant in the security problem. Section 3 gives a classification of attacks on watermarking schemes based on the their treatment of the secret key, and Section 4 reviews the evolution of watermarking security in the literature, introducing relevant definitions which help to link the classification of Section 3 to the concepts of robustness and security. Section 5 is slightly more technical, as it discusses how to measure security in a theoretical, quantitative manner, introducing also the main results so far on this direction. Section 6 gives a bird's-eye view on the works that have performed practical studies of the watermarking security problem, proposing tools for performing successful security attacks. Some countermeasures that can help to improve security are considered in Section 7, discussing their advantages and drawbacks, and finally the main challenges and achievements on this topic are summarized in Section 8. Throughout this paper we will use the terms watermarking/data hiding with no distinction, unless otherwise stated, and the same will apply to the terms detector/decoder. The discussion will be often referred to image watermarking, although it can be straightforwardly extended to digital signals in general.

2   The Role of the Secret Key

In most watermarking methods the key is used to determine certain parameters of the embedding function, such as the domain of embedding, the embedding direction, or the subset of image coefficients that will be watermarked, to list some examples. Key-dependent steganography can be traced to the ancient China, where a method to write a secret message using a paper mask with holes cut in it was developed. Such an idea was rediscovered in the Sixteenth century by Cardan, creating what is now known as Cardan grille [10]. More recently, with the advent of digital watermarking techniques, many different forms of secret communication have been proposed; the most popular of these are recalled in this section.

A number of methods that perform watermark embedding in a secret direction can be found in the literature. Van Schyndel et al. [11] suggested the use of m-sequences [12] commensurate to the image size to create a bipolar sequence that is added to the least significant bit (LSB) of the host image. This technique was later improved by Cox et al. [13] to enhance the invisibility of the watermark by modulating it with a perceptual mask that controls the embedding strength at every DCT coefficient, with the side effect of making it robust to simple LSB flipping attacks. In this method, commonly known as *additive spread-spectrum*, the watermark is a pseudorandom sequence (a.k.a. *spreading vector*) which is modulated by the bit to be embedded (± 1) in the case of data hiding applications. Cox et al. also recognized the advantages of generating a Gaussian-distributed watermark against collusion attacks as opposed to bipolar sequences. Further benefits of Gaussian watermarks in terms of detection and decoding performance are discussed in [14]. A similar procedure due to Hartung and Girod embeds the watermark in the spatial domain for data-hiding in video applications [15].

The foregoing schemes resemble spread-spectrum communications in that a pseudorandom carrier is chosen so that any other interfering signal (in the particular case of watermarking, the host) will be nearly orthogonal to the former. Other techniques are akin to pulse position modulations in that the secret key is used to select the set of indices of those coefficients that are modified by embedding. For instance, the technique known as *patchwork* [16] pseudorandomly selects two sets of pixels: the luminance is increased for those pixels in the first set, and decreased for those in the second. Detection simply consists in subtracting the sum of pixels in the second set from that corresponding to the first set. Notice that patchwork can be seen as a form of spread-spectrum where the watermark can take the values $\{-1, 0, 1\}$, the 0 value corresponding to those pixels that are left unaltered. The method by Koch *et al.* [17] works in the 8×8-block-DCT domain and selects a subset of blocks in a pseudorandom fashion. Within each block a triple of coefficients in the mid-frequencies range is selected according to the key from a set of 18 triples and modified to encode one bit of information. Hence, Koch et al.'s method can be regarded to as a combination of pulse position modulation (i.e., the selection of the block) and multipulse modulation (i.e., the selection of the triple) of a pseudorandom sequence.

An alternative to the embedding schemes mentioned above is the use of key-dependent transforms, which was proposed by Fridrich [18] to combat sensitivity-like attacks (see Section 6.4), since in this case the attacker would not know in which domain embedding takes place. Fridrich's method constructs a set of pseudorandom-vectors which are smoothed using a low-pass filter and orthogonalized by means of the Gram-Schmidt procedure. Fridrich went on to impose energy compaction constraints on the basis functions. Related techniques are [19], which constructs key-dependent sets of orthogonal or wavelet filters; [20], which pseudorandomly controls the lifting of the Daubechies 9-7 taps used in the JPEG-2000 standard, and [21], where a set of two-channel orthogonal filter banks is pseudorandomly generated using the host image as part of the embedding key.

Yeung and Mintzer's innovative scheme uses the key to select a detection function from a secret lookup table [22]. Embedding in a given pixel proceeds by determining which luminance modification will result in the desired value at the output of the detector. In this sense, this method can be considered a precursor of side-informed algorithms.

A potential problem with pseudorandomly generated watermarks in the spatial domain is their flat spectrum which makes them prone to compression and low-pass filtering attacks. A partial solution is the use of perceptual masking but, as Su and Girod showed in their *power-spectrum condition*, in order to resist filtering attacks, an energy-efficient watermark should match the spectral characteristics of the host signal [23]. Even though this can be achieved by low-pass filtering the watermark prior to its insertion, more sophisticated schemes which suggest new ways of generating the watermark from the key have been proposed. For instance, Voyatzis and Pitas use a one-dimensional chaotic map with a secret initial state [24]. The bipolar watermark is created by thresholding the chaotic sequence. By controlling the frequency of the trajectory oscillations, it is possible to impose the desired low-pass characteristics to the watermark. Finally, a two-dimensional watermark is constructed by using a Peano scan instead of a raster scan to preserve the low-pass characteristic. In a previous work by the same authors, the two-dimensional watermark was generated through a toral automorphism [25].

In the watermarking schemes mentioned so far (with exception of the Yeung-Mintzer scheme [22]) the watermark is independent of the host image, i.e. the latter is completely neglected during watermark generation, except for a possible perceptual masking which takes place a posteriori. The philosophy behind side-informed schemes is the opposite, since the host image is explicitly considered in the computation of the watermark. Nonetheless, in some side-informed methods the generation of the watermark is strongly related to that in spread-spectrum schemes; this is the case of the *Improved Spread-Spectrum* (ISS) technique by Malvar and Florêncio [26] and *Spread Transform - Dither Modulation* (ST-DM) originally proposed by Chen and Wornell [27,28]. In the former, the mapping from key to watermark is essentially the same as in [13], although it also accounts for a partial host interference removal in the secret direction of embedding. Similarly, the watermark in ST-DM is embedded in the subspace spanned by a key-dependent spreading vector, but its value is computed by quantizing the projection of the host image onto this subspace. In *quantization index modulation* (QIM) methods [27], the key is used to generate a secret codebook or set of centroids for quantizing the host image, and the watermark is basically the quantization error between the host and the secret quantizer. In the most popular implementation of QIM, known as dither modulation (DM) [27], as well as in its distortion-compensated version (DC-DM), the codebook consists of a certain lattice which is randomized by means of a key-dependent dither signal which introduces a secret shift in the embedding lattice. A more involved form of randomization of the lattice-based codebook has been recently proposed by Fei *et al* in [29], where only a subset of the lattice points (indexed by a keyed hash function) is valid for embedding. Rational Dither Modulation (RDM) methods [30] are also based on lattice quantization, but the quantization step varies as a certain function of the past watermarked samples; the codebook can be effectively randomized if this function is made key-dependent. The problem brought about by these last two randomization techniques is the difficulty of effectively controlling the embedding distortion. Yet another form of codebook randomization for DC-DM schemes which does not suffer from such drawback consists of a key-dependent rotation of the embedding lattice, as proposed by Moulin and Goteti in [31].

Other popular side-informed methods that are worth mentioning are JANIS (Just Another N-Order Side-Informed Scheme) by Furon *et al.* [32] and the trellis-based algorithm proposed by Miller *et al.* [33]. JANIS belongs to the group of methods that embed the watermark in a secret direction, but the generation of this direction is fundamentally different from the aforementioned methods; in JANIS, the direction of embedding is chosen so as to match the gradient of a key-dependent detection function evaluated in the host. As for the method by Miller *et al.*, the watermark generation is as follows: first, each message is mapped onto a set of paths on a trellis, and each transition in that trellis has associated a number of key-dependent spreading vectors. The decoding is performed by looking for the path on the trellis which maximizes the highest correlation between the received signal and all the spreading sequences related to that path.

3   Attacks on Watermarking Schemes

As seen in the previous section, the secret key (which hereinafter will be denoted by Θ) is an input to some mapping function $f(\Theta)$ that outputs the secret parameters (spreading vector, indices of watermarked coefficients, codebook, etc.) of the embedding and decoding functions. The aim of such parameterization is twofold: first, it is a way of protecting the contents from unauthorized embedding/decoding; second, it makes the watermarked contents more robust to attacks. The latter assertion is easy to see, for instance, in spread-spectrum-based methods: if the attacker ignores the secret subspace where the watermark lives, the best he can do is to perform his attack in a "random" direction of the space. However, if an accurate estimate of the spreading vector is available to the attacker, then he can put all the attacking power on the estimated subspace, so in that case the advantage brought about by spreading vanishes. Similar arguments hold for any method that performs watermark embedding in a secret subspace. As for the methods that rely on the secrecy of the codebook, it can be seen that an estimate of the latter would allow many harmful attacks to the robustness, including the possibility of recovering the original host image. Clearly, when evaluating attacks to watermarking systems it is important to consider the degree of knowledge about the secret key. Based on that amount of knowledge, the following classification of attacks to watermarking systems can be introduced.

1. **Blind watermark removal.** The attacker just tries to erase/modify the watermark without taking care of the secret key, even when the watermarking algorithm could be perfectly known. This is why these attacks are termed *blind*. These are the kind of attacks traditionally considered in the watermarking literature concerned with robustness assessment, and they include addition of noise, compression/filtering attacks, geometric distortions, etc. However, as suggested above, if the attacker manages to gain some knowledge about the secret key, he could devise more harmful attacks. In this sense, these *blind* attacks represent the most optimistic scenario for the watermarker.

2. **Attacks based on key estimation.** When the attacker has knowledge about the used watermarking scheme, he can try to obtain an estimate of $f(\Theta)$ through the observation of the outputs of the embedder (i.e., the watermarked images) and/or the decoder. As discussed above, this estimate can help him in succeeding in his task of defeating the system. Notice that we are talking about estimation of $f(\Theta)$ instead of Θ itself; this is so because even when $f(\Theta)$ and the mapping function $f(\cdot)$ are perfectly known, it may not be possible to recover the secret key Θ, since $f(\cdot)$ is (or should be) designed so as not to be easily invertible. However, the knowledge of $f(\Theta)$ is enough for the attacker's purposes, in general. The computation of the estimate of $f(\Theta)$ is a central issue of the attack: similarly to cryptographic scenarios, the watermarker is usually given his own secret key, that he will use repeatedly for watermarking images; hence, all the contents watermarked by the same user will contain information about the same secret key. Typically, a reliable computation of $f(\Theta)$ will require a large number of images watermarked with the same secret key, but once an estimate has been obtained it can be used for attacking more contents of the same user without additional effort, i.e., the information learned by the attacker can be reused in subsequent attacks.

3. **Tampering attacks.** If the attacker manages to get perfect knowledge about Θ, this implies a complete break of the watermarking system because the attacker could perform the same actions as any authorized user. As mentioned above, the observation of the outputs of the embedder or the decoder only gives information about $f(\Theta)$ but not about Θ; however, the attacker can try other ways for obtaining such information. For instance, when the watermark embedder/decoder is part of an electronic device which is publicly available (such as a DVD player), the attacker can try to tamper with it in order to disclose the secret key. If the detector is thought of as a black box, the attacker would try to break this box, inspect what is inside, and determine the secret key by reverse engineering. One countermeasure at the hardware level against these kind of attacks is the use of tamper-proofing devices, as proposed in the literature [34]. On the "soft" level, other countermeasures based on protocol approaches have been proposed, such as the so-called zero-knowledge schemes [35] (see Section 7).

It is clear that the first category of attacks just introduced (blind watermark removal) is concerned with the classical concept of robustness in watermarking. In the next section we will see how the second category can be related to the concept of *watermarking security*. As for the last one, it also pertains to security, but hardware implementations are out of the scope of this paper; however, zero-knowledge and related concepts will be discussed in Section 7.

4   Review of Watermarking Security in the Literature

In the 90's, when the digital watermarking problem arose, researchers were almost exclusively focused on the robustness of the proposed methods; simple attacks such as additive noise, coarse quantization, or even the interference due to the host signal itself, were already too harmful to the first watermarking schemes, so more elaborated attacks were almost paid no attention at all. At most, there was the distinction between *intentional* and *non-intentional* attacks. An example of this type of classification can be found in [36], where *signal transformations* (affine transformations, noise addition, compression) are distinguished from *intentional attacks*, introducing at a qualitative level concepts like the *sensitivity attack*, the *statistical averaging attack* (which is closely related to the *collusion attack* [37]) and attacks based on the availability of embedding devices. The sensitivity attack belongs to the category of *oracle attacks*, which are those where the attacker exploits his access to a watermark detector. *Statistical averaging attacks* are based on the fact that, if multiple images with the same embedded watermark are available, it is possible to estimate the watermark by averaging all those images: if $\mathbf{x}_i$ denotes the i-th zero-mean host image, $\mathbf{w}$ denotes the watermark, and there are N different watermarked images, then the sum $N\mathbf{w} + \sum_i \mathbf{x}_i$ tends to $N\mathbf{w}$. A similar attack may be performed to estimate the original image when a great number of versions of the same image with different watermarks are available.

Probably the fact that raised the issue of watermarking *security* was the proposal of the sensitivity attack [38]. This attack showed that if a binary-output detector were available, the watermark embedded by means of spread-spectrum [13], which was the most popular watermarking algorithm at that time, could be removed in just $O(n)$ attempts, where n is the dimensionality of the watermarked image. This removal is based on estimating the boundary of the decision region by observing the outputs of the detector. Furthermore, the knowledge of the decision region implies the disclosure of the secret spreading vector, meaning that the attacker could also forge contents at will. Therefore, a watermarking system susceptible of being defeated by this kind of attacks could be barely thought of as being *secure*.

The first attempt at proposing a theoretical framework for analyzing the security of a watermarking scheme was performed by Mitthelholzer in [39], inspired by the works of Cachin [40] and Zöllner *et al.* [41] in the field of steganography. Mitthelholzer studies the trade-off between *secrecy* of the embedded message and robustness from a mutual information approach; in fact, a system is said to achieve perfect secrecy when the mutual information between the watermarked signal and the embedded message is null whenever the secret key is unknown. This definition of perfect secrecy clearly resembles that proposed by Shannon in his seminal work [42], where he established the information-theoretic fundamentals of cryptanalysis.

Although the security issue was becoming more relevant in the watermarking research, the first attempt at clarifying this concept is due to Kalker, who in his work [43] provided the following definitions:

- *"Robust watermarking is a mechanism to create a communication channel that is multiplexed into original content"*, and whose capacity *"degrades as a smooth function of the degradation of the marked content"*.

- *"Security refers to the inability by unauthorized users to have access to the raw watermarking channel".* Such an access refers to trying to *"remove, detect and estimate, write and modify the raw watermarking bits".*

Notice that, according to these definitions, there is not a clear relationship between the intentionality of the attacks and the security; in fact, they suggest that intentionality and robustness/security can be regarded as independent concepts. Therefore, following Kalker's definitions, both intentional and non-intentional attacks may result in a threat to security.

Based on the above definitions of security and robust watermarking, a classification of watermark attacks according to different criteria is proposed in [43]. The main classification coincides with that given in [7], and it establishes the division in unauthorized watermark removal, detection (estimation), writing, and modification. Furthermore, other attack classifications are also proposed in [43] based on the degree of success of the attacks, the amount of information available to the attacker, the availability of embedding and/or detection engines, the degree of knowledge of the watermarking algorithms, and the degree of *universality* of the attack (ranging from the removal of the watermark from a certain document, to the knowledge of global secrets of the system under attack, such as the secret key).

The definitions by Kalker [43] are reviewed by Furon *et al.* in [44], where the difference between security and robustness is also emphasized; in this sense, it is said that security has a broader scope, since it does not only deal with watermark removal but also with unauthorized embedding and detection. Concerning the intentionality of the attack, [44] argues that intentionality is inherent to security attacks, whereas it is irrelevant to robustness attacks. Furon's work makes also a clear distinction between robustness and security: robustness deals with blind attacks (offering a partial break of the used watermarking technique), whereas security deals with intentional attacks where information about the data hiding scheme is known by the attacker (offering a complete break). This is clearly an evolution of the concept of security from the approach by Kalker in [43].

In [44] Furon *et al.* also translate Kerckhoffs' principle [45] from cryptography to watermarking: all functions (encoding/embedding, decoding/detection ...) should be declared public except for the secret key. The *security level* is said to be the effort required for disclosing this secret key, obtaining that definition as a corollary of Kerckhoffs' principle. Moreover, Furon *et al.* propose a classification of attacks to security based on another classical cryptography paper by Diffie and Hellman [46]. This classification is based on the amount of information relevant for the attack that is revealed to attackers; hence, one can consider the following scenarios (just to mention a few)

- the watermarked images are the only information at hand;
- the pairs original-watermarked are available (this corresponds to clear text - cypher text in cryptography);
- a watermark embedder or decoder is available to the attacker.

Although the above classification does not cover all the possible watermarking applications, it can be extended to account for other important scenarios as needed. The goodness of a classification like this is that it allows to separate at a great extent the security analysis from the specific watermarking applications. Finally, the authors of [44] adapted Shannon's cryptographic framework to watermarking. It differs from the previous translation by Mitthelholzer [39] in that the secrecy is not measured as the information leakage between the watermarked content and the corresponding message, but as the leakage between the set of available watermarked contents and the secret key, achieving *perfect secrecy* when that information leakage is null.

A different approach to watermarking security was proposed by Barni *et al.* in [47]. The authors consider the watermarking problem as a game with some rules that determine the publicly available information. If the attacker uses only this information, the attack is said to be *fair*; if he tries to learn more information about the system, the attack is said to be *unfair*. The publicly available information can range from *no knowledge*, that clearly collides with Kerckhoffs' principle, *knowledge of embedding and detection algorithms*, *knowledge of the detection key* (for asymmetric schemes), to *knowledge of both embedding and detection keys, and the algorithms*. Similarly to [44], the mutual information is used in [48] to measure the knowledge gained by the attacker. Finally, Barni *et al.* introduce a definition of security level similar to that in [44], although in this case the authors focus on the purpose of removing the watermark, not on disclosing the secret key.

One of the most recent and outstanding works on watermarking security is [49] by Cayre *et al.*. The first point emphasized in [49] is the recognition of the difficulty of distinguishing between security and robustness. A significant evolution from [44] is that in [49] the intentionality of the attack is not enough for deciding if it targets the security or the robustness of the system. In order to define robustness, the authors complete Kalker's definition in [43], establishing that the cause of the degradation of the marked document is a classical content processing. On the other hand, to define security the authors turn again to Kalker's definition in [43], but excluding from the removal attacks *"those already encompassed in the robustness category"*. Similarly, the classification of attacks to security proposed in [44] is the basis for that introduced in [49], where three different categories are introduced, depending on the knowledge available to the attacker:

- Watermarked Only Attack (WOA): the attacker has access only to watermarked contents.
- Known Message Attack (KMA): the attacker has access to pairs of watermarked contents and the corresponding embedded message.
- Known Original Attack (KOA): the attacker designs his attack based on the knowledge of pairs original-watermarked contents.

Probably one of the main contributions of Cayre *et al.* in [49] is the proposal of the Fisher Information Matrix [50] to quantify the security. This topic will be further discussed in Section 5.

This work by Cayre *et al.* [49] is also used as inspiration for [51,52,53,54], where new definitions of security and robustness are proposed. In those works the

authors propose that attacks to robustness are those whose target is to increase
the probability of error of the data-hiding channel, whereas attacks to security
are those aimed at gaining knowledge about the secrets of the system; obviously,
in a model where Kerckhoffs' principle holds the only secret parameters are
the key Θ and its mapping $f(\Theta)$. In this sense, attacks to security can be
related to the last two categories introduced in Section 3. We will stick to this
definition of security in the remaining of this paper. Finally, in [51] and [52]
some considerations are made in order to further clarify the boundary between
security and robustness, on the basis of the former definitions:

- Attacks to security are intentional, but not all intentional attacks are threats
  to security.
- Attacks to security are necessarily not blind, but there are non-blind attacks
  that are not aimed at attacking the security.
- The information gained by means of attacks to security can be used as a
  first step towards performing attacks to robustness.

5   Tools for Measuring Security

A consequence of the last definition of attacks to security given in the previous
section is that the security of a watermarking system is directly related to the
difficulty in estimating the key (or the mapping from the key to the secret parameters) based on the *observations*, where this term refers to all the information
made available to the attacker (watermarked signals, embedded messages, etc.),
according to the classification of security attacks given in Section 4. Thus, a natural question is how can we quantify the hardness of such estimation problem.
In order to obtain fundamental security limits, one can address this question
from a theoretical point of view: the first step is to check whether information
about the secret key leaks from the observations; if this is the case, the second step is to quantify the amount of information that can be learned from
each observation. Intuitively, a large information leakage implies that the system is potentially less secure. Shannon, in his paper on the theory of secrecy
systems [42] proposed the mutual information $I(\Theta; \mathbf{Y}_1, \ldots, \mathbf{Y}_N)$ [55] as a measure of information leakage, where $\mathbf{Y}_1, \ldots, \mathbf{Y}_N$ are ciphered texts. Although the
application of this approach to the watermarking field had been already sug-
gested by Hernández and Pérez-González in [56], it was applied for the first time
by Cayre *et al.* in [49], but relying on the Fisher information [50] instead of the
mutual information, arguing that the former is more suited to the watermarking
problem. Shannon's approach is finally recovered for watermarking security by
Comesaña *et al.* in [52], computing $I(f(\Theta); \mathbf{O}_1, \ldots, \mathbf{O}_N)$, where $\mathbf{O}_i$ stands for
the i-th observation. The reason for computing the mutual information between
the observations and $f(\Theta)$ is that the observations do not provide information
about Θ, but about $f(\Theta)$, as discussed in Section 3. The work presented in [52]
is largely based on [49], and the main difference turns out to be the information
leakage measurement, i.e. the mutual information, whose suitability for evaluating watermarking security is justified.

The information-theoretic framework for watermarking security requires a statistical modeling of all the variables involved in the problem: the host image, the secret key, and the embedded messages. Computation of the Fisher information needs the existence and differentiability of the log-likelihood function of the observations given the key, precluding its application to the analysis of some practical methods (dither modulation watermarking, for instance); fortunately, these problems do not appear when using the mutual information for quantifying the security. The adaptation of Shannon's measure to the watermarking security framework is straightforward, but one must be aware of a subtle difference: the paper by Shannon [42] deals with discrete random variables, whereas watermarking deals usually with continuous ones; this implies replacing the entropies in the computation of the mutual information by *differential* entropies [55]. Note that, as opposed to the entropy, the differential entropy can take negative values, yet it is still a useful measure of the uncertainty of a random variable. In the information-theoretic framework proposed by Shannon [42], the *equivocation* is defined as the remaining uncertainty about the secret key after observing the cyphertexts; in our case, the equivocation is redefined as the differential entropy of $f(\Theta)$ conditioned on the observations, i.e.,

$$h(f(\Theta)|\mathbf{O}_1,\ldots,\mathbf{O}_N) = h(f(\Theta)) - I(f(\Theta);\mathbf{O}_1,\ldots,\mathbf{O}_N), \qquad (1)$$

where $h(f(\Theta))$ is the *a priori* entropy of the secret parameters. The mutual information and the equivocation are the basis for the definition of some fundamental concepts:

Perfect secrecy: a watermarking system is said to achieve perfect secrecy whenever the observations do not provide any information about the secret key, that is, $I(f(\Theta);\mathbf{O}_1,\ldots,\mathbf{O}_N) = 0$.[1] This means that all efforts by the attacker for to disclose the secret key will be useless, even if he could afford infinite computational power. Clearly, the construction of watermarking systems complying with this definition may be an extremely difficult task, or lead to unpractical systems (due to complexity requirements or length of the key, for instance).

$\varepsilon - N$ **security:** a watermarking system is said to be $\varepsilon - N$ secure if

$$I(f(\Theta);\mathbf{O}_1,\ldots,\mathbf{O}_N) \leq \varepsilon, \qquad (2)$$

for a positive constant ε. Anyway, one must be careful with the definition of $\varepsilon - N$ security and perfect secrecy: maybe the information leakage is small (null), but this might be due to a small (null) *a priori* entropy of the secret key; to see this, consider the extreme case where the secret key is deterministic: in this situation, the information leakage is null, but in turn the system completely lacks security, since no secret parameterization takes place. This consideration gives rise to the notion of *security level*, defined next, as a more convenient measure of security.

---

[1] Notice that this and the subsequent definitions based on the mutual information can be adapted to the measures based on the Fisher information.

γ-**security level:** for those systems with $I(f(\boldsymbol{\Theta}); \mathbf{O}_1, \ldots, \mathbf{O}_N) \neq 0$, the γ-security level is defined as the number of observations N_γ needed to make

$$h(f(\boldsymbol{\Theta})|\mathbf{O}_1, \ldots, \mathbf{O}_{N_\gamma}) \leq \gamma, \tag{3}$$

where the threshold γ (which can be negative) is established according to some criteria, as discussed below.

Unicity distance: it is defined as the number of observations N_u needed to yield a deterministic key, i.e., $h(f(\boldsymbol{\Theta})|\mathbf{O}_1, \ldots, \mathbf{O}_{N_u}) = -\infty$.[2] In the case of an a priori deterministic key, the unicity distance would be the 0; however, it can approach ∞ in a general case, thus making useful the definition of the γ-security level. Furthermore, many attacks to the robustness can be performed without having perfect knowledge of $f(\boldsymbol{\Theta})$; instead, an accurate estimate may be enough for the attacker's purposes.

As mentioned above, it is not possible in general to construct perfectly secure watermarking systems; hence, the question is whether the achievable security levels are good enough for practical scenarios. The required security level will be determined by the specific application and the computational power of the attacker; in video watermarking, for instance, the large number of observations available [57] imposes severe restrictions in terms of security. As pointed out in [58], the information-theoretic models for watermarking security capture the worst case for the watermarker, i.e., they quantify the maximum amount of information about the key that is provided by each observation. An interesting question is the gap between theoretical and practical security, since the complexity of extracting all such information may be unaffordable, in general. In this sense, the mutual information $I(f(\boldsymbol{\Theta}); \mathbf{O}_1, \ldots, \mathbf{O}_N)$ must be regarded to as the *achievable rate* in a hypothetical communications problem, where the information to be transmitted is the secret key, and both the host and the embedded messages play the role of interfering channel. In other words, the information-theoretic analysis will provide a lower bound on the security level, a bound which is achievable by means of an infinite computational power, in general. Of course, the watermarker will be interested in minimizing the achievable rate about the secret key while simultaneously maximizing $I(\mathbf{Y}; M|\boldsymbol{\Theta})$, i.e., the achievable rate about the embedded message for a fair user.[3] For given embedding function and embedding distortion, this can be posed as an optimization problem where the variable to be optimized is the statistical distribution of the secret key.[4] The parameters of the embedding function affect both the security and the robustness of the scheme; their influence and the relation between security and robustness can be made patent by the representation of $I(\mathbf{Y}; M|\boldsymbol{\Theta})$ vs. $I(f(\boldsymbol{\Theta}); \mathbf{O}_1, \ldots, \mathbf{O}_N)$,

---

[2] The unicity distance was originally defined by Shannon in [42], but dealing with discrete random variables; hence, the N_u in the discrete case is such that $H(\boldsymbol{\Theta}|\mathbf{O}_1, \ldots, \mathbf{O}_{N_u}) = 0$.

[3] $I(\mathbf{Y}; M|\boldsymbol{\Theta})$ denotes the mutual information between the watermarked image $\mathbf{Y}$ and the embedded message M when the secret key $\boldsymbol{\Theta}$ is known.

[4] In this optimization problem, a constraint on the a priori entropy of the secret key must be imposed in order to avoid a trivial solution, such as a deterministic key.

yielding a sort of *achievable regions* similar to those in classical broadcast channels [55].

One of the main criticisms [58] to information-theoretic models for watermarking security is how can they be related to practical security levels, or equivalently, what should be the criteria for establishing the threshold γ in Eq. (3). From a practical point of view, the success of an attack based on the estimate of the secret mapping $f(\boldsymbol{\Theta})$ is closely related to the estimation error attainable by the attacker: the more reliable the estimate, the easier for the attacker to achieve his goals. Thus, it seems natural to fix the threshold γ in accordance with this estimation error. Fortunately, information-theoretic quantities and estimation errors are strongly related; for instance, the well known Cramèr-Rao lower bound [59] used in [49] relates the Fisher Information Matrix (FIM) to the minimum variance σ_E^2 achievable by an unbiased estimator:

$$\sigma_E^2 \geq \mathrm{tr}(\mathrm{FIM}(f(\boldsymbol{\Theta}))^{-1}). \tag{4}$$

Likewise, a similar bound can be arrived at by means of the equivocation [52,54]

$$\sigma_E^2 \geq \frac{1}{2\pi e} e^{\frac{2}{n} h(f(\boldsymbol{\Theta})|\mathbf{O}_1,...,\mathbf{O}_N)}. \tag{5}$$

The strong relation between information-theoretic and statistical measures has been recently reinforced by some works, where exact relations between mutual information and minimum mean squared error are established for a variety of additive channels [60,61,62].

Besides the information-theoretic models, there have been very few additional attempts at establishing theoretical measures of watermarking security: in fact, the authors of this paper are only aware of the so-called *computational* security model proposed in [58], directly inspired by computational models commonly used in cryptography. This model imposes a complexity constraint to the attacker in the sense that only polynomial time computations are allowed, and the security is related to the probability of successfully inferring (after an interaction between watermarker and attacker) which secret key out of two was used for watermarking a certain object. Nevertheless, as recognized in [58], the application of the computational model to existing watermarking schemes may be very difficult, and no results in this direction have been published so far. In contrast, the information-theoretic model has been already applied for assessing the security of the two main classes of watermarking methods: spread-spectrum and quantization-based ones. The main results are summarized below.

5.1   Theoretical Results on Spread-Spectrum Methods

Using the Fisher information, the authors of [49] quantified for the first time the security of additive spread spectrum methods under the KMA, WOA and KOA attacks. As mentioned in Section 2, in spread spectrum methods the secret key is mapped to a pseudorandom spreading sequence (the watermark itself). This implies that all the images watermarked with the same key contain the same pseudorandom pattern, a fact that can be exploited for estimation purposes. The Fisher information measures the information that the observations provide about the spreading sequence. The main conclusions of the analysis presented in [49] are:

- The difficulty of the estimation depends on the relative powers between the host signal and watermark (i.e., the Document to Watermark Ratio, DWR), in such a way that more embedding distortion implies a larger information leakage.
- Perfect estimation of the spreading sequence is only possible in the KMA case; for both the KOA and WOA cases, a sign ambiguity will remain independently of the number of observations.
- The information leakage is linear with the number of observations, i.e. all the observations provide the same amount of information about the spreading sequence.

The former conclusions are completed in [51,52], showing that the information leakage grows as a concave function of the number of observations.

Recently, a modified spread-spectrum embedding function named Natural Watermarking (NW) has been introduced by Bas and Cayre in [63]. The proposed method is shown to achieve perfect secrecy in the WOA scenario by means of information-theoretic tools, although a more intuitive explanation in terms of blind source separation (BSS) theory [64] is also given. However, the advantage of perfect secrecy of NW comes at the price of a significant degradation of the robustness with respect to the original spread-spectrum method. Another version more robust than NW is proposed in the same paper, although it does not preserve the perfect secrecy property.

5.2 Theoretical Results on Quantization-Based Methods

The most popular quantization-based methods are those with a codebook constructed by means of lattice quantizers, and they are commonly known as Distortion Compensated - Dither Modulation (DC-DM) [27,65]. In the security analysis carried out so far for this kind of methods, the only form of secret randomization of the codebook that has been considered is by means of a secret dither signal (see Section 2), which on the other hand is the case of virtually all implementations of DC-DM. As noted in [66], the security of these methods is determined by their host-rejecting nature and the boundedness of the support set of the secret dither given the observations. The main conclusions that can be extracted from the security analysis [53,54,66] based on the mutual information between the observations and the secret dither are the following:

- The security depends largely on the distortion compensation parameter α. Values of α close to 1 make the scheme extremely vulnerable to security attacks. However, in certain scenarios such as WOA, DC-DM can be made highly secure by choosing the appropriate value of α (for instance $\alpha \approx 1/2$

in binary transmission schemes with self-similar lattice partitions). This implies the existence of a trade-off between security and achievable rate in information transmission.

– When the embedding distortion is sufficiently small (as it is the case in scenarios of practical interest) the information leakage is virtually independent of the DWR, contrarily to spread-spectrum methods; nonetheless, it is still concave in the number of observations.

– The embedding lattice plays an important role in the security of the DC-DM scheme. The security level can be increased by increasing the dimensionality of the embedding lattice and choosing that lattice with the best mean-squared error quantization properties. In fact, the best security level achievable for DC-DM is conjectured to be given by those lattices whose Voronoi cells are the closest (in the normalized second order moment sense) to hyperspheres.[5]

– The security level of DC-DM schemes has been found to be fairly lower than for spread spectrum methods. Indeed, few tens of watermarked images may be enough for obtaining a sufficiently accurate estimate of the secret dither.

Some closed-form results have been obtained for the Known Message Attack and Watermarked Only Attack scenarios. However, computations with arbitrary lattices require Monte-Carlo integration most of the times.

Costa's theoretical construction [68] is closely related to DC-DM methods. A theoretical security analysis of the former was accomplished in [53], and a comparison between Costa and DC-DM was given in [53] and [66], concluding that the structure imposed to the codebook in DC-DM is responsible for its security weaknesses.

Substitutive schemes [69] can be seen as weakly related to quantization-based methods. They have been theoretically analyzed in [49], where they have been shown to provide perfect secrecy in the WOA scenario.

6   Attacks to Security

This section gives an overview of the main practical methods that have been proposed so far for performing security attacks. These methods are aimed at estimating the secret parameters of the system; the usefulness of the obtained estimates is discussed in [49, Sect. IV] and [54, Sect. V] in the context of spread-spectrum and quantization-based methods, respectively. As mentioned in Section 3, the attacker can aspire at disclosing, at most, the mapping $f(\Theta)$. Nevertheless, this knowledge may be enough for getting access to the raw watermarking channel [49],[54], i.e., to read the embedded bits, but this may not be enough for reading the actual message if a cryptographic layer is placed upon the watermarking channel (the *physical* layer). One must be aware of these considerations when dealing with security attacks.

---

[5] The reader interested in a detailed discussion about lattices is referred to the classical text by Conway and Sloane [67].

6.1   Attacks on Spread-Spectrum Methods

Attacks to the security of spread-spectrum methods are aimed at estimating the pseudorandom spreading vector which is derived from the secret key. In detection applications, the watermark signal just consists of this plain spreading vector, although in data hiding applications the spreading vector is modulated by the sign of the embedded message. A consequence of this correspondence between watermark and spreading vector is that most attacks previously proposed for watermark estimation are indeed attacks to security, such as the *Wiener filtering* attack [70] and the statistical averaging attack [36] (which typically needs a large number of watermarked signals to succeed) mentioned in Section 4. Related approaches using denoising techniques besides averaging are discussed in [57]. Another attempt at performing watermark estimation is due to Mıhçak *et al.* in [71], where the authors estimate the watermark based on the fact that the components of the watermark vector take discrete values ($\pm\Delta$), paying special attention to the case where these values are repeated in blocks of a certain length. Under the assumption of Gaussian host, the maximum a posteriori (MAP) estimate of the watermark is computed. The final aim of estimation attacks is to provide the information necessary to perform a *remodulation* attack [72] in order to remove the watermark.

The problem of watermark estimation in general scenarios (continuous-valued watermarks, decoding applications instead of detection) remained unaddressed for some time. A maximum likelihood (ML) watermark estimator (assuming Gaussian-distributed host signals) is proposed in [49] for the KMA case, whereas BSS techniques, namely Principal Component Analysis (PCA) and Independent Component Analyis (ICA) [64,73] are used in more involved scenarios. The rationale behind PCA and ICA-based estimation is that the energy of the watermark is concentrated in one particular subspace; moreover, the latter takes advantage of non-gaussianity of the message distribution and the independence between the embedded messages and the host images. An extension of this approach (focused on the WOA scenario) is considered in [74] using ICA jointly with the Expectation-Maximization (EM) algorithm [75] in order to reduce the computational complexity of the attack when the dimensionality of the spreading vector is very large. It is also pertinent to mention a simultaneous work, [76], in which the subspace generated by the secret key is estimated with PCA in order to remove the watermark. A previous work which used ICA to estimate the watermark signal, although without taking into account security considerations, is given in [77].

6.2   Attacks on Quantization-Based Methods

Two major approaches can be distinguished: those dealing with lattice DC-DM schemes, and those based on Spread Transform - Dither Modulation (ST-DM) [27,28]. Contrarily to spread-spectrum, for this kind of methods the watermark depends both on the secret key and the host signal; thus, a simple watermark estimation does not necessarily provide information about the secret key or the codebook.

For lattice DC-DM methods, the objective is to estimate the dither signal involved in the codebook parameterization. Dither estimators are addressed by Pérez-Freire *et al.* in [66] from a geometrical point of view, by means of set-theoretic (set-membership) estimators [78,79] that can be applied to generic embedding lattices. These estimators exploit the boundedness of the support set (which is, indeed, a polytope) of the secret dither given the observations. Results about the practical performance of these estimators (up to 8 dimensions) are shown in [54,66], confirming the feasibility of attacks with affordable computational complexity. Set-theoretic estimators turn out to be optimal in certain instances, but the simplifications needed to reduce the complexity of the attack (approximations with ellipsoids, for example [80]) introduce a loss of optimality which is not negligible in general; the performance gap with the optimal dither estimator (as predicted by the information-theoretic analysis) in that case is also considered in [66].

In ST-DM methods, the aim of the attacker is to disclose the secret subspace where quantization takes place. PCA and ICA have been proposed for attacking such schemes in [49] and [81]. Particularly, the good performance of ICA-based estimators was shown in [81], where a large ensemble of natural images watermarked with the same secret key are taken as input to the ICA algorithm, which outputs an estimate of the spreading vector. This estimate is used in a subsequent stage for attacking the robustness of the ST-DM scheme, and the results are compared to other attacks that do not exploit the estimate of the spreading vector at hand.

6.3 Attacks on Other Methods

A cryptanalytic approach for estimating the secret key was applied to steganographic methods by Fridrich *et al.* in a number of papers. In [82], JPEG steganography was addressed, considering two LSB-like steganographic methods (F5 [83] and OutGuess [84]). In these methods, the secret key determines the DCT coefficients that will be chosen for conveying the *stego message*. The estimate for the *stego key* (or better to say, the subset of coefficients used for embedding) is based on an exhaustive search, taking advantage of the characteristic statistical distribution of the DCT coefficients induced by the LSB embedding. The approach proposed in [82] was extended in [85] to steganography in the spatial domain, focusing again on LSB embedding.

It is worth noting that in the former works only one observation (or *stego image*) is exploited for performing key estimation. This is different from the approach followed in [86], where the Yeung-Mintzer authentication scheme [22] is attacked under the hypotheses given in the present paper: availability of multiple images watermarked with the same secret key (adding in this case the restriction that all the images contain the same watermark). By combining several watermarked images, the secret lookup table used in the Yeung-Mintzer scheme can be easily reconstructed, and consequently the embedded watermark can be read off. As a countermeasure for invalidating this attack, the use of additional lookup tables that depend on the pixel position is recommended in [86].

6.4 Sensitivity Attack

According to the definition given in Section 4, attacks to security are those which try to learn information about the secret key Θ or the secret parameters $f(\Theta)$, which completely determine the decision/decoding regions. Given that there is quite a number of examples in the literature of attacks which try to perform such estimate, and that they have been shown to be effective in removing the watermark from watermarked contents, in view of the discussion in Section 4, it is reasonable to consider whether those attacks are targeted to security.

Probably the best known in this family are the so-called *oracle attacks* where the estimate of the detection region is based on the observation of the detector output, which is available to the attacker. Just a subgroup of oracle attacks are *sensitivity attacks*, originally proposed in [36,38], and further analyzed in [87] and [88]; in those attacks the boundary of the detection region is estimated by modifying a watermarked image component-wise and analyzing the sensitivity of the detector to those changes on its input. The oracle attacks in general and the sensitivity attacks in particular are formulated as iterative processes; this implies that they require a large number of calls to the detector[6] in order to provide a good approximation to the detection region.

The initial proposal of the sensitivity attack, as well as subsequent papers on this topic [36,38,87,88] were concerned with the correlation-based detector used by spread spectrum. In that case the boundary of the detection region is simply given by a hyperplane, so the attacker only needs to estimate n points on that boundary for entirely determining it. This is, for example, the strategy followed by El Choubassi and Moulin in [89]. Once one has estimated the hyperplane, removing the watermark from any watermarked content or creating false positives from any other content is straightforward. Due to such effectiveness, several countermeasures have been proposed:

- Use of non-parametric decision regions: Mansour and Tewfik [90] suggest the use of fractals for complicating the estimate of the detection function.
- Randomization of the detection boundary: Linnartz and van Dijk [87] studied the impact on the sensitivity attack of randomizing the output of the detection function in the closeness of the former decision boundary based on a hyperplane.
- Randomization of the detection output when similar signals are successively fed [91]: Venturini designed a scheme where the detector randomly generates its output whenever a signal with a similar hash has been already input; in this way the attacker can not perform the iterative process inherent to the sensitivity attack.
- Randomization of the detection function: proposed by El Choubassi and Moulin in [92], it is based on performing detection over a random subset of image coefficients using a *mismatched* detector. The idea of performing detection in random subsets was previously proposed in [93].

---

[6] In fact, $O(n)$ calls are needed for spread-spectrum methods [36], being n the dimensionality of the watermarked image.

Nevertheless, it seems clear that one could always try to estimate the envelope of the actual detection boundary, obtaining a coarse estimate that in most of cases is enough for attacking the watermarking system. As long as this holds true, sensitivity attacks can be considered as security attacks for spread spectrum schemes.

Despite of their impressive performance, sensitivity attacks were not adapted to more generic kinds of detectors until recently. Attempts for doing so are due to El Choubassi and Moulin [89] and Comesaña et al. [94]. Both algorithms are based on locally approximating the detection boundary. Nevertheless, given the local nature of the approximation, the impact of these new versions of the sensitivity attack on security is rather limited. Hence, it is perhaps more adequate to say that sensitivity attacks for a general detection function are on the boundary between attacks to security and to robustness; in any case, a formal characterization of these attacks from a security point of view is still a pending question.

7   Countermeasures

In view of the security weaknesses inherent to some watermarking methods, a number of countermeasures against security attacks have been proposed in the literature. As discussed in Section 5.1, the main flaw of spread-spectrum schemes in terms of security is the repeated embedding of the same pseudo-random pattern. Enhanced security can be achieved by adopting the scheme proposed by Doërr and Dugelay in [57] for video watermarking, which consists of randomly alternating between several watermarks in order to prevent averaging attacks; advantages and limitations of this approach are discussed in the same paper. Another possible solution has been suggested by Holliman et al. [95] and Fridrich and Goljan [96], who recognized the advantages in terms of security of using image-dependent keys (this is equivalent to the use of a mapping function $f(\mathbf{x}, \boldsymbol{\Theta})$, where $\mathbf{x}$ represents the host image, i.e., the host image is part of the key). In [96], for instance, the authors present a method for generating a Gaussian vector depending on both a secret key and a robust hash function of the host image. However, one major issue for watermarking schemes based on image-dependent keys is that of key synchronization at the decoder side, since the transformations suffered by the watermarked signal may avoid the exact recovery of the mapping, i.e, it may occur that $f(\mathbf{x}, \boldsymbol{\Theta}) \neq f(\mathbf{y}, \boldsymbol{\Theta})$, where $\mathbf{y}$ is the attacked image available to the decoder; thus, it seems clear that the security improvement can be made at the expense of robustness loss. As discussed in the previous sections, the success of security attacks is based on the availability of a number (large, in general) of images watermarked with the same key. The use of a mapping function like $f(\mathbf{x}, \boldsymbol{\Theta})$ is indeed aimed at reducing the number of images which are useful for the security attack; nevertheless, due to the reasons of synchronization introduced above, the mapping function applied on perceptually similar images must yield exactly the same result, i.e., $f(\mathbf{x}_1, \boldsymbol{\Theta}) = f(\mathbf{x}_2, \boldsymbol{\Theta})$ whenever $\mathbf{x}_1$ and $\mathbf{x}_2$ are perceptually similar. This still implies the existence of a potential security hole in certain applications, such as video watermarking, where the attacker could exploit the existence of a number of perceptually similar frames (in still scenes, for instance).

In side-informed methods the watermark is already host-dependent, thus circumventing some of the security weaknesses of spread-spectrum methods. However, the existing information leakage still makes feasible attacks to security, as those mentioned in Section 6.2. One of the major disadvantages of lattice DC-DM schemes in terms of security is the use of a highly structured codebook: due to the lattice structure imposed, disclosure of one codeword implies disclosure of the whole codebook. One of the aims of the authentication scheme proposed by Fei *et al.* [29], based on lattice-quantization, is indeed the improvement of the security by making the codebook dependent on the host image. As mentioned in Section 2, the codebook in Rational Dither Modulation (RDM) watermarking [30] is also host-dependent, although this dependence is parameterized in a totally different manner.

The above countermeasures are targeted at making more difficult the estimation of $f(\Theta)$. However, there is another important group of countermeasures whose primary objective is to protect the secret key Θ. Up to now it has been shown that the most sensitive part of watermarking schemes is the embedding key; once this key is disclosed, the whole system is compromised, so the less information about this key the watermarking scheme leaks, the better for security. Nevertheless, symmetric schemes (as those we discussed up to now in this paper) require the embedding key also for detection/decoding of the inserted watermark, and this represents a security hole. There are two approaches for protecting the embedding key during the detection/decoding process, namely *asymmetric watermarking* and *zero-knowledge watermarking*.

7.1   Asymmetric Watermarking

The goal of asymmetric schemes is to make the process of detection/decoding independent of the embedding, by using different keys in these two steps. Although sometimes the terms public-key and asymmetric watermarking are used indistinctly, they have a different meaning, pointed out in most of the works in this area

- *Asymmetric watermarking*: The keys used for embedding and for extraction are different.
- *Public-key watermarking*: The key used for extraction (public key) holds enough information to accomplish the detection/decoding, while not allowing to remove the watermark or forge illegal contents if the key used for embedding (private key) is kept secret.

In [97], Smith and Dodge differentiate also between strong and weak public key watermarking; in the former, performing the extraction with the public key gives no advantage in stripping the watermark above that provided by the access to a watermark reading oracle, while a weak public key only deals with recovering the original image. They also present a very simple asymmetric method based on periodic watermarks.

Currently, there is no truly public-key watermarking method, although many efforts have been done in order to achieve an asymmetric scheme that fulfils also the requirements of public-key watermarking. In [98], Miller states that key asymmetry is not sufficient to achieve a valid public-key scheme, and he wonders whether it would even be necessary if some scheme applicable in an open-cards scenario existed. Current asymmetric schemes can be classified in two groups: linear and quadratic.

Linear Schemes. These are schemes based on classical spread-spectrum watermarking techniques, with linear detection functions. The first asymmetric scheme was developed in 1997 by Hartung and Girod [15], as an extension to their symmetric scheme [99]. They obtain the public key by substituting some bits of the private key by a random sequence. This scheme is not secure when disclosing the public key, as it can be used to make the watermark undetectable even when the private part can still be detected.

Two more linear schemes were presented in 2004 by Choi *et al.* [100] and Kim *et al.* [101]. The first one is based on a linear transform on the secret key to generate both the watermark and the public key; it has the same drawback as the previous scheme, but it is also susceptible to erasure of the watermark through the estimation of the linear transform when having a large set of private keys. The scheme by Kim *et al.* uses the same public watermark for a set of private watermarks, using the phase-shift-transform, that allows to have control over the correlation between the public and the secret watermark.

Quadratic Schemes. The first quadratic scheme was presented in 1999 by van Schyndel *et al.* [102], and it was based on invariance properties of Legendre sequences with respect to the DFT. This method was later improved by Eggers *et al.* [103,104], by using a watermark that is an eigenvector of a given linear transform matrix.

Later, Furon and Duhamel [105,106] presented an scheme that modifies the spectrum shape of an interleaved image to perform embedding of the watermark.

The three previous schemes, as well as the one presented by Smith and Dodge, can be described following the unified approach given by Furon *et al.* [107], that concludes that all these detection functions can be written using a quadratic form; furthermore, all of them have lower efficiency than symmetric schemes for the same DWR, although they are more robust against oracle attacks.

Nevertheless, [107,108] also show a statistical attack that allows to eliminate an embedded watermark relatively easily when the public key is known by the attacker.

This proves that the previous schemes are not really public-key, and their improved security when not publishing any keys comes from the higher complexity of the watermarking regions [48], leading to better security when increasing the order of the detection function [32,109]. This increase produces more complex embedders, what propitiates the use of different regions for embedding and extraction, so that detection regions are much more complicated than embedding ones; an example is the method presented by Mansour and Tewfik [110], that uses fractal theory for building a complex decision region from a simpler embedding region. Taking into account that fractal functions can give an indicator function of the detection region without revealing the boundary [48], these schemes might be seen as a way to achieve a truly public-key watermarking method, although nowadays there is no approach that can be envisaged as securely usable in a public-key scenario.

7.2 Zero-Knowledge Watermarking

Zero-knowledge watermark has arisen as a solution to conceal all the security parameters needed for detection/decoding in symmetric schemes. This way, when using a zero-knowledge watermarking protocol between two parties (Prover and Verifier), only the fact that a watermark is present or not is disclosed to the Verifier, but all the security parameters remain secret. This solves the problem posed by tampering attacks (Section 3), and provides a better protection against sensitivity attacks (Section 6.4), as only blind attacks may succeed.

The concept of zero-knowledge was introduced by Goldwasser *et al.* [111] in 1985. It basically consists in convincing an adversary of an assertion without giving him any knowledge but the assertion whose validity is proven. Zero-knowledge protocols are widely used in cryptography, generally to force a malicious adversary to behave as stated by a determined protocol.

These protocols are based on interactive proofs [111,112] and arguments [113], and especially on proofs of knowledge [114]. All of them are based on the intuitive notion that it is easier to prove a statement through an interaction between both parties (Prover and Verifier), than to write a proof that can be verified by any party without interaction. The concealment of data involved in this interaction is measured in terms of knowledge complexity [115], related to the similarity between random sequences and the sequences produced by the interaction. Zero-knowledge is the result of the indistinguishability of both types of sequences.

The first attempt of application of zero-knowledge to watermark detection was undertaken by Gopalakrishnan [116]; it consists in a protocol that allows to detect an encrypted watermark in an encrypted image, through the use of RSA [117]. Later, Craver [118] proposed several schemes of watermark detection with minimal disclosure, based on permutations using Pitas's scheme [119], or ambiguity attacks to generate a set of watermarks indistinguishable from the real one.

Adelsbach *et al.* [120] proved afterwards that all the preceding works had some flaws that made them non zero-knowledge, as they give information about the embedded watermark when using the detector as an oracle.

The formalization of zero-knowledge watermark detection was given by Adelsbach and Sadeghi [35]; they proposed the use of commitment schemes [121,122] for concealing the secret parameters of the detector; also in this work, they presented a truly zero-knowledge detection protocol for Cox's additive spread spectrum watermarking algorithm [13], as a high level protocol that uses existing zero-knowledge proofs as subblocks; it benefits from the homomorphic properties of some commitment schemes [123,124] for alleviating the communication complexity. Following the same philosophy, Piva *et al.* [125] also presented a zero-knowledge detection protocol for ST-DM.

Nevertheless, there are some security issues that must be taken into account when developing zero-knowledge watermarking protocols; they have been pointed out by Katzenbeisser in [126], and are mainly related to the correct concealing of protocol inputs and the problem of guaranteeing the correct generation of a concealed watermark. To overcome the latter issue, Adelsbach *et al.* [127] proposed several new zero-knowledge protocols that can be used to prove that a given sequence follows a determined probability distribution.

Although zero-knowledge protocols could seem an utopical solution to many security problems, they have advantages and also drawbacks [128]. Their main advantages are their null security degradation when used several times, and their resistance against clear-text attacks; their main drawback is their efficiency, as they commonly produce communication and complexity overheads that are much bigger than those presented by public-key protocols; as an example, a complete complexity study of the zero-knowledge version of Cox's non-blind detection scheme [13] is developed in [129]. Moreover, many techniques that are based on zero-knowledge lack a formal proof of zero-knowledge or even validity, due to the choices of parameters to improve efficiency; actually, many of the concepts related to zero-knowledge are asymptotic and cannot be directly applied to practical protocols.

8   Conclusions and Open Problems

We have made in this survey a thorough revision of the security problem in the watermarking literature. On the theoretical side, several definitions and measures have been given in order to clarify the concept of security and to establish formal models for security assessment. However, many important problems remain open, such as:

- Quantification of the gap between theoretical and practical security. As mentioned in Section 5, information-theoretic models for security represent the worst-case for the watermarker, and practical security may well be greater.
- Security assessment of a wider variety of watermarking methods, such as [30], [33], and [130]. So far, only the two major groups (spread-spectrum and quantization-based ones) have been analyzed in a few particular scenarios.
- Security assessment of oracle attacks. As said in Section 6.4, the impact of this kind of attacks on watermarking security needs to be clarified.
- The results published so far suggest that there is a trade-off between robustness and security. It is still an open question whether this trade-off is inherent to the considered problem or not.

On the practical side, we have seen that several methods for performing security attacks have been successfully tested. We have introduced also several countermeasures for improving the security level. In this regard, the main research directions appear to be the following:

- Rigorous assessment of the proposed countermeasures. As discussed in Section 7, some of them present serious drawbacks (such as the use of host-dependent keys).

- Development of zero-knowledge protocols with simplified interaction between prover and verifier. Nowadays, zero-knowledge protocols have not yet succeeded as a practical alternative due to their excessive communication complexity.
- Security assessment of watermarking schemes jointly using watermarks and cryptographic primitives, as suggested in [58]. The successful integration of cryptography and watermarking is still a pending issue.
- Development of *true* public-key watermarking schemes. As we have seen, none of the schemes proposed so far can be considered as a truly public-key scheme.

As a final comment, we would like to remark that no special attention was paid in this survey to the steganography scenario because, according to the security definition we have stuck to, steganographic security would be already encompassed by our discussion. This is true whenever secret keys are used in the secret communication process, as shown in Section 6.3, and constitutes a major difference with the survey in [9], where security for steganography has the meaning of *detectability*, according to some previous works [131,132]. Under this last point of view, a steganographic system is secure if it is impossible to distinguish between innocuous and stego images, since the secret of the system is the very existence of the embedded message. In our model, the secrecy of the message is not considered in the definition of security. One possibility for conciliating these two different approaches is to add the existence of the message to the set of secret parameters in our model (so far, only the secret key). Needles to say that this last point must be subject of further discussion.

Acknowledgments

This work was partially funded by *Xunta de Galicia* under projects PGIDT04 TIC322013PR and PGIDT04 PXIC32202PM; MEC project DIPSTICK, reference TEC2004-02551/TCM; FIS project IM3, reference G03/185 and European Comission through the IST Programme under Contract IST-2002-507932 ECRYPT, and Fundación Caixa Galicia grant for postgraduate studies. ECRYPT disclaimer: The information in this paper is provided as is, and no guarantee or warranty is given or implied that the information is fit for any particular purpose. The user thereof uses the information at its sole risk and liability.

References

1. Bartolini, F., Barni, M., Furon, T.: Security issues in digital watermarking. In: Proc. of 11th European Signal Processing Conference (EUSIPCO). Volume 1., Toulouse, France (2002) 282–302,441–461
2. Barni, M., Pérez-González, F.: Special session: watermarking security. In Edward J. Delp III, Wong, P.W., eds.: Security, Steganography, and Watermarking of Multimedia Contents VII. Volume 5681., San Jose, California, USA, SPIE (2005) 685–768

3. Barni, M., Pérez-González, F.: Tutorial: Security issues in digital watermarking. In: IEEE International Conference on Image Processing (ICIP), Genova, Italy (2005)
4. Pérez-González, F., Furon, T.: Special session on watermarking security. In Barni, M., Cox, I., Kalker, T., Kim, H.J., eds.: Fourth International Workshop on Digital Watermarking. Volume 3710., Siena, Italy, Springer (2005) 201–274
5. CERTIMARK: Certification of Watermarking Techniques (2000-2002) http://www.certimark.org.
6. ECRYPT: European Network of Excellence in Cryptology (2004-2008) http://www.ecrypt.eu.org.
7. Cox, I.J., Miller, M.L., Bloom, J.A.: Digital watermarking. Multimedia Information and Systems. Morgan Kauffman (2002)
8. Barni, M., Bartolini, F.: Watermarking Systems Engineering. Signal Processing and Communications. Marcel Dekker (2004)
9. Furon, T.: A survey of watermarking security. In Barni, M., ed.: Proc. of Int. Work. on Digital Watermarking. Volume 3710 of Lecture Notes on Computer Science., Siena, Italy, Springer-Verlag (2005) 201–215
10. Petitcolas, F., Anderson, R., Kuhn, M.: Information hiding-a survey. Proceedings of the IEEE **87** (1999) 1062–1078
11. van Schyndel, R.G., Tirkel, A.Z., Osborne, C.F.: A digital watermark. In: Proc. IEEE Int. Conference on Image Processing, Austin, Texas, USA (1994) 86–89
12. Viterbi, A.: CDMA: principles of spread spectrum communication. Addison Wesley Longman Publishing Co., Inc. Redwood City, CA, USA (1995)
13. Cox, I.J., Kilian, J., Leighton, F.T., Shamoon, T.: Secure spread spectrum watermarking for multimedia. IEEE Transactions on Image Processing **6** (1997) 1673–1687
14. Hernández, J.R., Pérez-González, F., Rodríguez, J.M., Nieto, G.: Performance analysis of a 2d-multipulse amplitude modulation scheme for data hiding and watermarking of still images. IEEE J. Select. Areas Commun. **16** (1998) 510–524
15. Hartung, F., Girod, B.: Fast public-key watermarking of compressed video. In: Proc. IEEE ICIP'97. Volume I., Santa Barbara, California, USA (1997) 528–531
16. Bender, W., Gruhl, D., Morimoto, N.: Techniques for data hiding. In: Proc. of the SPIE, San Jose, CA (1995) 2420–2440
17. Koch, E., Rindfrey, J., Zhao, J.: Copyright protection for multimedia data. In: Digital Media and Electronc Publishing. Academic Press (1996) 203–213
18. Fridrich, J.: Key-dependent random image transforms and their applications in image watermarking. In: Proc. International Conference on Imaging Science, Systems, and Technology, Las Vegas, NV, USA (1999) 237–243
19. Dietl, W., Meerwald, P., Uhl, A.: Protection of wavelet-based watermarking systems using filter parametrization. Elsevier Signal Processing **83** (2003) 2095–2116
20. Seo, Y., Kim, M., Park, H., Jung, H., Chung, H., Huh, Y., Lee, J., Center, V., ETRI, T.: A secure watermarking for JPEG-2000. In: Proc. IEEE Int. Conf. Image Processing. Volume 2., Thessaloniki, Greece (2001) 530–533
21. Wang, Y., Doherty, J., Dyck, R.V.: A wavelet-based watermarking algorithm for ownership verificationof digital images. IEEE Trans. on Image Processing **11** (2002) 77–88
22. Yeung, M., Mintzer, F.: An invisible watermarking technique for image verification. In: Proc. IEEE Int. Conf. Image Processing. Volume 2. (1997) 680–683
23. Su, J., Girod, B.: Power-spectrum condition for energy-efficient watermarking. Multimedia, IEEE Transactions on **4** (2002) 551–560

24. Voyatzis, G., Pitas, I.: Chaotic watermarks for embedding in the spatial digital image domain. In: Proc. IEEE Int. Conf. Image Processing. Volume 2., Chicago, IL, USA (1998) 432–436

25. Voyatzis, G., Pitas, I.: Applications of toral automorphisms in image watermarking. In: Proc. IEEE Int. Conf. Image Processing. Volume 2., Laussane, Switzerland (1996) 237–240

26. Malvar, H.S., Florencio, D.A.F.: Improved spread spectrum: a new modulation technique for robust watermarking. IEEE Transactions on Signal Processing **51** (2003) 898–905

27. Chen, B., Wornell, G.W.: Quantization index modulation: A class of provably good methods for digital watermarking and information embedding. IEEE Trans. on Information Theory **47** (2001) 1423–1443

28. Eggers, J.J., Bäuml, R., Tzschoppe, R., Girod, B.: Scalar Costa Scheme for information embedding. IEEE Transactions on Signal Processing **51** (2003) 1003–1019 Special Issue on Signal Processing for Data Hiding in Digital Media and Secure Content Delivery.

29. Fei, C., Kundur, D., Kwong, R.H.: Analysis and design of secure watermark-based authentication systems. IEEE Transactions on Information Forensics and Security **1** (2006) 43–55

30. Pérez-González, F., Mosquera, C., Barni, M., Abrardo, A.: Rational Dither Modulation: a high-rate data-hiding method robust to gain attacks. IEEE Trans. on Signal Processing **53** (2005) 3960–3975 Third supplement on secure media.

31. Moulin, P., Goteti, A.K.: Minmax strategies for QIM watermarking subject to attacks with memory. In: IEEE International Conference on Image Processing, ICIP 2005. Volume 1., Genova, Italy (2005) 985–988

32. Furon, T., Macq, B., Hurley, N., Silvestre, G.: JANIS: Just Another N-order side-Informed watermarking Scheme. In: IEEE International Conference on Image Processing, ICIP'02. Volume 3., Rochester, NY, USA (2002) 153–156

33. Miller, M.L., Doërr, G.J., Cox, I.J.: Applying informed coding and embedding to design a robust high-capacity watermarking. IEEE Transactions on Image Processing **13** (2004) 792–807

34. Anderson, R., Kuhn, M.: Low cost attacks on tamper resistant devices. In: International Workshop on Security Protocols. Volume 1361 of Lecture Notes in Computer Science., Paris, France, Springer Verlag (1997) 125–136

35. Adelsbach, A., Sadeghi, A.R.: Zero-knowledge watermark detection and proof of ownership. In: Information Hiding, Fourth International Workshop. Volume 2137 of Lecture Notes in Computer Science., Springer (2001) 273–288

36. Cox, I.J., Linnartz, J.P.M.G.: Some general methods for tampering with watermarks. IEEE Journal on Selected Areas in Communications **16** (1998) 587–593

37. Killian, J., Leighton, F.T., Matheson, L.R., Shamoon, T., Tarjan, R.E.: Resistance of watermarked documents to collusional attacks. Technical report, NEC Research Institute, Princeton, NJ (1997)

38. Cox, I.J., Linnartz, J.P.M.G.: Public watermarks and resistance to tampering. In: Proc. IEEE Int. Conf. on Image Processing. Volume 3., Santa Barbara, California, USA (1997) 3–6

39. Mitthelholzer, T.: An information-theoretic approach to steganography and watermarking. In Pfitzmann, A., ed.: 3rd Int. Workshop on Information Hiding, IH'99. Volume 1768 of Lecture Notes in Computer Science., Dresden, Germany, Springer Verlag (1999) 1–17

40. Cachin, C.: An information-theoretic model for steganography. In Aucsmith, D., ed.: 2nd Int. Workshop on Information Hiding, IH'98. Volume 1525 of Lecture Notes in Computer Science., Portland, OR, USA, Springer Verlag (1998) 306–318

41. Zöllner, J., Federrath, H., Klimant, H., Pfitzmann, A., Piotraschke, R., Westfeld, A., Wicke, G., Wolf, G.: Modeling the security of steganographic systems. In Aucsmith, D., ed.: Information Hiding International Workshop. Volume 1525 of Lecture Notes in Computer Science., Portland, OR, USA, Springer (1998) 344–354

42. Shannon, C.E.: Communication theory of secrecy systems. Bell system technical journal **28** (1949) 656–715

43. Kalker, T.: Considerations on watermarking security. In: IEEE International Workshop on Multimedia Signal Processing, Cannes, France (2001) 201–206

44. Furon, T., et al.: Security Analysis. European Project IST-1999-10987 CERTI-MARK, Deliverable D.5.5 (2002)

45. Kerckhoffs, A.: La cryptographie militaire. Journal des sciences militaires **9** (1883) 5–38

46. Diffie, W., Hellman, M.: New directions in cryptography. IEEE Transactions on Information Theory **22** (1976) 644–684

47. Barni, M., Bartolini, F., Furon, T.: A general framework for robust watermarking security. Signal Processing **83** (2003) 2069–2084 Special issue on Security of Data Hiding Technologies, invited paper.

48. Barni, M., Bartolini, F., Rosa, A.D.: Advantages and drawbacks of multiplicative spread spectrum watermarking. In Delp III, E.J., Wong, P.W., eds.: Security and Watermarking of Multimedia Contents V. Proceedings of SPIE (2003) 290–299

49. Cayre, F., Fontaine, C., Furon, T.: Watermarking security: Theory and practice. IEEE Trans. Signal Processing **53** (2005) 3976–3987

50. Fisher, R.A.: On the mathematical foundations of theoretical statistics. Philosophical Transactions of the Royal Society **222** (1922) 309–368

51. Comesaña, P., Pérez-Freire, L., Pérez-González, F.: An information-theoretic framework for assessing security in practical watermarking and data hiding scenarios. In: 6th International Workshop on Image Analysis for Multimedia Interactive Services, Montreux, Switzerland (2005)

52. Comesaña, P., Pérez-Freire, L., Pérez-González, F.: Fundamentals of data hiding security and their application to spread-spectrum analysis. In: 7th Information Hiding Workshop, IH05. Lecture Notes in Computer Science, Barcelona, Spain, Springer Verlag (2005) 146–160

53. Pérez-Freire, L., Comesaña, P., Pérez-González, F.: Information-theoretic analysis of security in side-informed data hiding. In: 7th Information Hiding Workshop, IH05. Lecture Notes in Computer Science, Barcelona, Spain, Springer Verlag (2005) 131–145

54. Pérez-Freire, L., Pérez-González, F., Furon, T., Comesaña, P.: Security of lattice-based data hiding against the Known Message Attack. IEEE Transactions on Information Forensics and Security (2006) Accepted for publication.

55. Cover, T.M., Thomas, J.A.: Elements of Information Theory. Wiley series in Telecommunications (1991)

56. Hernández, J.R., Pérez-González, F.: Shedding more light on image watermarks. In Aucsmith, D., ed.: 2nd Int. Workshop on Information Hiding, IH'98. Volume 1525 of Lecture Notes in Computer Science., Portland, OR, USA, Springer Verlag (1998) 191–207

57. Doërr, G., Dugelay, J.L.: Security pitfalls of frame-by-frame approaches to video watermarking. IEEE Trans. Sig. Proc., Supplement on Secure Media **52** (2004) 2955–2964

58. Katzenbeisser, S.: Computational security models for digital watermarks. In: Workshop on Image Analysis for Multimedia Interactive Services (WIAMIS), Montreux, Switzerland (2005)

59. Cramér, H.: Mathematical methods of statistics. Landmarks on Mathematics. Princeton University Press (1999) Reprint.

60. Guo, D., Shamai, S., Verdú, S.: Mutual information and minimum mean-square error in Gaussian channels. IEEE Transactions on Information Theory **51** (2005) 1261–1282

61. Guo, D., Shamai, S., Verdú, S.: Additive non-Gaussian noise channels: Mutual information and conditional mean estimation. In: IEEE International Symposium on Information Theory (ISIT), Adelaide, Australia (2005) 719–723

62. Palomar, D.P., Verdú, S.: Gradient of mutual information in linear vector Gaussian channels. IEEE Transactions on Information Theory **52** (2006) 141–154

63. P.Bas, Cayre, F.: Natural Watermarking: a secure spread spectrum technique for WOA. In: 8th Information Hiding Workshop, IH06. Lecture Notes in Computer Science, Old Town Alexandria, Virginia, USA, Springer Verlag (2006)

64. Hyvärinen, A., Karhunen, J., Oja, E.: Independent Component Analysis. Adaptive and learning systems for signal processing, communications and control. John Wiley & Sons (2001)

65. Moulin, P., Koetter, R.: Data hiding codes. Proceedings of IEEE **93** (2005) 2083–2126

66. Pérez-Freire, L., Pérez-González, F., Comesaña, P.: Secret dither estimation in lattice-quantization data hiding: a set-membership approach. In Edward J. Delp III, Wong, P.W., eds.: Security, Steganography, and Watermarking of Multimedia Contents VIII, San Jose, California, USA, SPIE (2006)

67. Conway, J., Sloane, N.: Sphere Packings, Lattices and Groups. 3rd edn. Volume 290 of Comprehensive Studies in Mathematics. Springer (1999)

68. Costa, M.H.: Writing on dirty paper. IEEE Trans. on Information Theory **29** (1983) 439–441

69. Burgett, S., Koch, E., Zhao, J.: Copyright labeling of digitized image data. IEEE Communications Magazine **36** (1998) 94–100

70. Su, J., Girod, B.: Power-spectrum condition for energy-efficient watermarking. IEEE Transactions on Multimedia **4** (2002) 551–560

71. Mıhçak, M.K., Venkatesan, R., Kesal, M.: Cryptanalysis of discrete-sequence spread spectrum watermarks. In Petitcolas, F.A.P., ed.: 5th International Workshop on Digital Watermarking, Noordwijkerhout, The Netherlands, Springer-Verlag (2002) 226–246

72. Voloshynovskiy, S., Pereira, S., Iquise, V., Pun, T.: Attack modeling: Towards a second generation benchmark. Signal Processing, Special Issue on Information Theoretic Issues in Digital Watermarking **81** (2001) 1177–1214

73. Hyvärinen, A., Oja, E.: Independent component analysis: Algorithms and applications. Neural Networks **13** (2000) 411–430

74. Cayre, F., Fontaine, C., Furon, T.: Watermarking security: application to a WSS technique for still images. In Cox, I.J., Kalker, T., Lee, H., eds.: Third International Workshop on Digital Watermarking. Volume 3304., Seoul, Korea, Springer (2004)

75. Dempster, A.P., Laird, N.M., Rubin, D.B.: Maximum likelihood from incomplete data via the em algorithm. Journal of the Royal Statistical Society, Series B (Methodological) **39** (1977) 1–38

76. Doërr, G., Dugelay, J.L.: Danger of low-dimensional watermarking subspaces. In: IEEE International Conference on Acoustics, Speech, and Signal Processing. Volume 3., Montreal, Canada (2004) 93–96

77. Du, J., Lee, C., Lee, H., Suh, Y.: Watermark attack based on blind estimation without priors. In: Proc. International Workshop on Digital Watermarking, IWDW. Volume 2613 of Lecture Notes in Computer Science., Seoul, Korea, Springer (2002)

78. Combettes, P.L.: The foundations of set theoretic estimation. Proceedings of the IEEE **81** (1993) 182–208

79. Deller, J.R.: Set membership identification in digital signal processing. IEEE ASSP Magazine **6** (1989) 4–20

80. Cheung, M.F., Yurkovich, S., Passino, K.M.: An optimal volume ellipsoid algorithm for parameter set estimation. IEEE Transactions on Automatic Control **38** (1993) 1292–1296

81. Bas, P., Hurri, J.: Security of DM quantization watermarking schemes: a practical study for digital images. In Barni, M., Cox, I., Kalker, T., Kim, H.J., eds.: Fourth International Workshop on Digital Watermarking. Volume 3710., Siena, Italy, Springer (2005) 186–200

82. Fridrich, J., Goljan, M., Soukal, D.: Searching for the stego-key. In: Proc. of Security and Watermarking of Multimedia Contents VI. Proceedings of SPIE, San Jose, CA, USA (2004) 70–82

83. Westfeld, A.: High capacity despite better steganalysis (F5-A steganographic algorithm). In: Int. Workshop on Information Hiding, IH'01. Volume 2137 of Lecture Notes in Computer Science., New York, NY, USA, Springer Verlag (2001) 289–302

84. Provos, N.: Defending against statistical steganalysis. In: 10th USENIX Security Symposium, Washington DC, USA (2001) 323–336

85. Fridrich, J., Goljan, M., Soukal, D., Holotyak, T.: Forensic steganalysis: determining the stego key in spatial domain steganography. In: Proc. of Security and Watermarking of Multimedia Contents VII. Proceedings of SPIE, San Jose, CA, USA (2005)

86. Fridrich, J., Goljan, M., Soukal, D., Memon, N.: Further attacks on Yeung-Mintzer fragile watermarking scheme. In: Proc. of Security and Watermarking of Multimedia Contents II. Proceedings of SPIE, San Jose, CA, USA (2000) 428–437

87. Linnartz, J.P.M.G., van Dijk, M.: Analysis of the sensitivity attack against electronic watermarks in images. In Aucsmith, D., ed.: 2nd International Workshop on Information Hiding, IH'98. Volume 1525 of Lecture Notes in Computer Science., Portland, OR, USA, Springer Verlag (1998) 258–272

88. Kalker, T., Linnartz, J.P., van Dijk, M.: Watermark estimation through detector analysis. In: IEEE International Conference on Image Processing, ICIP'98, Chicago, IL, USA (1998) 425–429

89. El Choubassi, M., Moulin, P.: New sensitivity analysis attack. In Edward J. Delp III, Wong, P.W., eds.: Security, Steganography and Watermarking of Multimedia contents VII, SPIE (2005) 734–745

90. Mansour, M.F., Tewfik, A.H.: LMS-based attack on watermark public detectors. In: IEEE International Conference on Image Processing, ICIP'02. Volume 3. (2002) 649–652

91. Venturini, I.: Oracle attacks and covert channels. In Barni, M., Cox, I., Kalker, T., Kim, H.J., eds.: Fourth International Workshop on Digital Watermarking. Volume 3710 of Lecture Notes in Computer Science., Siena, Italy, Springer (2005) 171–185

92. Choubassi, M.E., Moulin, P.: On the fundamental tradeoff between watermark detection performance and robustness against sensitivity analysis attacks. In III, E.J.D., Wong, P.W., eds.: Security, Steganography, and Watermarking of Multimedia Contents VIII. Volume 6072., SPIE (2006)

93. Venkatesan, R., Jakubowski, M.H.: Randomized detection for spread-spectrum watermarking: defending against sensitivity and other attacks. In: IEEE International Conference on Acoustics, Speech and Signal Processing (ICASSP). Volume 2., Philadelphia, USA (2005) 9–12

94. Comesaña, P., Pérez-Freire, L., Pérez-González, F.: The return of the sensitivity attack. In Barni, M., Cox, I., Kalker, T., Kim, H.J., eds.: International Workshop on Digital Watermarking. Volume 3710 of Lecture Notes in Computer Science., Siena, Italy, Springer (2005) 260–274

95. Holliman, M., Memon, N., Yeung, M.: On the need for image dependent keys for watermarking. In: Proceedings of IEEE Content Security and Data Hiding in Digital Media, Newark, NJ, USA (1999)

96. Fridrich, J., Goljan, M.: Robust hash functions for digital watermarking. In: Proceedings of the International Conference on Information Technology: Coding and Computing, Las Vegas, Nevada, USA (2000) 173–178

97. Smith, J.R., Dodge, C.: Developments in steganography. In: Information Hiding. (1999) 77–87

98. Miller, M.L.: Is asymmetric watermarking necessary or sufficient? In: Proc. XI European Signal Processing Conference, EUSIPCO'02. (2002) 291–294

99. Hartung, F., Girod, B.: Watermarking of uncompressed and compressed video. Signal Processing **66** (1998) 283–301

100. Choi, H., Lee, K., Kim, T.: Transformed-key asymmetric watermarking system. IEEE Signal Processing Letters **11** (2004) 251–254

101. Kim, T.Y., Choi, H., Lee, K., Kim, T.: An asymmetric watermarking system with many embedding watermarks corresponding to one detection watermark. IEEE Signal Processing Letters **11** (2004) 375–377

102. van Schyndel, R.G., Tirkel, A.Z., Svalbe, I.D.: Key independent watermark detection. In: IEEE International Conference on Multimedia Computing Systems (ICMCS99), Florence (1999) 580–585

103. Eggers, J., Su, J., Girod, B.: Public key watermarking by eigenvectors of linear transforms. In: Proceedings of the European Signal Processing Conference, Tampere, Finland (2000)

104. Eggers, J.J., Su, J.K., Girod, B.: Asymmetric watermarking schemes. In: Sicherheit in Mediendaten, Springer Reihe: Informatik Aktuell (2000) Invited paper.

105. Furon, T., Duhamel, P.: An asymmetric public detection watermarking technique. In Pfitzmann, A., ed.: Proc. of the third Int. Workshop on Information Hiding, Dresden, Germany, Springer Verlag (1999) 88–100

106. Furon, T., Duhamel, P.: An asymmetric watermarking method. IEEE Trans. on Signal Processing **51** (2003) 981–995 Special Issue on Signal Processing for Data Hiding in Digital Media and Secure Content Delivery.

107. Furon, T., Venturini, I., Duhamel, P.: An unified approach of asymmetric watermarking schemes. In P.W. Wong, E. Delp, eds.: Security and Watermarking of Multimedia Contents III, San Jose, Cal., USA, SPIE (2001)

108. Furon, T.: Use of watermarking techniques for copy protection. PhD thesis, Ecole Nationale Supérieure des Télécommunications. (2002)

109. Hurley, N.J., Silvestre, G.C.M.: Nth-order audio watermarking. In III, E.J.D., Wong, P.W., eds.: Security and Watermarking of Multimedia Contents IV. Volume 4675 of Proc. of SPIE., San José, CA, USA (2002) 102–109

110. Mansour, M.F., Tewfik, A.H.: Secure detection of public watermarks with fractal decision boundary. In: Proc. XI European Signal Processing Conference, EU-SIPCO'02, Toulouse, France (2002)

111. Goldwasser, S., Micali, S., Rackoff, C.: The knowledge complexity of interactive proof-systems. In: Proceedings of the 17th Annual ACM Symposium on the Theory of Computing. (1985) 291–304

112. Goldwasser, S., Micali, S., Rackoff, C.: The knowledge complexity of interactive proof-systems. In: SIAM Journal of Computing. Volume 18. (1989) 186–208

113. Brassard, G., Chaum, D., Crépeau, C.: Minimum disclosure proofs of knowledge. Journal of Computer and System Sciences **37** (1988) 156–189

114. Mihil Bellare, O.G.: On defining proofs of knowledge. In: Proceedings of Crypto'92. Volume 740 of Lecture Notes in Computer Science., Springer-Verlag (1992) 390–420

115. Goldreich, O., Petrank, E.: Quantifying knowledge complexity. Computational Complexity **8** (1999) 50–98

116. Gopalakrishnan, K., Memon, N.D., Vora, P.: Protocols for watermark verification. In: Multimedia and Security Workshop at ACM Multimedia. (1999) 91–94

117. Rivest, R.L., Shamir, A., Adleman, L.: A method for obtaining digital signatures and public-key cryptosystems. Communications of the ACM **21** (1978) 120–176

118. Craver, S.: Zero knowledge watermark detection. In: Information Hiding: Third International Workshop. Volume 1768 of Lecture Notes in Computer Science., Springer (2000) 101–116

119. Pitas, I.: A method for signature casting on digital images. In: Proceedings of ICIP. Volume 3. (1996) 215–218

120. Adelsbach, A., Katzenbeisser, S., Sadeghi, A.R.: Cryptography meets watermarking: Detecting watermarks with minimal- or zero-knowledge disclosure. In: XI European Signal Processing Conference. Volume I. (2003) 446–449

121. Damgård, I.: Commitment schemes and zero-knowledge protocols. In: Lectures on data security: modern cryptology in theory and practise. Volume 1561 of Lecture Notes in Computer Science., Springer-Verlag (1998) 63–86

122. Schneier, B.: Applied cryptography. Computer Networking and Distributed Systems. John Wiley & Sons (1994)

123. Fujisaki, E., Okamoto, T.: A practical and provably secure scheme for publicly verifiable secret sharing and its applications. In: Proceedings of EUROCRYPT'98. Volume 1403 of Lecture Notes in Computer Science., Springer (1998) 32–46

124. Damgård, I., Fujisaki, E.: A statistically-hiding integer commitment scheme based on groups with hidden order. In: ASIACRYPT 2002: 8th International Conference on the Theory and Application of Cryptology and Information Security. Volume 2501 of Lecture Notes in Computer Science., Spriger-Verlag (2002) 125–142

125. Piva, A., Corazzi, D., Rosa, A.D., Barni, M.: Zero knowledge st-dm watermarking. In III, E.J.D., Wong, P.W., eds.: Security, Steganography, and Watermarking of Multimedia Contents VIII, SPIE, San José, California, USA (2006)

126. Katzenbeisser, S.: On the integration of watermarks and cryptography. In: International Workshop on Digital Watermarking. (2003) 50–60

127. Adelsbach, A., Rohe, M., Sadeghi, A.R.: Overcoming the obstacles of zero-knowledge watermark detection. In: Proceedings of Multimedia and Security Workshop. (2004) 46–55

128. Menezes, A.J., van Oorschot, P.C., Vanstone, S.A.: Handbook of Applied Cryptography. CRC Press (2001) 5th reprint.

129. Adelsbach, A., Rohe, M., Sadeghi, A.R.: Non-interactive watermark detection for a correlation-based watermarking scheme. In: Communications and Multimedia Security: 9th IFIP TC-6 TC-11International Conference, CMS 2005. Volume 3677 of Lecture Notes in Computer Science., Spriger-Verlag (2005) 129–139

130. Abrardo, A., Barni, M.: Informed watermarking by means of orthogonal and quasi-orthogonal dirty paper coding. IEEE Transactions on Signal Processing **53** (2005) 824–833

131. Katzenbeisser, S., Petitcolas, F.A.P.: Defining security in steganographic systems. In Edward J. Delp III, Wong, P.W., eds.: Security, Steganography, and Watermarking of Multimedia Contents IV. Volume 4675., San Jose, California, USA, SPIE (2002) 50–56

132. Cachin, C.: An information-theoretic model for steganography. Information and Computation **192** (2004) 41–56

Efficient Implementation of Zero-Knowledge Proofs for Watermark Detection in Multimedia Data

André Adelsbach[1], Markus Rohe[2], and Ahmad-Reza Sadeghi[2]

[1] Chair for Network and Data Security, Ruhr-Universität Bochum, Germany
andre.adelsbach@nds.rub.de
[2] Applied Data Security Group, Ruhr-Universität Bochum, Germany
{rohe, sadeghi}@crypto.rub.de

Abstract. Robust digital watermarking systems are important building blocks in applications such as fingerprinting, dispute resolving or direct proofs of authorship, where the presence of a watermark serves as evidence for some fact, e.g., illegal redistribution or authorship. A major drawback of (symmetric) watermarking schemes in this context is that proving the presence of a watermark requires disclosing security critical detection information (watermark, detection key, original data) to a (potentially malicious) verifying party. This may completely jeopardise the security of embedded watermarks once this information is revealed. To overcome this problem recent work on secure watermark detection proposes cryptographic proofs that perform the detection on concealed detection information. The proposed solutions focus on correlation-based detection and can be applied to any watermarking scheme whose detection criteria can be expressed as a polynomial relation between the quantities required for the detection.

In this paper, we present in-depth guidelines for the adoptions required to transform well-established watermarking schemes by Cox et al and Piva et al into secure cryptographic proofs in the non-interactive setting. Moreover, we present our implementation, its performance results and the corresponding tool we have developed for this purpose. Our results underpin the practicability of the cryptographic approach.

Keywords: watermark, detection, implementation, zero-knowledge.

1 Introduction

Digital watermarks are proposed to be deployed in various applications. Some applications require a proof that a certain watermark is present in the underlying digital content. Examples are fingerprinting [1], dispute resolving [2] or direct authorship proofs [3,4]. In typical scenarios the proof is done to potentially untrusted party such as a dispute resolver or a customer. However, proving the presence of the watermark in digital data requires sensitive information such as the watermark, the detection key[1] and the original data in case of non-blind

---

[1] Note that most existing watermarking schemes are symmetric, i.e., they use the same key for embedding the watermark as for its detection or extraction.

Y.Q. Shi (Ed.): Transactions on DHMS I, LNCS 4300, pp. 73–103, 2006.

watermark schemes. This information can be misused by a malicious verifier attempting to remove the watermark.

In [4] the authors propose a cryptographic proof, more precisely, a zero-knowledge watermark detection scheme, to overcome this problem. In this proof a proving party commits to the security critical detection information and applies a zero-knowledge protocol proving to a verifier that the committed watermark is detectable in the stego-data. Other proposals such as [5,6], however, either do not achieve the strong security we require, or have security flaws as discussed in [7].

The zero-knowledge property of the protocol guarantees that the verifier gains no useful information on the sensitive information (embedded watermark, detection key, original data) beyond the fact that the watermark can be detected.[2]

The zero-knowledge watermark detection paradigm can be applied to *any* watermarking scheme whose detection criterion is expressible as a polynomial relation among the required detection inputs. This also includes more advanced embedding and detection strategies to improve robustness and imperceptibility with respect to the HVS (Human Visual System) as cited in [8]. In this paper we restrict our consideration to two well-known watermarking schemes representative enough to demonstrate the practical feasibility of zero-knowledge watermark detection. We present concrete ZKWMD constructions for the correlation-based non-blind watermarking scheme proposed by Cox et al. [9] and the correlation-based blind watermarking scheme by Piva et al. [10]. Furthermore, we give a precise quantisation of the computation and communication complexities of the protocols. After minor transformations, the correlation value can be computed as a polynomial expression such that the entire zero-knowledge watermark detection protocol can be composed from elementary zero-knowledge sub-protocols.

This paper extends and complements the previous work presented in [11] and [12] with a ZKWMD protocol for the watermarking scheme of Piva et al. [10]. Furthermore, compared to the previous prototype implementation the running time of the corresponding protocols is significantly improved. The communication and computation complexities of the constructed protocols mainly depend on the number of required zero-knowledge sub-protocols. The properties of the applied cryptographic primitive concealing the watermark or the original data, however, allow both the prover and the verifier to perform some computations autonomously – mostly on publicly known values. This supersedes interaction and saves expensive computations. The performance of different protocols is therefore not comparable in a linear manner to the number of watermarking coefficients.

Additionally, we discuss different system setup issues (Section 8.1), and for better understanding we review the details of a concrete zero-knowledge sub-protocol to illustrate the communication steps between prover and verifier.

---

[2] Obviously, the watermarked data itself reveals information about the watermark. However, this issue concerns the security of the embedding procedure, and the zero-knowledge watermark detection (ZKWMD) should only guarantee that the verifier gains no additional information after the run of ZKWMD.

1.1   Related Work

Since the first proposals in 1999 [5,6] there has been a lot of work on zero-knowledge watermark detection protocols, but only few of them can be considered to be reasonably secure. In this section we give a short overview of the relevant existing related work published so far, where we categorise and assess previous results regarding their strengths and limitations.

Before, we informally review the basic security requirements on zero-knowledge watermark detection protocols. They should ideally fulfil the following main requirements:

- *Hiding secret information:* The inputs required by the detection protocols do not reveal any information about the watermark, the detection key and the reference data. The "hiding"-requirement is of great importance, as it determines the information already leaked a-priori by the hidden detection inputs (without even running the protocol). A large class of proposed schemes uses only weakly hidden inputs, mainly because this significantly eases the design of the actual detection protocol.
- *Zero-knowledge:* A run of the protocol does not disclose any *new* information, i.e., information *beyond* the *positive detection result* and the *information already leaked by the protocol inputs.*
- *Soundness:* A dishonest prover should not be able to make a verifier falsely believe that the watermark, concealed in the input, is detectable in the given data.

The protocol proposed by Gopalakrishnan, Memon and Vora [6] encrypts each coefficient of the watermark using naive, i.e., non-probabilistic RSA encryption. As the message space of each coefficient is quite small (in the order of at most 2^{32} values) it is quite easy to compute a dictionary, mapping each coefficient to its ciphertext under the public key. Using this dictionary, an attacker can reverse lookup the plaintext of each watermark coefficient. Furthermore, a run of the protocol itself leaks a good approximation on the correlation value, which allows an attacker to mount sensitivity attacks.

The schemes proposed by Craver [5] do not even encrypt the watermarks, but only hide the plain-text watermark in a list of "fake" watermarks or permute the watermark coefficients. For the latter protocol, permuting the watermark coefficients, the hiding requirement is obviously only weakly fulfilled, because it leaks statistical properties like mean value or minimum coefficient value. The protocol hiding the real watermark in a list of fake watermarks faces a giant storage problem. Let us illustrate this fact by considering the following example: when hiding the plain-text watermark in a list of 2^{40} fake (indistinguishable) watermarks, a concealed real watermark, having 1000 coefficients (each of 16 bit length), would have a size of $2^{40} \cdot 1000 \cdot 16$ bit (=2048000 GB) and the detection protocol would require to perform 2^{40} watermark detections!

The advantage of using a weak encryption is that the verifier can simply detect the concealed watermark on his own by applying the standard detection algorithm and without requiring any interactive proof. An interactive proof is only used to prove that one of the detected watermarks (or its permutation) is *legal*, which is either defined as knowing the discrete logarithm of the watermark or knowing a graph isomorphism.

Furthermore, it is easy to see that the protocol hiding the watermark in a list of fake watermarks is *not zero-knowledge*: To break this scheme the attacker simply runs the protocol several times with the prover, each time removing *all but one watermark* WM_i in the list. Once the prover succeeds in proving that one of the detected watermarks, i.e., WM_i, is valid, the legal watermark has been identified and can be removed. Summarising, both the computation and the communication complexities of this protocol are impractical and unreasonably bad compared to the achieved level of security.

In a paper by Craver, Liu and Wolf [13] the authors attempt to improve the protocol's zero-knowledge property by embedding several $(l > 1)$ watermarks and hiding them in a list of f fake watermarks. However, applying the same attack as above allows the attacker to remove all legal watermarks by running the protocol $l + f$ times, each time deleting all but one watermark. Applying this attack in the context of dispute resolution would allow an attacker to remove all legal watermarks by loosing at most l lawsuits, which is significantly less than what is stated in [13]. l is a quite small number, as each embedded legal watermark adds significant noise to the data. To make it even worse, there is another issue with this protocol: the authors propose a concrete method to generate the fake watermarks by decomposing the original image. To make these fake watermarks indistinguishable from the legal watermarks, the fake watermarks should be whitened. Craver, Liu and Wolf propose to whiten the fake watermarks by permuting their coefficients. However, the authors overlooked that detection of permuted watermarks requires the data to be permuted in the same way, which leaks information about the whitening permutation. This may allow an attacker to revert the whitening process and, thereby, to distinguish fake from legal watermarks.

The approach proposed by Adelsbach and Sadeghi [4], which we follow in this paper, is to hide the detection inputs (watermark) in perfectly hiding commitments[3], which conceal the detection inputs even from strong attackers, having arbitrary computation power at their disposal. Building upon cryptographic zero-knowledge proofs, which prove relations on the committed detection inputs, these protocols prove in zero-knowledge that the detection statistic holds. As the sequential composition of zero-knowledge proofs is zero-knowledge again the overall protocol is zero-knowledge.

Jin [15] follows the same approach by Adelsbach and Sadeghi [4] and describes a protocol construction with the corresponding implementation of a zero-knowledge detection protocol for blind watermarking schemes. The main objective is to minimise the amount of exchanged communication traffic between prover and verifier. Unfortunately, this strategy requires the construction

---

[3] Commitments are cryptographic primitives to bind a party to a value, while at the same time concealing this value from another party [14].

and storage of a square matrix $W_{m,m}$ whose entries consist of the commitments of all possible binary products of the watermark coefficients, i.e., consider the vector of m watermark coefficients $WM = (WM_1, \ldots, WM_m)$, then the entry of the i-th row and the j-th column is $w_{i,j} = C_{WM_i \cdot WM_j}$. This leads to an asymptotically square order of storage and computation complexity when executing the protocol. Since practical instantiations of blind watermarking schemes often require more than 1000 coefficients (for example Piva et al. [16] suggests 16000) an enormous amount of storage and computation becomes necessary. For this reason, Jin's prototype implementation works on a 16×16 pixels image with a watermark of the same size.

Furthermore, Jin constructs a watermark detection protocol for the setting where the prover has no access to the alleged stego data while, normally, this data belongs to the common input of both prover and verifier. This case can occur if one single watermark has to be detected in many different alleged stego data sets[4]. As a drawback, the protocol assumes at least a *trusted* verifying party. The verifier computes the operations between committed watermarking coefficients and the public alleged stego data and passes the result to the prover. In this setting the prover has no opportunity to check whether commitment containing the correlation value was generated correctly such that an untrusted verifier can easily generate a commitment on an arbitrary correlation value, either larger or smaller than a publicly given detection threshold.

1.2   Some Limitation

Finally, we straighten out an important fact: Zero-knowledge watermark detection is still vulnerable against the same attacks as in the plaintext domain. The protocol is zero-knowledge in the cryptographic sense which means that the verifier is assured that some predicate (here presence of a concealed watermark) is fulfilled and gains no further information during a protocol run. For ZKWMD, one provides a detection result without revealing the underlying computation results. However, even being convinced of the validity of a predicate *is* some information in this special case if a verifier wants to perform some kind of *oracle* or so-called *sensitivity attacks* (see [17,18] or [19,20] for some recent publications). In our setting, a malicious verifier can try to manipulate the alleged stego-work W^* and ask for a proof of the presence of the watermark WM until this proof fails. However, it depends on the prover to recognize such an attempt and – for example – to restrict the number of runs of a proof protocol on a few image modifications per verifier – instead of arbitrary many trials. Acting this way a misuse of the prover as a stateless oracle can be avoided.

---

[4] Consider, for example, the case where the presence of a certain watermark is supposed to indicate to a DVD recorder that it is not allowed to record a copy of this given movie. It is expensive for the proving authority to keep a database containing all versions of all protected movies. Furthermore, transferring the entire movie to the proving instance to run the standard ZKWMD protocol causes too much communication traffic over the network.

1.3   Outline

Section 2 recapitulates the invoked watermarking scheme while Section 3 introduces the cryptographic primitives. In Section 5 and Section 6 we discuss all considerations and modifications of the original watermarking scheme when it is efficiently transform it into the zero-knowledge setting. In Sections 7 and 8 we present theoretical estimations and practical results of a prototype implementation concerning the expense of computation and the amount of exchanged data between prover and verifier.

2   Watermarking Schemes

This section provides a brief review of correlation-based watermarking schemes. We consider two well-established schemes by Cox et al. [9] and Piva et al. [16] which serve as representatives for two different flavours of correlation-based watermarking schemes.

2.1   Correlation-Based Watermarking Schemes

We describe a family of watermarking schemes that shares the common principle of *correlation-based* watermark detection. Most operations are processed in the frequency domain[5] $\hat{W}$ of the original data W that is derived by the transformation $\mathcal{T}$ as $\hat{W} := \mathcal{T}(W)$. In fact, any frequency domain transformation can be applied; of course, it depends on the concrete application which transformation is most suitable. The watermarking scheme consists of three components:

Generation: A vector WM of m watermark coefficients is generated as required in the concrete scheme.

Embedding: Let $\hat{W}^{[m]}$ denote the vector of m entries determined from $\hat{W}$ according some specific algorithm. The embedding of the watermark WM into the original data W is done in manipulating $\hat{W}^{[m]}$ by means of WM's entries. $\hat{W}'^{[m]}$ is the m-dimensional vector containing the result of the processing among $\hat{W}^{[m]}$ and WM. If one substitutes all manipulated coefficients $\hat{W}'^{[m]}$ in $\hat{W}$ one obtains the transformed *watermarked data* $\hat{W}'$ which results in the *watermarked data* W' when applying the inverse transformation $\mathcal{T}^{-1}$ on $\hat{W}'$ pursuant to $W' := \mathcal{T}^{-1}(\hat{W}')$.[6]

Detection: If a certain watermark WM has to be detected in a so-called *alleged stego-data* W^*, we usually compute some *correlation value corr* between WM and $\hat{W}^*$ (blind detection) respectively WM and the so-called *extracted watermark* WM^* from $\hat{W}^*$ (non-blind). This depends on the concrete detection method. If *corr* exceeds some predetermined threshold value S, the watermark is considered to be present ($corr \geq S$), otherwise absent ($corr < S$).

---

[5] However, there exist some watermarking schemes working in the spatial domain as well.

[6] However, there are watermarking schemes where applying transformation $\mathcal{T}$ and its inversion $\mathcal{T}^{-1}$ are not exactly a $1:1$ operation.

This general concept is applicable on any type of multimedia data which permits the transformation into the frequency domain: audio, video and still-image data.

2.2 Watermarking Scheme by Piva et al.

This watermarking system is suggested by Piva et al. in [16] and extensively described in [10]. It is a blind detection scheme designed to work on black and white still-images. However, it can be extended to coloured images [21] by combining the particular correlations of each colour space to one single correlation value. The experimental results presented in [16] demonstrate robustness against several signal processing techniques and geometric distortions, including JPEG compression, low pass and median filtering, histogram equalisation and stretching, Gaussian noise addition and cropping.

Generation: The WM vector consists of $m = 16000$ [16] coefficients of $N(0,1)$ distributed real values.

Embedding: To embed the watermark WM into a $N \times N$ picture W, we compute $\hat{W} := DCT(W)$ and determine the vector $\hat{W}^{[m]}$ applying the following strategy: In the DCT transformation of a $N \times N$ image the coefficient $\hat{W}_{0,0}$ represents the DC coefficient (see Figure 1). For most[7] pictures, the low frequency coefficients have the highest magnitude and are, therefore, most significant such that we have to consider them when we require robustness for the watermarking scheme. If the components for $\hat{W}^{[m]}$ are chosen from $\hat{W}_{i,j}$ in a zig-zag sequence as illustrated in Figure 1 we obtain these coefficients in an approximately decreasing magnitude, respectively significance. Embedding WM is proceeded according to the following Equation:

$$\hat{W'}_i^{[m]} = \hat{W}_i^{[m]} + \alpha \cdot \left| \hat{W}_i^{[m]} \right| \cdot WM_i \quad ; \quad i = 0, \ldots, m-1 \qquad (1)$$

Piva et al. [16] suggest to start the embedding of the coefficients at some position l of the zig-zag walk, respectively some diagonal d, in the zig-zag walk ($l = 25000$, which corresponds approximatively to the first position in diagonal $d = 223$) and, furthermore, to adopt the following m coefficients from $\hat{W}_{i,j}$ for $\hat{W}^{[m]}$ to achieve a tradeoff between imperceptibility and robustness.[8]

---

[7] There also exist counter-examples: The frequency transformation (e.g. FFT) of a screened photography, commonly used in newspapers, contains high-magnitude coefficients in the frequencies determined by the raster points' distance. Hence, here also exist high-magnitude (relevant) coefficients in the high frequency part of $\hat{W}$.

[8] After this processing step there exist a further method to enhance the robustness of the watermark by exploiting the characteristics of the Human Visual System (HVS), called *visual masking*. This approach represents a weighting strategy for the embedding factor α at each pixel in the spatial domain. In this way it is possible to increase the marking level α without compromising the watermark's imperceptibility. On the other hand, this visual masking has no influence on the detection equation such that for demonstration purposes we omitted this step and embedded WM with a constant factor of $\alpha = 0.2$ and without the masking procedure.

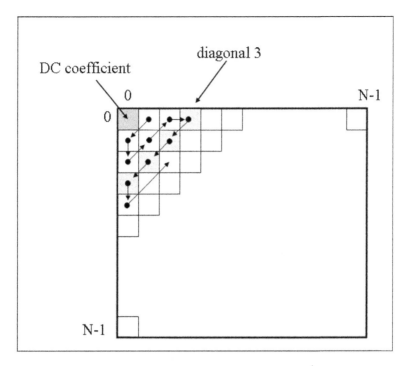

Fig. 1. Zig-zag selection for coefficients in $\hat{W}_{i,j}$

Detection: During watermark detection, the DCT is applied on some possibly modified work W^* and the same frequency coefficients are selected as in the embedding process to form the vector $\hat{W}*^{[m]}$. Since detection is blind, the correlation value is computed as

$$corr = \frac{1}{m} \cdot \sum_{i=0}^{m-1} \hat{W}*_{i}^{[m]} \cdot WM_i. \tag{2}$$

In comparing the correlation $corr$ to a predefined threshold value S we decide whether the given watermark WM is considered to be present ($corr \geq S$) or absent ($corr < S$). Piva et al [16] suggest the following estimation term for S which can be directly determined from W^*:

$$S = \frac{\alpha}{3m} \sum_{i=0}^{m-1} \left| \hat{W}*_{i}^{[m]} \right|. \tag{3}$$

2.3   Watermarking Scheme by Cox et al.

The following watermarking scheme was introduced by Cox et al. [9] for black and white still-images as the basis for our detection protocol. The authors claim that their proposed watermarking scheme is robust enough to survive the following image manipulations: low-pass filtering, JPEG compression, cropping, dithering and printing-xeroxing-scanning and several others.

Generation: The watermark vector WM consists of m (in the order of 1000) independently chosen $N(0, 1)$-distributed coefficients.

Embedding: The discrete cosine transformation (DCT) is applied to the original image, resulting in $\hat{W}$. Let $\hat{W}^{[m]}$ denote the m coefficients carrying the watermark information which corresponds here to the m highest magnitude AC-coefficients in $\hat{W}$. Cox et al. originally propose three different equations[9] to embed the watermark, yielding the m-dimensional vector $\hat{W'}^{[m]}$ of marked coefficients $\hat{W'}_i^{[m]}$ for $i = 0, \ldots, m - 1$:

$$\hat{W'}_i^{[m]} = \hat{W}_i^{[m]} + \alpha \cdot WM_i \tag{4}$$

$$\hat{W'}_i^{[m]} = \hat{W}_i^{[m]} \cdot (1 + \alpha \cdot WM_i) \tag{5}$$

where the constant α denotes the strength of embedding.

Substituting $\hat{W'}^{[m]}$ in $\hat{W}$ (at the corresponding positions) and applying the inverse discrete cosine transformation DCT^{-1} results in the watermarked image W'.

Detection: To decide whether a given watermark WM is contained in image W^* we extract a watermark candidate WM^* whose correlation value is computed against the watermark WM. In this extraction we first compute $\hat{W} = DCT(W)$ and $\hat{W}^* = DCT(W^*)$. Afterwards, we choose $\hat{W}^{[m]}$ as the m-highest magnitude coefficients of $\hat{W}$. $\hat{W}^{*[m]}$ is determined as the coefficients of $\hat{W}^*$ at the same positions as for the choice of $\hat{W}^{[m]}$. Then WM^* is obtained by inverting the embedding equation (see Section 5.1). Finally, we compute the correlation

$$corr = \frac{< WM, WM^* >}{\sqrt{< WM^*, WM^* >}} \tag{6}$$

and compare it to some given threshold S. If $corr \geq S$ then WM is considered to be present. Otherwise it is considered to be absent.

3   Cryptographic Primitives and Notation

This section offers an overview of the main cryptographic primitives which are applied to construct the detection protocols: zero-knowledge proof systems and homomorphic commitment schemes.

---

[9] As the third embedding equation $\hat{W'}_i^{[m]} = \hat{W}_i^{[m]} \cdot \left(e^{\alpha \cdot WM_i}\right)$ is commonly not used in practice, we omit its further discussion.

3.1 Commitment Schemes

A *commitment scheme* is a cryptographic protocol that allows one party, the so-called *committer* C, to commit himself to a message $s \in M$ from the message space M, such that the *recipient* R of the commitment is assured that C is unable to change the value of s afterwards (*binding property*). At the same time s is kept secret from the recipient R (*hiding property*).

Protocols. A commitment scheme consists of two main protocol steps:

1. Commit(): To commit to a certain message $s \in M$, C runs the algorithm $(C_s, sk_{C_s}) \leftarrow \mathsf{commit}\,(s)$ to obtain the commitment C_s to s and the corresponding *secret key* sk_{C_s} that allows C to open C_s correctly in the Open() protocol. The committer passes C_s to the recipient who saves it for further use.
2. Open(): To open C_s to R, C sends the message s and the corresponding secret key sk_{C_s} to the recipient. With this information R is able to verify s regarding the previously received commitment C_s. If the verification has been successful, R outputs the message s, otherwise he rejects. We denote such a successful protocol run[10] as $(C : -; R : s) \leftarrow \mathsf{Open}(C : s, sk_{C_s}; R : -; C_s)$

We refer to [14] for a detailed introduction to commitment schemes.

A concrete scheme. We use the Damgård-Fujisaki (DF) integer commitment scheme [22] in our protocol. A commitment to a message $s \in \mathbb{Z}$ is computed as $C_s := g^s h^{sk_{C_s}} \mod n$, where n is the product of two safe primes, h is the generator of a large subgroup of $\mathbb{Z}_n^*$, i.e. $g \in \langle h \rangle$ and $\log_h g$ is unknown to C. g, h and n form together with some other public (security) parameters (cf. Section 7) in the so-called *commitment description* $descr_{com}$. Instantiated in this manner, the DF commitment scheme is *statistically hiding* and *computationally binding* under the *strong RSA assumption*[11].

Homomorphic property. The structure of the DF commitment scheme allows R to perform computations on secret values without knowledge of opening information. This feature permits a higher efficiency in the watermark detection

---

[10] This notation is motivated the following way: A *protocol* Prot consists of two or more parties, each of them performing local computations and exchanging messages with other participants. A protocol with the two participants A and B is characterised by the following input and output parameters: The *common input* c is known to both parties while the *individual input* in_A respectively in_B is only available to A and B. After the execution of the protocol each party outputs its *individual message* out_A and out_B. A protocol run is denoted as

$$(A : out_A; B : out_B) \leftarrow \mathsf{Prot}(A : in_A; B : in_B; c)$$

[11] Given an RSA modulus n and an element $u \in \mathbb{Z}_n^*$, the strong RSA assumption states that it is hard to compute values $e > 1$ and v such that $v^e \equiv u \mod n$.

protocol. Let C_x and C_y be two commitments to the secret values x and y and γ be some publicly known integer.

1. The product $C_x \cdot C_y$ can be opened as $x + y$ as follows:

$$(\mathcal{C} : -; \mathcal{R} : x + y) \leftarrow \texttt{Open}(\mathcal{C} : x + y, sk_{C_x} + sk_{C_y}; \mathcal{R} : -; C_x \cdot C_y),$$

   i.e., $\mathcal{R}$ can autonomously compute C_{x+y}.
2. $(C_x)^\gamma$ can be opened as $\gamma \cdot x$ as follows:

$$(\mathcal{C} : -; \mathcal{R} : \gamma \cdot x) \leftarrow \texttt{Open}(\mathcal{C} : \gamma \cdot x, \gamma \cdot sk_{C_x}; \mathcal{R} : -; C_x^\gamma),$$

   i.e., $\mathcal{R}$ can autonomously compute $C_{\gamma \cdot x}$.
3. $C_x \cdot g^\gamma$ can be opened as $\gamma + x$ as follows:

$$(\mathcal{C} : -; \mathcal{R} : \gamma + x) \leftarrow \texttt{Open}(\mathcal{C} : \gamma + x, sk_{C_x}; \mathcal{R} : -; C_x \cdot g^\gamma),$$

   i.e., $\mathcal{R}$ can autonomously compute $C_{\gamma+x}$.

3.2   Zero-Knowledge Proof Systems

Interactive two-party proof systems involve a *prover* $\mathcal{P}$ and a *verifier* $\mathcal{V}$ where each of them has its own *private input* and both have access to some given *common input*. In our context, the common input consists of commitments of which $\mathcal{P}$ is aware of the secret messages and the corresponding secret keys as its private input. Applying such proof systems $\mathcal{P}$ convinces $\mathcal{V}$ that he is indeed able to open the commitments, provided as common input, correctly and that certain relations hold among their secret messages. There exist three security requirements for these proof systems: *Completeness:* If $\mathcal{P}$ and $\mathcal{V}$ act honestly, every run of the proof system will be accepted by $\mathcal{V}$. *Soundness* guarantees that a cheating prover (who is not able to open the underlying commitments) can make $\mathcal{V}$ accept the proof protocol only with a negligible probability. Finally, the *zero-knowledge* requirement guarantees that $\mathcal{V}$ gains no new knowledge from a protocol run beyond the assertion that has been proven.

We will make use of several elementary zero-knowledge proof protocols shown in Table 1, which prove the multiplicative relation ($\texttt{PoK}_{mult}()$), the square relation ($\texttt{PoK}_{sq}()$) and the equality relation on committed values ($\texttt{PoK}_{eq}()$). We use the multiplication protocol proposed by Damgård and Fujisaki [22], while the square and the equality proof are adapted from Boudot [23]. Finally, we use a proof system $\texttt{PoK}_{\geq 0}()$ which proves that a committed value is greater or equal to zero. An elegant proof system has been suggested by Lipmaa [24] and is based on a number theoretical result by Lagrange [25,26], which states that every positive integer x can be represented as a sum of four squares, i.e. $x = x_1^2 + x_2^2 + x_3^2 + x_4^2$. Hence, the proof system $\texttt{PoK}_{\geq 0}()$ can be composed by 4 square proofs, the homomorphic addition of $C_{x_1^2}, \ldots, C_{x_4^2}$ and the proof of an equality relation for $C_{x_1^2+x_2^2+x_3^2+x_4^2}$ and C_x. $\texttt{PoK}_{open}()$ convinces a verifier that the prover is able to successfully run an open protocol step on C_x. All other

Table 1. Elementary sub-protocols and relations

Relation	Abbreviation	Application
open	$\mathsf{PoK}_{open}()$	$\mathsf{PoK}_{open}(C_x)$
equality	$\mathsf{PoK}_{eq}()$	$\mathsf{PoK}_{eq}(C_x, C_y)$
multiplication	$\mathsf{PoK}_{mult}()$	$\mathsf{PoK}_{mult}(C_c; C_a, C_b)$
squaring	$\mathsf{PoK}_{sq}()$	$\mathsf{PoK}_{sq}(C_{x^2}, C_x)$
greater or equal zero	$\mathsf{PoK}_{\geq 0}()$	$\mathsf{PoK}_{\geq 0}(C_x)$

elementary proofs convince a verifier that the corresponding relation hold and furthermore implicitly include that the prover is aware of all corresponding secret keys of the commitments provided as common input.

Typically, zero-knowledge proofs are executed as interactive challenge-response protocols. However, there exists an efficient transformation to convert the interactive protocol version into a non-interactive setting in the random oracle model [27] where the prover performs a complete precomputation of a proof and passes it to the verifier. Our implementation uses the elementary sub-proofs in this efficient proof mode.

We will give the computational complexity of all protocols in terms of modular exponentiations (E), modular inversions (I) and modular multiplications (M), as these operations dominate their complexities. With $\mathsf{Comp}_{\mathcal{P}}$ we denote the *computational complexity* of the prover, whereas $\mathsf{Comp}_{\mathcal{V}}$ refers to that of the verifier. L denotes the computation expense of a 4-square Lagrange decomposition, for which an efficient probabilistic algorithm can be found in [28]. With $\mathsf{Comm}_{(\mathcal{P}, \mathcal{V})}$ we denote the *communication complexity*, measured as the number of bits exchanged between $\mathcal{P}$ and $\mathcal{V}$.

The complexities of the basic protocols mainly depend on the security parameters of the DF commitment scheme, namely $|n|$, k, T, B and $C(k)$ (which we will denote in the following as ℓ_n, $\ell_\varnothing$, ℓ_T, ℓ_B and ℓ_F). The security parameters are related to each other in the following way: $\ell_n = |n|$, $\ell_\varnothing = k$, $\ell_T = |T|$, $\ell_F = |C(k)|$ and $\ell_B = B$. ℓ_n denotes the binary length of the strong RSA modulus. ℓ_B is an estimator for the upper bound of the order of $\langle h \rangle$, such that $ord(\langle h \rangle) \leq 2^{\ell_B}$, while ℓ_T specifies the message space $\mathcal{M} = [-2^{\ell_T}, 2^{\ell_T}]$. We use the parameter $\ell_\varnothing$ to limit the maximum statistical distance (statistical zero knowledge property) between an accepting real and a simulated[12] protocol run which is less than $2^{-\ell_\varnothing}$. ℓ_F determines the binary length of the challenge size and therefore the

---

[12] The zero-knowledge property is defined by the conception of a so-called *simulator* as follows: A simulator is a probabilistic polynomial-time algorithm that is able to generate an accepting protocol run given the common input of *without* the prover's secret input and having black box access to the verifier. It is indistinguishable, whether a given protocol run was obtained during an interaction between prover and verifier or was computed by the simulator. For the statistical zero-knowledge property, the statistical distance between the probability distributions of the simulated and the real protocol runs is negligible small. A more detailed explanation can be found for example in [29].

security parameter for the proof's soundness. As such, it limits the probability that a cheating prover is able to carry out an accepting proof[13] to $< 2^{-\ell_F}$. For further details regarding these parameters we refer to [22].

Table 2 gives an overview of $\mathsf{Comp}_\mathcal{P}$, $\mathsf{Comp}_\mathcal{V}$ and $\mathsf{Comm}_{(\mathcal{P},\mathcal{V})}$, including the communication complexity for reasonably chosen security parameters (cf. Section 7). The binary length of exchanged messages $\mathsf{Comm}_{(\mathcal{P},\mathcal{V})}$ is the summary of the binary length of all exchanged messages which is determined by the security parameters. The value for $\mathsf{PoK}_{eq}()$ indicated in column 4 of Table 2 can be verified by inspecting the detailed protocol run in the Appendix. As a matter of fact, $\mathsf{Comm}_{(\mathcal{P},\mathcal{V})}$ indicates a lower bound that any practical implementation cannot fall below.

Table 2. Communication and computation complexities in the non-interactive proof mode

Relation	$\mathsf{Comp}_\mathcal{P}$	$\mathsf{Comp}_\mathcal{V}$	$\mathsf{Comm}_{\mathcal{P},\mathcal{V}}$	[KBytes]
$\mathsf{PoK}_{open}()$	$2E + 3M$	$3E + I + 2M$	$3\ell_F + \ell_T + 3\ell_\varnothing + \ell_B + 2$	0.23
$\mathsf{PoK}_{mult}()$	$6E + 9M$	$9E + 3I + 6M$	$6\ell_F + 3\ell_T + 8\ell_\varnothing + 3\ell_B + 5$	0.66
$\mathsf{PoK}_{sq}()$	$4E + 6M$	$6E + 2I + 4M$	$4\ell_F + 2\ell_T + 5\ell_\varnothing + 2\ell_B + 3$	0.44
$\mathsf{PoK}_{eq}()$	$4E + 5M$	$6E + 2I + 4M$	$4\ell_F + \ell_T + 5\ell_\varnothing + 2\ell_B + 3$	0.38
$\mathsf{PoK}_{\geq 0}()$	$38E + 42M + L$	$30E + 10I + 23M$	$8\ell_n + 20\ell_F + 9\ell_T + 25\ell_\varnothing$ $+10\ell_B + 15$	3.13

Technical Remark. Watermarking schemes require computations on real numbers, while the applied DF commitment scheme supports integers. However, by scaling all real values by an appropriate factor λ (in our implementation we chose $\lambda = 10^{10}$) and discarding additional decimal places we can perform all required computations in the integer domain. For instance, the relation $a \cdot b = c$ is scaled as $\lfloor \lambda_a a \rfloor \cdot \lfloor \lambda_b b \rfloor = \lfloor \lambda_a \lambda_b \cdot c \rfloor$.

A concrete example: Let $a = 1.345$, $b = 57.387$ and employ a scaling factor of $\lambda = 10^6$ for both a and b then the result c has to be scaled by 10^{12} in further computations according to the following equation: $(10^6 \cdot 1.345) \cdot (10^6 \cdot 57.387) = 1345000 \cdot 57387000 = 77185515000000 = 10^{12} \cdot 77.185515$.

4   General Steps for Protocol Construction

To incorporate a watermarking scheme into a zero-knowledge protocol one has to consider the following issues:

1. Inverting the embedding equations as a preparation step for computing the correlation has to be performed in an efficient way.

---

[13] The challenge is chosen randomly from $[0, 2^{\ell_F}[$ (cf. Appendix). In fact, the prover can convince the verifier without knowing the claimed secret if and only if the challenge is 0. Otherwise he is able to break some cryptographic assumptions which is considered to be computationally infeasible.

2. The recovery of the positions where the watermark vector is embedded and which is normally derived from the original data is not possible anymore in a straightforward manner.
3. The detection criterion has to be transformed into a polynomial expression to be efficiently processed by the elementary zero-knowledge protocols presented in Section 3.

4.1 Proving the Absence of a Given Watermark

Both of the two watermark detection protocols presented in Section 5 and Section 6 can be turned into a proof of knowledge that a given committed watermark is *not* contained in some given alleged stego-work W^*. A watermark is considered to be present if $corr \geq S$ respectively $corr - S \geq 0$. Hence, the absence is shown as $corr - S \leq 0$ respectively $S - corr \geq 0$ since this relation can be proven by $\mathrm{PoK}_{\geq 0}()$. The modifications in the protocols are straightforward.

5 Constructing Proof for Cox's Scheme

5.1 Embedding Equations

The first step of the detection algorithm is to extract WM^* from the alleged stego-image $\hat{W}^*$, which, in non-blind detection, additionally involves the original image $\hat{W}$. In zero-knowledge watermark detection, $\mathcal{V}$ is only aware of the committed version $C_{\hat{W}}$ of $\hat{W}$ such that, after the extraction, he has to be convinced in zero-knowledge that the content of $C_{WM^*} := (C_{WM^*_1}, \ldots, C_{WM^*_m})$ has been obtained correctly.

Equation 1: If WM was embedded according to Equation (4)

$$\hat{W'}_i^{[m]} = \hat{W}_i^{[m]} + \alpha \cdot WM_i$$

then WM^* is obtained[14] as

$$\Delta_i := \alpha \cdot WM^*_i = \hat{W}^*{}_i^{[m]} - \hat{W}_i^{[m]} \tag{7}$$

such that Δ_i is a difference of committed values, which can be easily computed in the committed domain by taking advantage of the homomorphic property of the commitment scheme.

Equation 2: In this case

$$\hat{W'}_i^{[m]} = \hat{W}_i^{[m]} \cdot (1 + \alpha \cdot WM_i).$$

Δ_i is obtained as the quotient

---

[14] We invert to $\Delta_i := \alpha \cdot WM^*_i$ instead of WM^*_i because with Δ_i in the detection inequality the construction of an efficient protocol is easier to achieve, cf. Section 5.3.

$$\Delta_i := \alpha \cdot WM^*{}_i = \frac{\hat{W}^*{}_i^{[m]} - \hat{W}_i^{[m]}}{\hat{W}_i^{[m]}}. \tag{8}$$

To convince $\mathcal{V}$ in the committed domain that Δ_i in C_{Δ_i} has been computed correctly as $\Delta_i = \hat{W}^*{}_i^{[m]} \cdot \left(\hat{W}_i^{[m]} \right)^{-1} - 1$ an additional zero-knowledge proof has to be performed. Therefore, the computation of C_{Δ_i} at the beginning of the detection protocol described in Section 5.4 has to be extended by an additional multiplication subproof and a proof that $\left(\hat{W}_i^{[m]} \right)^{-1}$ was computed correctly.[15] Clearly, the entire detection protocol can be extended by the described subproofs, but this introduces additional overhead. Hence, embedding the watermark with Equation (4) yields a more efficient zero-knowledge watermark detection protocol.

5.2 Determination of $\hat{W}^*{}^{[m]}$

The original methodology in Cox's watermarking scheme (see Section 2.3) requires to select the coefficients of $\hat{W}$ with the m-highest magnitudes to construct $\hat{W}^*{}^{[m]}$ and $\hat{W}^{[m]}$. In the context of zero-knowledge watermark detection, this cannot be done in a straightforward way, since $\mathcal{V}$ only knows the committed version $C_{\hat{W}^{[m]}}$ of the original transformed image $\hat{W}$. We describe two possible viable solutions to overcome this problem:

Solution 1: This method provides a generic solution which is applicable to *every* correlation-based watermarking scheme whose detection criterion can be expressed as a polynomial of the inputs required for the detection. The general idea of this solution is that WM is chosen as large as the image size (e.g., $m = N \cdot N$) and that all positions i, not supposed to be marked, are set to value $WM_i := 0$. In this case no selection for $\hat{W}^*{}^{[m]}$ and $\hat{W}^{[m]}$ is required at all and *corr* remains unaffected as well. Unfortunately, this general approach involves a significant computation overhead, as the number m of coefficients that have to be processed becomes quite large.

Solution 2: Here we consider the *special case* where the embedding positions are public parameters of the watermarking scheme and, therefore, can be given as common input to both parties, thus yielding more efficient detection protocols. One possibility to obtain these fixed embedding positions has been proposed by Piva et al [16] and works as follows: Embed WM along a zig-zag scan of the AC coefficients similar to the walk in the JPEG compression algorithm (but on the entire $N \times N$ DCT-transformed image). Embedding of the watermark begins at a predetermined diagonal d (cf. Figure1), which becomes part of the common

---

[15] This can be achieved by proving the multiplicative relation $\text{PoK}_{mult}(C_z, C_{\left(\hat{W}_i^{[m]}\right)^{-1}},$ $C_{\hat{W}_i^{[m]}})$ and that z is close enough to 1. The latter can be proven by an interval proof [23] that $z \in [1 - \delta, 1 + \delta]$ for a reasonable small δ.

input. d is chosen such that a sufficient number of low-frequency AC coefficients is used for embedding. This methodology matches the required choice of significant coefficients in $\hat{W}$ for embedding WM, since for most images the low-frequency coefficients mainly coincide with the highest magnitude coefficients of $\hat{W}$. One obtains a watermarking scheme to Cox's methodology but the corresponding ZKWMD protocol is far more efficient.

5.3   The Detection Relation

We have to transform the detection criterion $corr \geq S$ respectively $corr - S \geq 0$ such that the computation of $corr$ can be expressed as a polynomial term. Substituting Equation (6) into $corr - S \geq 0$ leads to

$$\sum_{i=0}^{m-1} WM_i \cdot WM^*{}_i \; - \; S \cdot \sqrt{\sum_{i=0}^{m-1} (WM^*{}_i)^2} \; \geq \; 0.$$

The detection threshold S can be chosen as $S \geq 0$ [9]. For the committed setting it is important to know that if WM is present, then $\sum_{i=0}^{m-1} WM_i \cdot WM^*{}_i \geq 0$ also holds. In this case one could square the inequality to dispose the root term. This is because otherwise the protocol would become more costly since one cannot efficiently process the square root with the given zero-knowledge protocol primitives. Otherwise, it is already evident in this protocol stage that WM is not present and can omit further computations (cf. Section 5.4).

Now the resulting term has a polynomial form which allows us to apply the zero-knowledge protocol primitives. A multiplication with α^2 enables us to use $\Delta_i := \alpha \cdot WM_i$ directly from Equation (7 - 8) which leads to

$$\underbrace{\left(\sum_{i=0}^{m-1} WM_i \cdot \Delta_i \right)^2}_{=:A} \; - \; S^2 \cdot \underbrace{\sum_{i=0}^{m-1} \Delta_i^2}_{=:B} \; \geq \; 0. \tag{9}$$

An intermediate computation of C_{Δ_i}, C_{A^2} and C_B and a proof that $A^2 - B \geq 0$ in C_{A^2-B} convinces a verifier that a given committed watermark C_{WM} is present in W^*.

Certainly, the entire protocol becomes less sophisticated if one assumes a detection criterion $S \geq WM \cdot WM^*$ without any denominator. However, in the zero-knowledge setting, one cannot simply multiply Equation (6) by $\sqrt{< WM^*, WM^* >}$ because this value is obtained from $\hat{W}^{[m]}$, which is cryptographically concealed from the verifier by $C_{\hat{W}^{[m]}}$. Making it public as a new detection threshold $S \cdot \sqrt{< WM^*, WM^* >}$ would leak knowledge about WM^*.

5.4   The Entire Protocol

The common input to the protocol shown in Figure 2 consists of the commitments C_{WM}, $C_{\hat{W}^{[m]}}$, the commitment description $descr_{com}$, W^*, the watermark

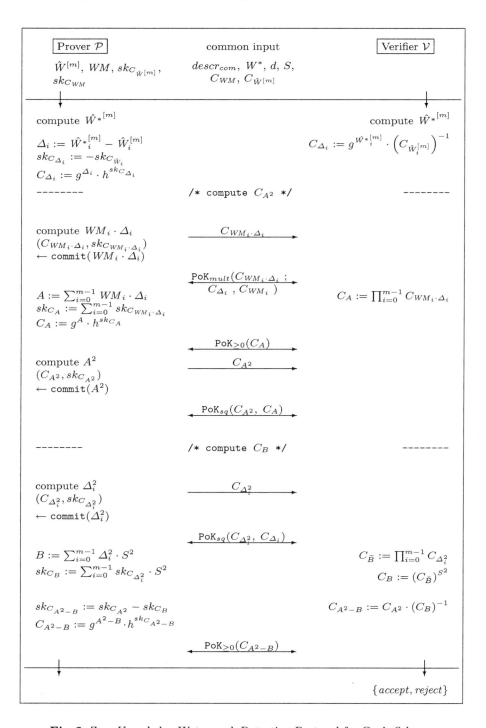

Fig. 2. Zero-Knowledge Watermark Detection Protocol for Cox's Scheme

position d and the detection threshold S. Furthermore, $\mathcal{P}$ knows the plain-text version of WM and $\hat{W}^{[m]}$ as well as the corresponding secret opening information of the commitments.

First, $\mathcal{P}$ and $\mathcal{V}$ compute $\hat{W}*^{[m]}$ according to the JPEG-analog zig-zag heuristic, starting at diagonal d. In several stages, $\mathcal{P}$ and $\mathcal{V}$ interactively compute the required committed intermediate results C_Δ, C_{A^2} and C_B. Finally, $\mathcal{P}$ proves to $\mathcal{V}$ that the detection equation (9) is satisfied. This is proceeded as follows:

1. $\mathcal{V}$ computes all m components C_{Δ_i} of C_Δ homomorphically as $C_{\Delta_i} := g^{\hat{W}*_i^{[m]}} \cdot \left(C_{\hat{W}_i^{[m]}}\right)^{-1}$.
2. The committed addends for C_A, i.e., $C_{WM_i \cdot \Delta_i}$, have to be provided by $\mathcal{P}$ and $\mathcal{P}$ initiates m subproofs $\mathsf{PoK}_{mult}()$ to convince $\mathcal{V}$ that the products contained in $C_{WM_i \cdot \Delta_i}$ are correct.
3. $\mathcal{V}$ can compute C_A homomorphically on his own as $C_A := \prod_{i=0}^{m-1} C_{WM_i \cdot \Delta_i}$.
4. Before the squaring step, $\mathcal{P}$ has to prove that A contained in C_A is greater or equal to zero. Otherwise, this would imply that $corr$ in Equation (6) is < 0 and $\mathcal{V}$ would be assured already in this stage of the protocol that WM is not present in W^* and aborts the protocol. Finally, $\mathcal{P}$ generates C_{A^2}, sends it to $\mathcal{V}$ and proves in zero-knowledge that C_{A^2} indeed contains the square of the value A contained in C_A.
5. The value B of Equation (9) is determined: $\mathcal{P}$ provides $C_{\Delta_i^2}$ and proves that $C_{\Delta_i^2}$ indeed contains the square of the value Δ_i contained in C_{Δ_i}.
6. $\mathcal{V}$ can compute C_B and C_{A^2-B} by making use of the commitment scheme's homomorphic property.
7. The watermark detection protocol is completed by a proof that the value $A^2 - B$, contained in C_{A^2-B}, is greater or equal to 0.

Completeness of the protocol follows from the completeness of all sub-protocols and the homomorphic property of the commitment scheme. The *soundness* of the entire protocol holds, because $\mathcal{P}$ would either have to break the soundness of at least one sub-protocol or the binding property of the commitment scheme. As both is assumed to be computationally infeasible, soundness of the overall protocol follows. The *zero-knowledge* property follows from the zero-knowledge property of the sub-protocols (composition theorem) and from the fact that additional communication consists of commitments, which are statistically hiding.

5.5   Remark

In some applications one may omit the first of the two subprotocols for a test greater or equal to zero of a committed value, i.e. $\mathsf{PoK}_{\geq 0}(C_A)$ before squaring A. For practical reasons the probability that an attacker is able to generate a negative correlated version of WM^* (which fulfils $corr^2 > S^2$) is considered as unlikely as the construction of a positive correlated fake watermark. This is a deviation of the original detection rule [9] and therefore the consequences for false positive detection have to be reconsidered, because additional watermarks fulfilling the modified correlation test occur. All in all, in an instantiation of the protocol with 1000 coefficients, leaving out one $\mathrm{PoK}_{\geq 0}()$ does hardly affect the performance results: $\mathrm{PoK}_{\geq 0}()$ causes 3.13 KBytes compared to 1.4 MBytes for a complete run (Table 2 and Table 3) and the dimensions for the computation complexity are similar.

6   Constructing Piva's Protocol

In contrast to the previous watermarking scheme only the watermark data is cryptographically concealed and its embedding position is determined by public constants. It turns out that only the transformation of the detection criterion into a polynomial form has to be considered. The resulting protocol becomes very simple which allows a fast and efficient implementation.

6.1   The Detection Relation

If WM is present in W^* then $corr \geq S$. This criterion can be rearranged such that all computations is verified applying the basic zero-knowledge protocols from Section 3 and taking advantage of the homomorphic property of the commitment scheme.

$$corr \geq S$$

We insert Equations (2) for $corr$ and (3) for S and obtain

$$\frac{1}{m} \cdot \sum_{i=0}^{m-1} \hat{W}*_i^{[m]} \cdot WM_i \geq \frac{\alpha}{3m} \sum_{i=0}^{m-1} \left| \hat{W}*_i^{[m]} \right|$$

$$\Longleftrightarrow \quad \underbrace{\sum_{i=0}^{m-1} \hat{W}*_i^{[m]} \cdot WM_i}_{=:corr'} \geq \underbrace{\frac{\alpha}{3} \sum_{i=0}^{m-1} \left| \hat{W}*_i^{[m]} \right|}_{=:S'}$$

$$\Longleftrightarrow \quad \underbrace{\sum_{i=0}^{m-1} \hat{W}*_i^{[m]} \cdot WM_i - \frac{\alpha}{3} \sum_{i=0}^{m-1} \left| \hat{W}*_i^{[m]} \right|}_{corr'-S'} \geq 0 \qquad (10)$$

6.2   The Concrete Protocol

The zero-knowledge protocol for the watermark detection by Piva et al. is shown in Figure 3. The common input consists of the committed watermark vector C_{WM}, the commitment description $descr_{com}$, the alleged stego-image W^* and the watermark embedding position l. Furthermore, $\mathcal{P}$ is aware of the plaintext watermark vector WM and all necessary secret commitment keys $sk_{C_{WM}}$ as its private input. The protocol is carried out as follows:

1. $\mathcal{P}$ and $\mathcal{V}$ construct $\hat{W}*^{[m]}$ and compute S'.
2. $\mathcal{P}$ proves that he knows how to open all C_{WM_i}.
3. All computation for $corr'$ and $C_{corr'-S'}$ is done autonomously by both parties via homomorphic operations offered by the commitment scheme. $\mathcal{P}$ is able to perform its computations directly on the secret values and the corresponding blinders (i.e., secret commitment keys sk) such that it saves most computationally expensive exponentiations.
4. A proof of knowledge is executed which proves that $corr'-S'$, contained in $C_{corr'-S'}$, is greater or equal to zero. If $\mathcal{V}$ accepts all sub-proofs then he is convinced that $corr'$ was computed correctly and that $corr'-S' \geq 0$, which implies that WM is indeed present in W^* just as required in Equation (10).

Completeness, soundness and the *zero-knowledge* property of the entire proof system hold analogously to Cox's protocol in Section 5.

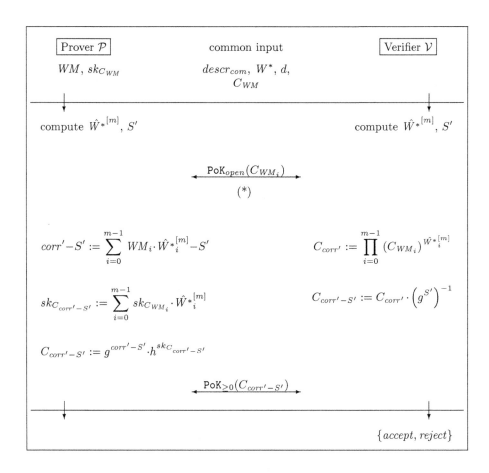

Fig. 3. Zero-Knowledge Watermark Detection Protocol for Piva's Scheme

6.3 Significant Speedup for Precomputation

We point out a remarkable optimisation in the protocol shown in Figure 3: After the proofs that all commitments on the watermarking coefficients C_{WM} can be opened correctly – marked by (*) – only homomorphic operations are performed, except the final $\mathsf{PoK}_{\geq 0}()$. The commitment scheme's special structure permits this construction. This brings an advantage for practical applications where the same watermark has to be detected in many different data. Hence, all proofs how to open $\mathsf{PoK}_{open}()$ can be executed once for all following detection processes. The homomorphic operations require much less time consuming operations as necessary for zero-knowledge sub-protocols such that the rest of the protocol can be terminated very quickly. Table 5 in Section 8 illustrates this result.

The construction for Cox's detection protocol is more sophisticated since here the committed values from the original image are involved as well.

7 Theoretical Bounds for Efficiency

Starting from the amount of transmitted bits and computations required for the deployed subprotocols and operations on commitments we are able to give estimations on the communication and computation complexity for the constructed protocols. The obtained estimation for the communication complexity indicates a lower bound of transmitted bits under which any practical implementation will not fall. It serves as a measure of quality of the obtained implementation.

7.1 Piva's Scheme

The communication complexity of Protocol 3, when implemented as a sequential composition of the non-interactive subproofs in the random oracle model is given by the following equation:

$$
\begin{aligned}
\mathsf{Comm}^{WM\,Piva} &= m \cdot \mathsf{Comm}^{\mathsf{PoK}_{open}()} + \mathsf{Comm}^{\mathsf{PoK}_{\geq 0}()} \\
&= m \cdot (3\ell_F + \ell_T + 3\ell_\varnothing + \ell_B + 2) \\
&\quad + (8\ell_n + 20\ell_F + 9\ell_T + 25\ell_\varnothing + 10\ell_B + 15) \\
&= 8\ell_n + (3m + 20)\ell_F + (m + 9)\ell_T \\
&\quad + (3m + 25)\ell_\varnothing + (m + 10)\ell_B + 2m + 15
\end{aligned}
$$

If we assume a watermark size of $m = 16000$ coefficients [16], then about 3710 KBytes $\approx$ 3.6 MBytes have to be transferred, excluding any network or implementation overhead. The protocol in Figure 3 demonstrates that a large amount of traffic can be saved when most of the computations are done taking advantage of homomorphic operations without any interaction.

The computation complexity is discussed separately for each party. The generation of $\hat{W}*^{[m]}$ will be neglected in computation complexity as it is not part of the very zero-knowledge watermark detection protocol. We first consider $\mathcal{V}$'s computation complexity: In addition to the computation steps within the zero-knowledge subprotocols, $\mathcal{V}$ executes m exponentiations and $m-1$ multiplications to obtain $C_{corr'}$ and one exponentiation, one multiplication and one inversion to compute $C_{corr'-S'}$, such that

$$
\begin{aligned}
\mathsf{Comp}_{\mathcal{V}}^{WM\,Piva} &= m \cdot \mathsf{Comp}_{\mathcal{V}}^{\mathsf{PoK}_{open}()} + \mathsf{Comp}_{\mathcal{V}}^{\mathsf{PoK}_{\geq 0}()} + (m+1)\cdot E + 1\cdot I + m\cdot M \\
&= m\cdot(3\cdot E + 1\cdot I + 2\cdot M) + (30\cdot E + 10\cdot I + 23\cdot M) \\
&\quad + (m+1)\cdot E + 1\cdot I + m\cdot M \\
&= (4m+31)\cdot E + (m+11)\cdot I + (3m+23)\cdot M
\end{aligned}
$$

During its homomorphic operations, $\mathcal{P}$ is able to directly process the secret values and blinders of their corresponding commitments such that the following operations are necessary:

- computation of $corr' - S'$ in plain-text: $m\cdot M$
- computation of $sk_{C_{corr'-S'}}$: $m\cdot M$
- computation of $C_{corr'-S'}$ as $(g^{corr'-S'}\cdot h^{sk_{C_{corr'-S'}}}) \mod n$: $2\cdot E + 1\cdot M$

Hence, $\mathcal{P}$'s computation complexity is:

$$
\begin{aligned}
\mathsf{Comp}_{\mathcal{P}}^{WM\,Piva} &= m\cdot\mathsf{Comp}_{\mathcal{P}}^{\mathsf{PoK}_{open}()} + \mathsf{Comp}_{\mathcal{P}}^{\mathsf{PoK}_{\geq 0}()} + 2\cdot E + (2m+1)\cdot M \\
&= m\cdot(2\cdot E + 3\cdot M) + (38\cdot E + 42\cdot M + L) + 2\cdot E + (2m+1)\cdot M \\
&= (2m+40)\cdot E + (5m+43)\cdot M + L
\end{aligned}
$$

This leads to a total computation complexity of

$$
\mathsf{Comp}_{(\mathcal{P},\mathcal{V})}^{WM\,Piva} = (6\cdot m + 71)\cdot E + (m+11)\cdot I + (8\cdot m + 66)\cdot M + L.
$$

7.2   Cox's Scheme

We discuss the communication complexity for the sequential composition of non-interactive elementary sub-protocols. All in all, in addition to the protocol communication of the sub-proofs, $\mathcal{P}$ transfers $2m+1$ commitments (namely $C_{WM_i\cdot\Delta_i}$, C_{A^2} and $C_{\Delta_i^2}$; $i = 0,\ldots,m-1$), which corresponds to approximately $(2m+1)\cdot\ell_n$ bits of traffic.

$$
\begin{aligned}
\mathsf{Comm}_{(\mathcal{P},\mathcal{V})}^{WM\,Cox} &= m\cdot\mathsf{Comm}_{(\mathcal{P},\mathcal{V})}^{\mathsf{PoK}_{mult}()} + 2\cdot\mathsf{Comm}_{(\mathcal{P},\mathcal{V})}^{\mathsf{PoK}_{\geq 0}()} + (m+1)\cdot\mathsf{Comm}_{(\mathcal{P},\mathcal{V})}^{\mathsf{PoK}_{sq}()} \\
&\quad + (2m+1)\cdot\ell_n \\
&= (2m+17)\ell_n + (10m+44)\ell_F + (5m+20)\ell_T \\
&\quad + (13m+55)\ell_\varnothing + (5m+22)\ell_B + 8m + 33
\end{aligned}
$$

Next we consider $\mathcal{V}$'s computation complexity: The homomorphic computations which provide the intermediate committed results require the following operations

- computation of C_{Δ_i} : $m \cdot E + m \cdot I + m \cdot M$
- computation of C_A : $(m-1) \cdot M$
- computation of C_B : $1 \cdot E + (m-1) \cdot M$
- computation of C_{A^2-B} : $1 \cdot I + 1 \cdot M$

such that we obtain a computation complexity of $(m+1) \cdot E + (m+1) \cdot I + (3m-1) \cdot M$. Together with the sub-protocols, we get

$$\mathsf{Comp}_{\mathcal{V}}^{WMCox} = m \cdot \mathsf{Comp}_{\mathcal{V}}^{\mathsf{PoK}_{mult}()} + 2 \cdot \mathsf{Comp}_{\mathcal{V}}^{\mathsf{PoK}_{\geq 0}()} + (m+1) \cdot \mathsf{Comp}_{\mathcal{V}}^{\mathsf{PoK}_{sq}()}$$
$$+(m+1) \cdot E + (m+1) \cdot I + (3m-1) \cdot M$$
$$= (16m + 67) \cdot E + (5m + 23) \cdot I + (13m + 49) \cdot M$$

$\mathcal{P}$ is able to follow $\mathcal{V}$'s homomorphic operations directly on the secret values and secret keys of the corresponding commitments. Therefore, we obtain a computation complexity of $(4m+4) \cdot E + (4m+5) \cdot M$. Hence, $\mathcal{P}$'s computation complexity including all sub-protocols is:

$$\mathsf{Comp}_{\mathcal{P}}^{WMCox} = m \cdot \mathsf{Comp}_{\mathcal{P}}^{\mathsf{PoK}_{mult}()} + 2 \cdot \mathsf{Comp}_{\mathcal{P}}^{\mathsf{PoK}_{\geq 0}()} + (m+1) \cdot \mathsf{Comp}_{\mathcal{P}}^{\mathsf{PoK}_{sq}()}$$
$$+ (4m+4) \cdot E + (4m+5) \cdot M$$
$$= (14m + 84) \cdot E + (19m + 95) \cdot M + 2 \cdot L$$

This leads to a total computation complexity of

$$\mathsf{Comp}_{(\mathcal{P},\mathcal{V})}^{WMCox} = (30m + 151) \cdot E + (5m + 22) \cdot I + (32m + 144) \cdot M + 2 \cdot L.$$

8   Practical Results

Our prototype implementation in JAVA is a proof of concept of the practicability of zero-knowledge watermark detection. Table 3, 4 and 5 show the results for the two protocols and different numbers of coefficients while the security parameters are fixed[16] as follows: $\ell_n = 1024$, $\ell_B = 1024$, $\ell_T = 512$, $\ell_F = 80$ and $\ell_{\varnothing} = 40$. The runtime was measured for a prover and a verifier process, running simultaneously on two Pentium IV 2400 desktop PCs connected via Ethernet. The estimated lower bound for the communication complexity $\mathsf{Comm}_{(\mathcal{P},\mathcal{V})}$ – without any implementation or network overhead – is obtained by summarising the theoretical results from Table 3 and 4 together with the transmission of the supplementary commitments. The last column of Table 4 and 3 shows that if the communication traffic exchanged by our implementation is compressed by a zip-packer, we come very close to the expected theoretical bound $\mathsf{Comm}_{(\mathcal{P},\mathcal{V})}$. Finally, the remarkable performance for Piva's method when all proofs how to open the committed watermark (cf. Section 6.3) are done in advance is displayed in Table 5.

---

[16] The dimensions of the security parameters are chosen according to [24] such that the message space for the secret value x in C_x is sufficiently large ($\ell_T = 512$) or such that factoring a n - bit number ($\ell_n = 1024$) is computationally infeasible to guarantee the binding property of the commitment scheme.

Table 3. Time [min:sec] and $\mathsf{Comm}_{(\mathcal{P},\mathcal{V})}$ [Bytes], for the Cox scheme. $\Delta\mathsf{Comm}$ is an abbreviation for $\mathsf{zip}(\mathsf{Comm}_{(\mathcal{P},\mathcal{V})})$ - $\mathsf{Comm}_{(\mathcal{P},\mathcal{V})}$.

Coeffs	time	$\mathsf{Comm}_{(\mathcal{P},\mathcal{V})}$	measured $\mathsf{Comm}_{(\mathcal{P},\mathcal{V})}$	zip ($\mathsf{Comm}_{(\mathcal{P},\mathcal{V})}$)	$\frac{\Delta\mathsf{Comm}}{\mathsf{Comm}_{(\mathcal{P},\mathcal{V})}}$ in %
100	0:17	144,168	221,614	161,879	12.3
200	0:29	282,368	413,808	303,825	7.6
400	0:58	558,768	801,080	587,493	5.1
800	1:51	1,111,568	1,572,529	1,154,695	3.9
1000	2:14	1,387,968	1,958,554	1,438,377	3.5

Table 4. Time [min:sec] and $\mathsf{Comm}_{(\mathcal{P},\mathcal{V})}$ [Bytes], for Piva's scheme. $\Delta\mathsf{Comm}$ is an abbreviation for $\mathsf{zip}(\mathsf{Comm}_{(\mathcal{P},\mathcal{V})})$ - $\mathsf{Comm}_{(\mathcal{P},\mathcal{V})}$.

Coeffs	time	$\mathsf{Comm}_{(\mathcal{P},\mathcal{V})}$	measured $\mathsf{Comm}_{(\mathcal{P},\mathcal{V})}$	zip ($\mathsf{Comm}_{(\mathcal{P},\mathcal{V})}$)	$\frac{\Delta\mathsf{Comm}}{\mathsf{Comm}_{(\mathcal{P},\mathcal{V})}}$ in %
1000	0:30	240,457	418,247	263,593	8.8
2000	0:45	477,707	808,513	509,286	6.2
4000	1:27	952,207	1,589,428	1,000,797	4.9
8000	2:56	1,901,207	3,150,823	1,983,738	4.2
16000	5:46	3,799,207	6,274,536	3,949,500	3.8

8.1   Accelerating Modular Operations

This section only deals with an efficient computation of the cryptographic building blocks. We point out that registration of a work and a watermark at a trusted party and the embedding process has to be considered separately.

Since the same bases g and h are used in all subproofs and intermediate commitments, the use of fixed-base exponentiation algorithms (see Chapter 14 of [30]), achieves a significant speed up (about factor 3) for the underlying modular exponentiations. The precomputation required by these exponentiation algorithms took 4 : 20 minutes and can be done during the setup of the commitment scheme and has to be done only once for all further executions of watermark detection protocol.

A further acceleration depends on the setup of the commitment scheme – either by the verifier [22] or by some trusted third party. It will turn out that in our trust model only the verifier can be accelerated if he is aware of some secret information. However, note that the prover is *not* allowed to set up the commitment scheme since otherwise the binding property (see Section 3) would not hold any more.

- **Taking advantage of the commitment's structure:** C_x has the following structure: $g^x h^r \mod n$. Since both bases g and h are generators of $\langle h \rangle$ there exists a unique exponent α such that $h^\alpha = g \mod n$. This value is chosen during the construction of the commitment description. Knowing this secret value, the computation expense to generate one commitment reduces from two modular exponentiations and one modular multiplication to one singe modular exponentiation. This reduction holds as well for the verifier to compute terms for verification in a zero-knowledge subproof (cf. Appendix). In this case C_x is obtained as $C_x := h^{x \cdot \alpha + r} \bmod n$ instead of $g^x h^r \bmod n$. However, one cannot give this crucial information to the prover since then the binding property of the commitment scheme does not hold any more. Assume that $\mathcal{P}$ has committed to some message x and is aware of the secret information α. Then C_x reduces for him to $C_x = h^{x \cdot \alpha + r}$. Hence, it is easy to open C_x as some value $x' \neq x$ by simply choosing an appropriate r' such that $x \cdot \alpha + r = x' \cdot \alpha + r'$ holds. If the verifier is setting up the commitment scheme for a two-party setting he chooses the modulus n and the bases g and h then he is aware of both the factorisation of n and the discrete logarithm $\alpha = \log_h(g)$ (cf. [22], in fact, the verifier proves in zero-knowledge to the committer that he knows such α to justify $g \in \langle h \rangle$). A trusted third party is trusted by both parties to generate n, g and h properly and therefore, only this necessary public information is distributed.

– **Speedup by using the Chinese Remainder Theorem:** The exponentiation modulo an RSA-modulus $n = p \cdot q$ can be significantly accelerated if it is performed *mod p* and *mod q* and then multiplying the results [30]. Again, this additional strategy is only applicable if the verifier sets up the commitment scheme, since then he knows the factorisation of n. An external trusted third party will only provide the modulus n without prime factors.

Our aim was to provide a general approach for the implementation such that we have not considered these speedup possibilities for the verifier yet.

8.2   Remarks on Running Time

The amount of coefficients does not necessary determine the running time of the detection protocol in a linear manner: Although Piva's protocol includes 16 times more watermark coefficients in a standard application ([16,9]) than the protocol by Cox et al., its execution time takes only about twice the time and three times more exchanged traffic. The reason is most operations are performed on publicly known values, here the alleged stego-work W^*.

The homomorphic property of the applied commitment scheme allows autonomous computations to the verifier which saves a large amount of elementary subprotocols causing communication and computation expense. The detection of Cox-type watermarks, in contrast, requires a committed version of the original cover data W such that the application of the expensive subproofs cannot be omitted, let alone a speedup analogously to the results shown in table 5 as for Piva's protocol. However, note that this acceleration is only feasible if the *same* watermark has to be detected in several different alleged stego-works.

Figure 4 shows the graphical user interface of a prover and a verifier client. The prover generates the watermark, embeds it and provides the committed versions of the watermark coefficients and – if necessary – of the original image. The verifier client has the chance to do some attack (adding some Gaussian noise) on the image (Fig. 4) to prevent the following proof from terminating

Table 5. Piva: Results for partly precomputed proofs

Coeffs.	time [m:s]	homomorphic time [s]
1000	0:30	3
2000	0:45	5
4000	1:27	9
8000	2:56	15
16000	5:46	27

Fig. 4. Screenshot of the prover and the verifier client

successfully. After sending back the manipulated image to the prover client, the preparation for the following zero-knowledge proof is finished.

9 Conclusion

We presented the entire technical details of cryptographic proofs for Zero-Knowledge Watermark Detection (ZKWMD) for two different correlation-based watermarking schemes by Cox et al [9] and Piva et al [10]. Both of them are well-established schemes and representative for many similar schemes and derivatives. The presented results of a prototype implementation show that this secure methodology can indeed be applied in practice.

Acknowledgement

We would like to thank Tomasz Kaszubowski and Christian Klimetzek for implementing a graphical user interface to visualise the implementation of the zero-knowledge watermark detection protocols.

References

1. Kilian, J., Leighton, F.T., Matheson, L.R., Shamoon, T.G., Tarjan, R.E., Zane, F.s.: Resistance of digital watermarks to collusive attacks. In: ISIT 1998, IEEE Press (1998) 271
2. Adelsbach, A., Sadeghi, A.R.: Advanced techniques for dispute resolving and authorship proofs on digital works. In Delp, E.J., Wong, P.W., eds.: Electronic Imaging 2003, Security and Watermarking of Multimedia Contents. Volume 5020., The Society for Imaging Science and Technology (IS&T) and the International Society for Optical Engineering (SPIE) (2003) 677 – 688
3. Adelsbach, A., Pfitzmann, B., Sadeghi, A.R.: Proving ownership of digital content. [31] 126–141
4. Adelsbach, A., Sadeghi, A.R.: Zero-knowledge watermark detection and proof of ownership. In: Information Hiding, IHW 2001. Volume 2137 of LNCS., Springer, Germany (2001) 273–288
5. Craver, S.: Zero knowledge watermark detection. [31] 101–116
6. Gopalakrishnan, K., Memon, N., Vora, P.: Protocols for watermark verification. In: Multimedia and Security, Workshop at ACM Multimedia. (1999) 91–94
7. Adelsbach, A., Katzenbeisser, S., Sadeghi, A.R.: Watermark detection with zero-knowledge disclosure. ACM Multimedia Systems Journal, Special Issue on Multimedia Security **9** (2003) 266–278
8. Hernandez, J., Perez-Gonzales, F.: Statistical analysis of watermarking schemes for copyright protection of images. In: Proceedings of the IEEE. Volume 87. (1999) 1142–1166
9. Cox, I., Kilian, J., Leighton, T., Shamoon, T.: A secure, robust watermark for multimedia. In: Information Hiding—First International Workshop, IH'96. Volume 1174 of LNCS., Springer Verlag (1996) 175–190
10. Barni, M., Bartolini, F., Cappellini, V., Piva, A.: A dct-domain system for robust image watermarking. Signal Processing - Special Issue in Copyright Protection and Access Control for Multimedia Services **66** (1998) 357–372
11. Adelsbach, A., Rohe, M., Sadeghi, A.R.: Security engineering for zero-knowledge watermark detection. In: Special Session on Media Security - WIAMIS 2005, Montreux, Switzerland (2005) 13–15
12. Adelsbach, A., Rohe, M., Sadeghi, A.R.: Non-Interactive Watermark Detection for a Correlation-Based Watermarking Scheme. In Dittmann, J., Katzenbeisser, S., Uhl, A., eds.: CMS 2005. Volume 3677 of LNCS., Springer (2005) 129–139
13. Craver, S., Liu, B., Wolf, W.: An implementation of, and attacks on, zero-knowledge watermarking. In Friedrich, J., ed.: Information Hiding—6th International Workshop, IHW 2004. Volume 3200 of LNCS., Springer Verlag (2004) 1–12
14. Damgård, I.: Commitment schemes and zero-knowledge protocols. In Damgård, I., ed.: Lectures on data security: modern cryptology in theory and practise. Volume 1561 of LNCS. Springer Verlag (1998) 63–86

15. Jin, Y.: Zero knowledge watermark detection. Master's thesis, Delft University of Technology and Philips Research Laboratories, Eindhoven (2004)
16. Piva, A., Barni, M., Bartolini, F., Cappellini, V.: Dct-based watermark recovering without resorting to the uncorrupted original image. In: Proceedings of ICIP97. Volume I., Santa Barbara, CA, USA, IEEE (1997) 520–523
17. Cox, I.J., Linnartz, J.P.M.G.: Some general methods for tampering with watermarks. IEEE Journal on Selected Areas in Communications **16** (1998) 587–593
18. Linnartz, J.P.M.G., van Dijk, M.: Analysis of the sensitivity attack against electronic watermarks in images. In Aucsmith, D., ed.: Information Hiding—Second International Workshop, IH'98. Volume 1525 of LNCS., Portland Oregon, USA, Springer Verlag (1998) 258–272
19. Comesaña, P., Pérez-Freire, L., Pérez-González, F.: The return of the sensitivity attack. In Barni, M., Cox, I., Kalker, T., Kim, H.J., eds.: Digital Watermarking: 4th International Workshop, IWDW 2005. Volume 3710 of Lecture Notes in Computer Science., Springer (2005) 260–274
20. Choubassi, M.E., Moulin, P.: New sensitivity analysis attack. In Delp, E.J., Wong, P.W., eds.: Security, Steganography, and Watermarking of Multimedia Contents. Volume 5681 of Proceedings of SPIE., SPIE (2005) 734–745
21. Piva, A., Barni, M., Bartolini, F., Cappellini, V.: Exploiting the cross-correlation of rgb-channels for robust watermarking of color images. In: Proceedings of 6th IEEE International Conference on Image Processing ICIP99. Volume I., Kobe, Japan, IEEE (1999) 306–310
22. Damgård, I., Fujisaki, E.: A statistically-hiding integer commitment scheme based on groups with hidden order. In: ASIACRYPT. Volume 2501 of LNCS., Springer (2002) 125–142
23. Boudot, F.: Efficient proofs that a committed number lies in an interval. In: Advances in Cryptology – EUROCRYPT '2000. Volume 1807 of LNCS., Springer Verlag (2000) 431–444
24. Lipmaa, H.: On diophantine complexity and statistical zero-knowledge arguments. In: ASIACRYPT. Volume 2894 of LNCS., Springer (2003) 398–415
25. Lagrange, J.L.: Démonstration d'un Théorème d'Arithmétique. Nouveaux Mémoires de l'Académie royale des Sciences et Belles-Lettres de Berlin (1770) 123–
26. Lagrange, J.L. In: Oeuvres de Lagrange. Volume III. Gauthier-Villars (1869) 189–201
27. Bellare, M., Rogaway, P.: Random oracles are practical: A paradigm for designing efficient protocols. In: Proceedings of the ACM CCS, ACM Press (1993) 62–73
28. Rabin, M.O., Shallit, J.O.: Randomized Algorithms in Number Theory. Communications on Pure and Applied Mathematics **39** (1986) S 239– S 256
29. Goldreich, O.: Foundations of Cryptography. Volume Basic Tools. Cambridge University Press (2001)
30. Menezes, A.J., van Oorschot, P.C., Vanstone, S.A.: Handbook of Applied Cryptography. CRC Press series on discrete mathematics and its applications. CRC Press (1997) ISBN 0-8493-8523-7.
31. Pfitzmann, A., ed.: Information Hiding—3rd International Workshop, IH'99. Volume 1768 of LNCS., Dresden, Germany, Springer Verlag (2000)
32. Schnorr, C.P.: Efficient identification and signatures for smartc cards. In Brassard, G., ed.: Advances in Cryptology - CRYPTO. Volume 435 of Lecture Notes in Computer Science., Springer (1989) 20–24
33. Poupard, G., Stern, J.: Short proofs of knowledge for factoring. In Imai, H., Zheng, Y., eds.: Public Key Cryptography. Volume 1751 of Lecture Notes in Computer Science., Springer (2000) 147–166

A   An Example: Proof of an Equality Relation

We added this appendix to give an impression how one single subproof is accomplished, what computations are performed and how the exchanged messages are constructed. Further details on the commitment scheme and corresponding zero-knowledge proof protocols can be found in [22].

The Interactive Version

This protocol is adapted from Boudot [23] and convinces a verifier that two commitments $\widetilde{C_x}$ and C_x given as a common input contain the same secret value $x \in [-2^{\ell_T}, 2^{\ell_T}]$ and, furthermore, that $\mathcal{P}$ is able to open C_x and $\widetilde{C_x}$ at all.

The general idea to prove the knowledge of the exponents in one or several commitments is to commit to some random values as a *first message*, obtaining a *challenge* uniformly chosen at random from the verifier. Finally, a so-called *response* involving the random value, the challenge and secret exponent is computed and sent to the verifier. The verification of this response is only successful if the correct secret value has been used in the response.

If two commitments contain the same secret value x then choosing the same random value for x in the first message leads to one single response and since this response works in both verification equations, $\mathcal{V}$ is convinced that both commitments contain the same secret.

In more detail: To run this proof, $\mathcal{P}$ chooses y from $[0, 2^{\ell_F + \ell_T + \ell_\varnothing}[$ and s_1, s_2 from $[0, 2^{\ell_F + \ell_B + 2\ell_\varnothing}[$ uniformly at random and commits to the first messages $d_1 := g^y h^{s_1} \mod n$ and $d_2 := g^y h^{s_2} \mod n$. After that, $\mathcal{V}$ chooses one challenge e for both first messages and receives the corresponding responses u, v_1 and v_2. It suffices to send one single response u instead of u_1 and u_2 because u_1 and u_2 would be identical since they refer to the same random value y, the same secret x and one single challenge e.

Non-interactive Form in the Random Oracle Model

To transform the three-step interactive into a non-interactive protocol by means of the random oracle model [27], both $\mathcal{P}$ and $\mathcal{V}$ have to obtain the challenge e by hashing the first messages d_1 and d_2 as $e = H(d_1 \| d_2)$. Furthermore, the structure of the commitments and the form of the verification equation allows to omit sending the first messages d_1 and d_2. This methodology is analogue to the so-called Schnorr-signatures of knowledge [32]. According to Poupard and Stern [33] the statistical zero-knowledge property is preserved under this transformation.

Instead of d_1, d_2, u, v_1 and v_2, $\mathcal{P}$ only sends e, u, v_1 and v_2 which is significantly shorter. To verify the proof, $\mathcal{V}$ has to check whether

$$d_1 \cdot (C_x)^e \overset{?}{=} g^u h^{v_1} \mod n \quad \text{and} \quad d_2 \cdot (\widetilde{C_x})^e \overset{?}{=} g^u h^{v_2} \mod n$$

which is equivalent to

$$d_1 \stackrel{?}{=} g^u h^{v_1} \cdot (C_x)^{-e} \mod n \quad \text{and} \quad d_2 \stackrel{?}{=} g^u h^{v_2} \cdot (\widetilde{C_x})^{-e} \mod n.$$

Instead of calculating $e = H(d_1 \| d_2)$ and verifying $d_1 \cdot (C_x)^e \stackrel{?}{=} g^u h^{v_1} \mod n$ respectively $d_2 \cdot (\widetilde{C_x})^e \stackrel{?}{=} g^u h^{v_2} \mod n$, $\mathcal{V}$ computes $\tilde{d}_1 := g^u h^{v_1} \cdot (C_x)^{-e}$ and $\tilde{d}_2 \stackrel{?}{=} g^u h^{v_2} \cdot (\widetilde{C_x})^{-e} \mod n$ and checks whether $H(\tilde{d}_1 \| \tilde{d}_2) \stackrel{?}{=} e$. In this case, $\mathcal{V}$ relies on the *collision intractability* assumption of H: The probability that a cheating prover succeeds in constructing a first message d' with $d' \neq d$ such that $H(d') = H(d)$ is assumed to be negligible (Here: d denotes $d_1 \| d_2$).

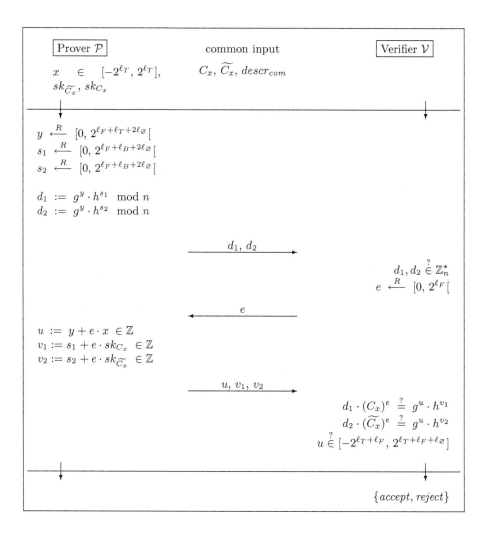

Fig. 5. Proof that two commitments contain the same secret value $\mathsf{PoK}_{eq}(C_x, \widetilde{C_x})$

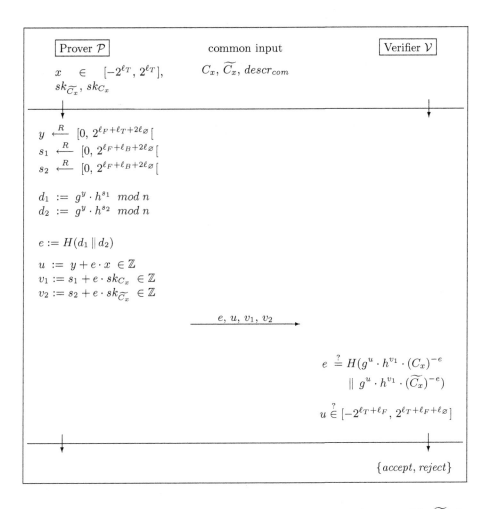

Fig. 6. Proof that two commitments contain the same secret value $\mathrm{PoK}_{eq}(C_x, \widetilde{C}_x)$ in the Random Oracle proof-mode

Identity-Based DRM: Personal Entertainment Domain

Paul Koster, Frank Kamperman, Peter Lenoir, and Koen Vrielink

Information and System Security Department, Philips Research
High Tech Campus 34, 5656AE Eindhoven, The Netherlands
{R.P.Koster, Frank.Kamperman, Peter.Lenoir,
Koen.Vrielink}@Philips.com

Abstract. Digital Rights Management (DRM) enforces the rights of copyright holders and enforces their business models. This imposes restrictions on how users can handle content. These restrictions apply specifically in networked environments. Authorized Domain (AD) DRM concepts remove several of these restrictions, while taking into account the content providers' need to limit the proliferation of content. This paper compares a number of alternative DRM concepts based on some criteria including control on content proliferation and user experience. We introduce a new concept called Personal Entertainment Domain (PED) DRM. PED-DRM binds content to a person. This person has a number of permanent domain devices. The person's content can be rendered on these permanent domain devices and temporarily on other devices after user authentication. This concept aims at providing a better user experience than current solutions by making it more person identity based. The concept builds upon the best aspects of device-based and person-based DRM. Furthermore, we present the architecture of a PED-DRM realization. We conclude that PED-DRM meets the criteria and is practical to implement, although it has the prerequisite of having an authentication infrastructure.

Keywords: Digital Rights Management, DRM, Authorized Domain.

1 Introduction

Digital Rights Management (DRM) is a much-discussed topic nowadays. The main reason for this is the rise of broadband Internet services and the online sales of digital multimedia content. Especially the availability of music services is rapidly increasing. These services all use content protection technology to avoid the large scale copying of their content on peer-to-peer networks as happened with for example content from CDs. DRM manages the digital rights associated with the content. Systems in place today are, for example Windows Media DRM, Apple FairPlay and OMA DRM.

In this paper we take as a starting point the concept of Authorized Domain (AD) DRM [8,22]. AD aims to fulfill some of the requirements of both the content owners and the users, which often appear to be conflicting. For an AD the general idea is that content can flow freely between the devices that belong to the domain, while content transactions between ADs are restricted. Various companies [4,5,10,17,21] and standardization bodies such as Digital Video Broadcasting (DVB) [22] and Open Mobile Alliance (OMA) [15] are investigating and developing the concept of Authorized

Y.Q. Shi (Ed.): Transactions on DHMS I, LNCS 4300, pp. 104–122, 2006.

Domains. The traditional approach with ADs is device-oriented where an AD groups a set of devices. These approaches have the intention to group the devices that belong to a certain household. However, the device-oriented approach does not allow for users to access their content anywhere, at any time and on any device. We present the Personal Entertainment Domain (PED) AD concept as the solution to this problem.

We consider the following motivating scenario. The user Aaron has a PC in his study and a media center is his living. When he installs the devices he configures them to be part of his AD, and ensures that all content he buys on either device is synchronized on these devices. At any moment in time he can render his content on both devices. He can also render the content of his girlfriend Jasmine on the media center because she also configured the media center for her content next to her portable player. When Aaron visits another place he can still enjoy his content stored at home by downloading it over the Internet. Naturally, third parties cannot access Aaron's or Jasmine's content and they cannot access each other's content except on their shared media center.

From this scenario we extract criteria for DRM for multimedia content: limited and controlled content proliferation, social flexibility in accessing content at any place and sharing between users, and user experience and transparency.

The outline of this paper is as follows. Section 2 presents the state of the art in DRM concepts and evaluates these. Section 3 introduces the PED concept. In section 4 we describe the architecture and operation of a realization of the PED-DRM concept with local domain management. Section 5 briefly presents the threat model and security analysis for PED-DRM. The paper ends with conclusions.

2 State of the Art DRM Concepts

Digital Rights Management targets electronic content delivery. It controls the use of content. Key concept of DRM is the license, which binds usage rights for digital content to one or more identities. Examples of identity include devices, groups of devices and persons. In this article we focus on these identity aspects.

To illustrate and validate the criteria extracted from the motivating scenario we apply them to copy protection. Copy protection is one area of content protection like DRM. The copy protection paradigm targets medium based content delivery such as DVD. Copy protection meets the criteria: *content proliferation* is strictly controlled, because it is not trivial to make an exact copy and thereby the scope of content distribution and access is limited, (2) *availability and social flexibility* is good since content can be played anywhere and by anyone, (3) *user experience and transparency* is good, because content renders on any player in which the medium fits.

These three criteria are not an exhaustive list of important criteria for DRM. However, these criteria relate to the identity component of DRM licensing. Furthermore, these are the criteria on which the DRM concepts that follow differentiate. For example, the DRM concepts would score similarly if we would consider the ability to sell or give away content.

The first generation DRM systems bound content to a single device. This DRM concept has been found to violate the availability criterion because availability on just one device is too restrictive. Therefore developments have taken place to make content available on more devices, e.g. in home networks and on portable devices. We present a classification of the alternatives and discuss these in the following sections.

2.1 Device-Based DRM with Tethered Devices

The networked DRM concept superseding the device-based DRM concept is the so-called device-based DRM with support for tethered devices. A tethered device is an end-point that can operate in stand alone mode. Key characteristics of this concept (see Fig.1) are (1) content is securely bound to one device on which it can be rendered, (2) content can be transferred from the first device to up to a maximum number (n) of tethered devices under some conditions, for example proximity of the two devices, and rendered on those devices, (3) content is securely locked, for example by a license, to the tethered devices and cannot be distributed further, (4) content on tethered devices is out of management scope of the original transaction and the first device, (5) tethered devices may accept content from a maximum number of (m) devices. An example is the Windows Media Player using Windows Media DRM (WM DRM) [14]. WM DRM distinguishes between two types of tethered devices, i.e. devices with and without persistent storage [12,13]. The transfer of content to tethered devices has many similarities with the copy protection approach. The concept of tethered devices is often justified by the argument that such tethered devices are resource constrained and cannot support the full DRM functionality.

The device-based DRM concept with tethered devices meets the content proliferation criterion because the transfer to tethered devices is subject to conditions and limitations. The concept scores less good on user experience and transparency because different rules and conditions apply for the main device and the tethered devices. The same reasons also contribute to a low score on availability and social flexibility, e.g. enjoying some content at another place distributing the content using a network instead of carrying devices is not supported.

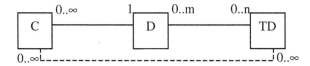

Fig. 1. Device-based DRM with tethered devices. C, D and TD represent an acquired content item, device and tethered device respectively. The relations C-D, D-TD and C-TD represent that content is bound to a device by means of a license, up to n tethered devices can be bound to up to m devices, and content bound to a device can be accessed on the tethered devices bound to that device, respectively.

2.2 Device-Based-AD

DVB introduced the concept of Authorized Domain (AD) in response to device-based DRM [22]. The AD concept introduces an explicit identity called AD that groups devices and replaces the direct binding between content and devices. This allows users to purchase, render and manage their content on more than one device. Key characteristics of the device-based AD concept (see Fig.2) are (1) content is bound to the AD when it is acquired, (2) content can be exchanged between and rendered on domain devices without external involvement, (3) an AD consists of a maximum number (n) of devices, (4) a device may be member of a number (m) of domains. Examples systems implementing this concept are OMA DRM 2.0 [15,16], SmartRight [21], PERM [5] and xCP [17]. Typically, solutions adhering to this solution distribute (domain) key(s) required to access domain content to devices when they become member of the AD.

The proliferation of content is strictly controlled by the entity or component that determines which devices belong to the domain. The user experience criterion is met by the simplicity of the concept. For example, it allows straightforward the peer-to-peer exchange of content between devices. Of course, there is a requirement for a user to manage his domain, but this can be limited to the installation procedure after acquiring a new device. Arrangements for exceptional cases such as loss of a device may require the user to go to more manual and explicit procedures. The concept partially meets the availability and social flexibility criterion. For example, if a maximum number (n) of devices is the only limitation then availability is good, while further requirements decrease its attractiveness. Rendering content just once at another location requires a registration followed by a deregistration of a device to the domain. This is not flexible and degrades availability. Social flexibility is hindered when multiple users bind content to the same domain. This problem especially arises when users later want to take their content and their devices with them. Some systems such as SmartRight force this behaviour, because devices can only be bound to one domain. Server based AD solutions like OMA DRM 2.0 and FairPlay [1] promote separate domains per user and do not suffer from this.

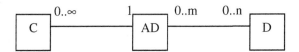

Fig. 2. Device-based AD. C, AD and D represent acquired content, (authorized) domain, and devices, respectively. The relations C-AD and AD-D represent that acquired content is bound to an AD, and that up to n devices are member of up to m ADs, respectively.

Apple FairPlay, depicted in Fig. 3 is a special instance of the device-based AD concept. It is based on the concept of a user account in a server backend. A user may register, or authorize in FairPlay terms, online a number (n) of devices. These devices thereby obtain the necessary (user) keys to render the bought content. On these devices users can buy, download and access his content, and transfer it to an unlimited amount of tethered devices. FairPlay's orientation at users avoids some typical drawbacks of device-based AD, because it is clear who owns the content. However, it is strongly coupled to the particular deployment with an online service. Incidental content access at another location still requires a registration and deregistration step, which does not make it very attractive for that purpose. The introduction of tethered devices reduces transparency and user experience similar to the device-based DRM with tethered devices concept.

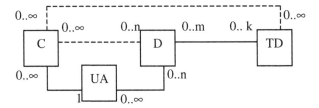

Fig. 3. FairPlay: device-based AD with tethered devices. C, D, TD and UA represent content, devices, tethered devices and a server based user account, respectively. The relations C-UA, UA-D and C-D represent that content is bound to a user account, that upto n devices can be bound to a user account on which the content can be accessed, and that content renders on upto n devices, respectively.

2.3 Person-Based DRM

Another example of an alternative concept is the person-based DRM concept. Key characteristics are (1) content is bound to a user, and (2) content is accessible after user authentication for the length of the authentication session. The concept has been known for some time. For example, rights expression languages as ODRL support the binding of content to identifiers representing users [9]. Currently, person-based DRM is not widely used for multimedia content. This is mainly due to its prerequisites on an authentication infrastructure [20]. Contrariwise, enterprise DRM is typically person-based and reuses the corporate IT infrastructure for authentication. The OPERA project explored person-based DRM for multimedia content [23]. Currently no DRM systems for multimedia content in the market are person-based. FairPlay comes near with its notion of a user account and authorization of PCs by end-users providing their username and password. However, the persistence of the authorization makes it more device-based AD than person-based DRM with authentication sessions.

Person-based DRM meets the criteria of controlled content proliferation when proper user authentication mechanisms and policies are used. Availability of the content is also good and sharing is possible when people come together. Transparency is good since there is one major rule, but user convenience is bad since reauthenticating often is cumbersome.

The biggest hurdle for person-based DRM is not that one of the criteria is not met, but the lack of a general authentication infrastructure that works on a broad range of devices. For example, username/password is considered as insufficient, because these are easily shared and hard to support in offline cases. This introduces the need for alternative authentication mechanisms.

A person-based DRM system puts the user in the centre of the content experience, i.e. content is licensed to him enabling play back on any compliant device. However, person-based DRM has some potentially undesired consequences in the area of privacy. Examples include (1) a service provider can easily monitor the purchases of individual users, (2) everyone having access to the licenses and knowing somebody's identity may find out what content he possesses, and (3) the location of the user might be tracked when using content on a device after user authentication. For the first problem an anonymous buying scheme can be used, e.g. based of a pre-payment scheme. In such a scheme a user buys a ticket anonymously, which then later can be used to acquire a license. To hide the relation between content and users identities may be concealed in licenses. More privacy aspects can be addressed using techniques found in privacy-enhancing technologies, such as pseudonymity services, roles or anonymous assertions. The basic approach is that each party only knows the relations with users that he needs. Therefore the real user identity is decoupled from his identifiers [2].

Person-based DRM also brings opportunities to give users more control on their content. For example, user attributed rights enable the user to control (after acquisition) who, when, and where content is consumed, e.g. for the purpose of parental control [18]. After acquisition the user attaches additional conditions to the license. These conditions stay within the limits of the original license that is paid for.

2.4 Summary

None of the above DRM concepts meet all criteria sufficiently, summarized in Table 1. Device-based with tethered devices fails amongst others the transparency criterion. Device-based AD fails to meet the availability and social flexibility criterion. Person-based DRM fails to offer user convenience in daily use.

Table 1. Summary evaluation for alternative DRM concepts

	device-based DRM (with tethered devices)	device-based AD	person-based DRM
content proliferation	+	+	+
user experience and transparency	-	+	o
content availability and social flexibility	-	o	+

3 Personal Entertainment Domain

PED-DRM is characterized by its structure and policy. The structure is depicted in Fig.4 and highlights the key concepts, namely that content is bound to the user identity and is accessible permanently on a domain of devices and temporarily on other devices. The policy defines the rules that govern domain management, content access and proliferation. The key characteristics of PED DRM are (1) a single user (P) is the member/owner of the domain, (2) content (C) is bound to that user representing possession of usage rights on the content, (3) a number (n) of devices (D) is bound to the user forming the domain (AD), (4) domain content can be accessed on the set of permanent domain devices (without further actions), (5) domain content can be accessed on other devices after user authentication for the length of the authentication session, (6) devices may exchange content directly, and (7) devices may be member of multiple domains. This allows convenient content usage at home on permanent domain devices, including the sharing of content among family members. Furthermore, it enables people to access their content anywhere and at any time after user authentication. In that case the device is called a temporary domain device.

PED-DRM meets the criteria. It meets the criterion on content proliferation by its structure and its policy that limit the number of devices on which content can be accessed in parallel. Availability and social flexibility with content is also supported since content can be rendered anywhere and the clear ownership of (usage rights on) content ease support of changing social relationships. Social flexibility is further increased by the ease of sharing content by sharing devices, as is typically done in families. In that case all family members include the shared device in their domain. User experience and transparency is good and intuitive, because the concept is simple with only one device class and two general rules to access content on devices. Furthermore, the binding of bought content to users leads to an intuitive form of ownership. Of course, a user must add one or more devices to his domain, but typically this is done only the first time content is rendered on a newly bought device. The prerequisite of an authentication infrastructure applies to PED-DRM as it does for person-based DRM in general. However, it is less an obstacle because PED-DRM includes an alternative to access content.

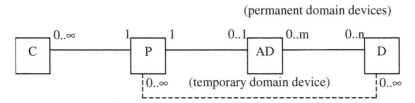

Fig. 4. Personal Entertainment Domain. C, P, AD and D represent content, person/user, (authorized) domain and devices, respectively. The relations C-P, P-AD, AD-D and P-D represent that acquired content is bound to a person who possesses certain usage rights on the content, a person may have a domain, this domain consists of up to n devices while a maximum m could hold for the number of domains a device can be member of, and a device can temporary belong to a person's domain and access the users content after authentication, respectively.

Current DRM systems do not meet all characteristics of PED. OMA DRM 2.0 supports the binding of content and devices to a domain. It also supports the explicit binding of content to a user identity in the rights expression, but only to restrict the access to content further in addition the domain mechanism. This means that content is restricted to a set of devices where also the user is authenticated, while in PED-DRM content is restricted to a set of devices or to a device where the user is authenticated. FairPlay also shares characteristics with PED since it is based on a user account and the persistent authorization of devices. However, FairPlay lacks a user authentication session of limited length.

In a straightforward PED-DRM implementation the content provider knows which type of domain is used and is assured that each person only has one domain. This may be the case for example when just one (system-defined) type of domain exists and thereby the content proliferation effects are clear when content is bound to a person. In other cases the (type of) domain is taken into account at the moment of content acquisition, resulting in an explicit relation between content and domain. This can be represented in the license.

By separating person identity from domain identity, PED-DRM anticipates that in the future support for domains with multiple persons may be required. This would allow that also at remote locations people could use their family member's content. The detailed requirements and allowed policies in this situation are currently unclear. The effects on the structure depicted in Fig. 4 would be that content is still bound to the user owning it, and the domain still belongs to one person, but another type of relationship between the AD and persons is added to represent the users that are member of the domain

4   A PED-DRM Realization

This section describes a realization of the PED-DRM concept covering the architecture and operations. We assume localized domain management based on a domain manager running on a token, i.e. a secure device with a compact form factor and suitable communication interface. However, many aspects are generic for the PED-DRM concept and hold also for other deployment scenarios, e.g. one with an online domain manager.

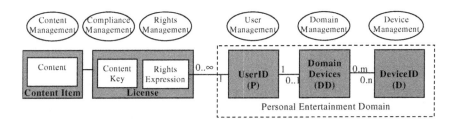

Fig. 5. PED-DRM overview of functions (ovals) and data objects (squares)

4.1   Functional Architecture and Design

We start discussing a realization of the PED-DRM concept by identifying the main functions and corresponding data objects, schematically depicted in Fig. 5. This is a refinement of Fig. 4 with typical DRM features added such as licenses [7,15]. We focus on the identity and domain aspects of PED-DRM that builds upon the user, device and domain management functions. Domain management concerns which devices belong to the domain of the user. The relation between PED and rights management is typically represented by means of a user identifier embedded in the license.

4.1.1   User Management
The main aspect of user management in PED-DRM consists of providing a user with an identity that he can use to obtain and access content. The user identity can have many representations such as a physical tokens with secrets, but also a user account with username/password, or a physical user in combination with biometrics. We opt for a physical token. The user identity has the form of a UserID certificate with

corresponding public/private key pair that can be used for authentication. The user is not granted access to the private key in order to prevent him from misusing or giving away his private key and enabling someone else to impersonate him. To enforce this, the user's private key is stored securely on a tamper-resistant non-clonable user identity token. Presence of this token represents the user's presence. This does not prevent the user from lending or sharing his token, but does limit parallel access to one person. In practical cases sharing of the token is inconvenient since it must be physically exchanged. Typical tokens are smartcards and mobile phones equipped with a SIM card.

The introduction of user identity tokens also implies management of the link between users and tokens, depicted in Fig. 6. In its basic form the token just stores the user certificate and related keys. Since tokens are devices but with a dedicated purpose and a smaller form factor, they have a device identity called token identity in Fig. 6. The separation between user and token identity is advantageous since they serve different purposes and also their lifecycle differs. A party or system manages the link according to the token policy. A typical policy limits each user identity to have a limited number of physical tokens that can be used for authentication. In the context of DRM this is typically set to one. A proof of the link may be stored explicitly in the form of an assertion. This may be of use later to support for example revocation of this link, i.e. the token can no longer authenticate the user.

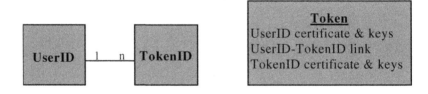

Fig. 6. User and token identities (left), and information stored on token (right)

Managing users and tokens is relatively straightforward if it is in the hands of one organisation. This is more complicated when the DRM user identity has to be related to some token managed by another organisation, e.g. a SIM card managed by a mobile operator. This can be very attractive for the PED-DRM concept since it contributes to the prerequisite of having an authentication infrastructure available. Naturally, trust needs to be established between both parties. Concepts and techniques known from federated identity management can be used to establish such trust and provide a part of the authentication infrastructure [11].

4.1.2 Device Management

Device management is concerned with giving devices an identity and ensuring that only trustworthy devices participate in the system. Devices participating in PED-DRM receive a DeviceID certificate. This certificate defines the device DRM identity, and also asserts that it is a trustworthy compliant device that respects the compliance and robustness rules of the PED-DRM system. The authority responsible for issuing the compliance certificate may also revoke it at some point in time. Therefore devices also have to deal with the distribution and verification of compliance status information. In addition to their identity, devices are also given explicit authorization to fulfill certain functions. This limits the effects in case of a security breach by preventing the certificate and keys of a hacked device from being misused for other functions, e.g. keys from a rendering device cannot be used to register other devices to the domain.

4.1.3 Domain Management

Domain management in PED-DRM concerns the relation between a UserID and a number of DeviceIDs, which is characterized by the DomainDevices (DD) data object depicted in Fig. 5. We propose an approach in which DD is a certificate containing a reference to the user of the domain, references to a number of devices, a version number and the signature of the domain manager.

$$DD = \{ \text{ DomainID, Version, UserID, DeviceID1, ..., DeviceIDn, SignDM } \} \qquad (1)$$

We identify the following advantages of this approach: (1) the signature shows who issued it, (2) all domain members in one certificate allows a simple but secure signaling mechanism of the devices in the domain, (3) it allows reporting of domain information to the user on any domain device at any time, and (4) it uniquely identifies the user owning the domain allowing easy evaluation in case of content access. The secure signaling contributes to an effective mechanism to inform deregistered devices and to obtain and distribute compliance status information. This is especially advantageous when not all devices are always online and reachable. In a more online setting like OMA DRM the domain devices list could be kept internal to the domain manager and only devices itself receive a notification of their domain membership. The advantages of the DD structure are then realized by means of online network connectivity.

Domain-based DRM systems typically base their security on domain key(s) [5,17,21]. In these systems the content key is typically encrypted with the domain key. This has security advantages if devices are hacked because the accessible content to these devices is limited to the domain content. PED-DRM addresses this threat differently by limiting license distribution to permanent and temporary domain devices.

The maximum of one domain per user is enforced by the authority that manages the user identity or by the token that represents the user identity. For this purpose the domain manager and this user identity authority or token interact during the creation of a domain.

4.1.4 System Components and Their Interaction

Fig. 7 presents the main components – ADMCore, ADClient, UserIdentity and ADMTerminal – that group PED-DRM functionality and the interaction between them. Also the typical connectivity means that enable interaction between the components are indicated: combined on the same device (local), connected through a network (IP) or via wired/wireless connection with a limitation on the distance (near-field). Typical examples of the latter are contactless smartcard or wired USB connections.

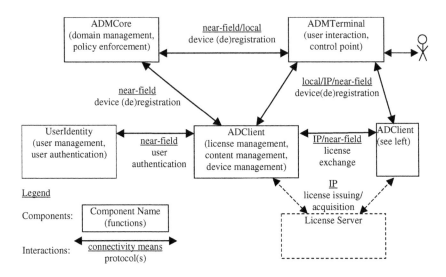

Fig. 7. Local PED-DRM components and their interaction

The ADMCore, ADClient and UserIdentity must run on a compliant device, because they manage domain or content related data. The ADMTerminal component is only responsible for UI and control aspects and ADMTerminal is therefore not subject to DRM compliance requirements. We foresee that the UserIdentity and ADMCore components are deployed on the same device, e.g. on a smartcard or mobile phone. Alternatively, ADMCore runs as a service on the Internet, an approach similar to OMA DRM 2.0 and Apple FairPlay. Local domain management may offer some advantages such as the ability to do proximity verification between components. On the other hand, central domain management in the network may offer features like centralized control and easy and direct audit facilities. In the remainder of this work we assume that ADMCore runs on a device. Ideally, each ADClient is deployed on a device together with an ADMTerminal component, allowing straightforward AD management operations using the user interface of the device for interaction with the user. Typical devices are hardware- and software-based media centers and connected renders (TVs).

4.1.5 Domain Policy

The domain policy specifies under which conditions entities are entitled to be part of the domain and thereby largely defines the scale of content proliferation in a domain-based DRM system. Users prefer a policy with a relaxed regime, while copyright holders prefer more tight regimes. As most other domain-enabled DRM systems, PED-DRM has a domain policy that is fixed for the system. An exception to this is OMA DRM 2.0, where the domain policy is left to the individual Rights Issuers. On one hand this is convenient since Rights Issuers control the domains to which they deliver content, while in PED-DRM they have less direct control and have to accept or deny the offered policy. On the other hand, a fixed policy contributes to transparency to the users.

We propose a simple and straightforward basic domain policy enforced by ADMCore. The policy is based on a maximum number of devices per domain. So far, the policy is very similar to Apple FairPlay's limit of 5 authorized PCs [1]. Furthermore, ADMCore only registers ADClients that are in direct proximity, i.e. directly connected. This limits the domain size and content proliferation to places the user (actually his token) visits. Devices may be a member of multiple domains to support sharing of content between people who share devices. The domain policy is enforced partially by other components such as ADClient. An example is the length of the authentication session. This approach has the advantage that enforcement is done local to certain components, avoiding complex distributed management.

Further policy rules may be required by the content owners, e.g. to counter some subtle attacks against limited content proliferation. A balanced set of policy rules should be selected such that in normal circumstances a user does not encounter them. The policy may also affect more than just domain management operations such as content access or license exchange. Examples include membership liveness meaning that domain membership must be confirmed regularly by the ADMCore; rate-limited domain management meaning that (de)registrations may not exceed a maximum level per time unit at either ADMCore or ADClient; a maximum number of domains of which an ADClient may be a member, which is unrestricted in pure PED-DRM; limiting the exchange of licenses between domain devices to distance-limited channels; a maximum number of authentications per ADClient or UserIdentity per time frame. Also for these policy rules it holds that they can be implemented and enforced by a single component. The exception is membership liveness which therefore better can be avoided.

4.2 Operations

4.2.1 Device Registration
The protocol for registering an ADClient to a domain starts when, under the user's control, the ADMTerminal instructs the ADClient to register itself at the ADMCore. This is done with its DeviceID reference. The ADMCore responds to the ADClient with a new DD certificate, including the ADClient DeviceID. The ADMCore processes the registration request using the following steps: it verifies the authenticity of ADClient request, it verifies that the device with DeviceID is not revoked and is not already a member, it executes the PED policy algorithm to determine whether the ADClient may be added to the domain, and it creates a new DD certificate with the DeviceID reference included and an increased version number, and reusing other fields such as UserID. In a final step, the ADClient verifies the validity of the DD certificate received and stores it. Subsequently, it is able to render domain content based on possession of the DD certificate.

The device registration protocol supports two deployment scenarios explicitly. The first is the trivial case where the ADClient and ADMTerminal are located on the same device with a near-field interface to the ADMCore. The second case concerns a device with limited UI capabilities and which must be controlled over the network by an ADMTerminal. Interests of the user in his role as domain and device owner must be addressed when domain management can be controlled over a network to prevent unwanted registrations by third parties. Device owner consent is addressed by involving user confirmation at the ADClient for registration such as putting it in a registration mode by pressing a button. Alternatively, it comprises authentication of the device or domain owner. Domain owner consent is implicitly assumed, because the ADMCore must be in physical proximity of ADClient.

The protocol is made robust by including acknowledgements, rollback procedures, and DD distribution as part of the protocol. This prevents the ADClient from considering itself a domain member while the ADMCore does not. The ADMCore has to implement the device registration protocol as a transaction due to the fact that communication could fail, for example when an ADMCore smartcard is removed prematurely from the reader. To speed up the distribution of the new domain composition, the registered ADClient should broadcast the latest DD certificate to other ADClients. The latter is a best-effort approach in addition to the forced synchronization as described later.

4.2.2 Device Deregistration

Device deregistration ends the domain membership of a device. The device deregistration protocol starts when the ADMTerminal under the control of the user instructs ADClient to deregister itself at the ADMCore. The ADClient sends a deregister request with its DeviceID to the ADMCore, which responds with a new DD certificate. If the ADClient is not available, e.g. if it has been stolen, broken or is offline, then the ADMTerminal may send the deregister request on its behalf. The ADMCore verifies that the DeviceID is listed in DD, it removes the device from the DD certificate and increases its version number. Subsequently, the ADClient checks the validity of the DD certificate and if it is no longer listed it deletes the DD certificate. Before ADMCore replaces its stored DD certificate, it expects a deregistration confirmation from ADClient to ensure that ADClient received the request and deregistered itself. Unconfirmed deregistrations, including deregistrations of offline devices, may be administered differently. This knowledge may be used in the domain policy for future device registrations, such that the protocol cannot be misused to allow on a large scale for new registrations while the old ones are effectively still present. The new DD certificate should be broadcasted so that other domain devices learn the new domain composition as quickly as possible. Stolen and offline devices are removed effectively over time when the new domain composition is distributed in the form of the DD certificate as a result of the forced DD synchronization described later.

The interests of the domain owner in the deregistration protocol are protected by requiring that the ADMCore and ADMTerminal must be in close proximity or in direct contact with each other. The presence of the ADMCore implies authorization for the deregistration action. Alternatively, the ADMCore is present at the ADClient that is removed in combination with an explicit user confirmation to thwart unwanted deregistrations from the network. The implementation must ensure that the user may not be subject to a denial of service attack consisting of many confirmation requests.

4.2.3 Local Deregistration Through ADClient Reset

A local deregistration stands for an ADClient that ends its domain membership without interaction with ADMCore. This required for example when someone gives his device away without having his ADMCore in the neighborhood but still wants to prevent the new owner from accessing his content. In this case he needs to perform an autonomous ADClient reset action whereby the ADClient deletes the DD certificate. This approach should not be advocated because there is no automatic means to ensure that ADMCore removes it from the DD certificate as well. A device should therefore indicate to the user that he needs to perform (offline) deregistration at ADMCore as well.

4.2.4 ADMCore Disaster

If the ADMCore device is broken or lost, a user is no longer able to change the composition of his domain. If the ADMCore is stolen, somebody else is able to add his own devices and access the content belonging to the original owner, assuming that no additional access control mechanisms are in place. To mitigate this problem, a user requests a new ADMCore device. As part of this process the old ADMCore is revoked, with the result that the devices will no longer engage in AD management protocols with the old ADMCore and DD certificates issued by the old ADMCore will not validate correctly, since the old ADMCore is blacklisted. In effect, the old ADMCore and the old domain are revoked. The user needs to register all his devices to a new domain managed by his new ADMCore.

The relation between a user and his domain is carefully managed. In this realization the user is supposed to have one domain. This is trivial to enforce when UserIdentity and ADMCore are deployed on the same token and are replaced at the same time, but in other cases special attention is required. In that case the revocation and replacement procedure for ADMCore also involves user management. Concretely, it means that the new domain is related to a specific user and replaces his old domain entry. This effectively also pairs the UserIdentity and ADMCore tokens. This allows the new ADMCore to create a DD certificate listing the userID but no ADClients.

4.2.5 Secure Authenticated Channel and Revocation

The domain management and license exchange protocols require confidentiality, integrity, authenticity and protection against replay attacks. These are provided by a Secure Authenticated Channel (SAC). We just highlight some specific features for PED-DRM given that many general purpose SACs exist such as TLS [3].

A first feature for PED-DRM is forced synchronization of the domain composition based on the exchange of DD certificates as part of the SAC setup phase. A device replaces the stored DD when it receives a valid DD certificate with a higher version number, provided that it is still listed, otherwise it removes its DD certificate completely. Inclusion of the DD certificate facilitates the correct functioning of the DRM system. Based on their accurate view on the domain, devices decide how they can exchange licenses with other devices and what kind of content access is allowed. The exchange of the DD certificate as part of SAC setup facilitates the update of a deregistered device that was deregistered from the domain while it was offline. The viral nature of the DD certificate distribution ensures that eventually the deregistered devices are no longer able to render any further domain content, except when a deregistered device no longer has any contact with its former domain members. This method is made more effective by requiring SAC usage for common operations such as license exchange, domain (de)registration and user authentication.

A second feature is the support for revocation. Devices only participate in domain management or license management interaction when the other party is still compliant. A general problem is the distribution of fresh compliance or revocation status information, especially for devices that have no direct Internet connectivity. We propose a scheme in which compliance status information for all domain devices is distributed over the domain devices, a method similar to the one presented in [19]. This can be done for example by piggy backing this information with DD certificates and the viral distribution nature thereof. A device with connectivity means obtains fresh compliance status information related to a given domain.

4.2.6 User Authentication

The user authentication protocol consists of unilateral authentication based on a straightforward challenge-response PKI protocol extended with proximity/presence assertions. Compliance and revocation should be verified as part of the user authentication protocol on three levels: user identity, user identity token, and the link between them that defines whether a token may be used to authenticate a particular user. The user identity is revoked when the private key of the user is compromised or when the user is banned from using the system for another reason. Tokens are revoked when it is not compliant anymore, e.g. when it is hacked or cloned. The link between a user and user identity token is revoked when it needs to be replaced and the old one may not be used anymore, e.g. in case of breakage, loss or theft. The user obtains a new token and can use both his old and new content. An additional measure could be that for new content the old token is specifically blacklisted in order to tackle cases where propagation of revocation status information may take some time. For all forms of revocation nothing needs to be done with either content or licenses.

4.2.7 License Management

License distribution and exchange is the main aspect of license management. We propose that ADClients exchange licenses with each other using the SAC. The properties of the SAC ensure that only and non-revoked compliant devices can obtain licenses. To reduce the effect in the case of hacked devices, licenses are only transferred to domain devices or devices that recently authenticated the user. Preferably the source device receives some proof by the user identity token before transferring the license. A pure form of the approach implies that domain licenses are removed from devices upon deregistration or upon expiry of an authentication session. However, this is impractical since it could unintentionally destroy the last domain license for a content item while not achieving any significant increase in security because the device already possesses it. A minor drawback of this approach is that licenses cannot be distributed upfront as they can when domain keys are used to protect the domain content.

5 Threat Model and Security Analysis

The typical threat model for DRM systems applies also to PED-DRM. This model assumes that users may be malicious and will attempt to gain unauthorized access to content. In this model, the attacker has full control of his local environment, including network and devices. It is assumed that compliant devices have some form of tamper resistance. Malicious users may use compromised and circumvention devices and software. Average attackers have limited computational resources to break cryptography, have only limited capability to disrupt external network communication outside his local environment and do not have access to professional tools. However, a small number of attackers have the skills, technology and resources to perform such attacks [6]. We continue with a brief overview of attacks and countermeasures related to domains and person-based DRM.

We start the security analysis from the perspective of the content owners. Focus is given to attacks and countermeasures that affect content proliferation, because that has the highest financial impact. The analysis is limited to the specific aspects of PED-DRM, i.e. domains and user management. The analysis of attacks and countermeasures covers all components from the architecture and their interactions:

☐ An attacker breaks an ADClient, ADMCore or UserIdentity implementation and extracts secret keys or makes changes to the operation of the device such that not all conditions are enforced. This attack is addressed by secure and robust implementations. Furthermore, the potential effects of the attack are contained by avoiding system-wide secrets in the design. As a result exposed secrets only affect a limited part of the content population, e.g. the domain content.

☐ Malicious users can interfere with the protocols in the local environment for domain management, license management or user authentication. The threats here relate to messages that represent value. Here these messages include the domain registration message that includes a domain devices certificate by ADMCore, the domain deregistration confirmation message by ADClient, and the authentication response message from UserIdentity. For example, a malicious user could replay the message that makes an ADClient, which was a former member of the domain again a domain member. Secure and robust protocols address this attack. Signing and encrypting all interactions between DRM components, ensuring freshness, and coupling all keys and credentials to the identity of the recipient address these attacks.

☐ Malicious users may interfere in the distribution of device compliance status information through the home network. Specifically, users may hinder distribution of revocation information. This attack is addressed by requiring that new content requires fresh compliance status information, otherwise an ADClient refuses rendering. The rationale here is that the older content is already exposed to the threat.

The above attacks relating to the security of the system and protocols are addressed by robust implementations and protocol design. There is also a range of attacks that relate to unintended use of the mechanisms and concepts. These are addressed by the right selection of policies:

☐ 'Content club' is the name for the attack where a large group of people share an account/identity/domain and obtain lots of content in such a way that it is accessible to all individual members, e.g. because they all have exactly one authorized device. The countermeasure consists of a tight domain policy limiting the amount of domain devices. This may be supplemented by mechanisms like regular re-registrations to prove membership liveness, but none of the considered mechanisms are considered both effective and user friendly at the same time. However, it is expected that even without taking additional measures that the attack only causes minor financial damage due to the inconvenience of circulating a physical domain management token in a group of people.

☐ 'Content cannibalization' is the name for the attack where many subsequent user authentications result in a large number of parallel temporary domain memberships just before some premium content is released. This attack is countered by putting some limit on the number of authentications per time frame enforced by the user authentication token.

☐ 'Content filling station' indicates the attack where a storage device with rendering capabilities is loaded with domain content followed by a transfer of ownership of the device, leaving the content available to the new and old owner. No countermeasures exist that do not affect user convenience severely, e.g. using time-outs on permanent domain memberships. In practice the financial loss is limited to a certain maximum due to the maximum number of devices in a domain. The old owner will try to deregister this device at the domain manager without affecting the device itself in order to register another device. However, this is subject to tight policy rules that put a cap on the financial effects, e.g. offer such deregistration only once a year.

Another class of attacks exist, which cannot be detected nor countered by technical means alone:

☐ Exploiting procedural processes for person management, e.g. malicious requests for replacement authentication tokens. To counter these three attacks one must ensure that the right (manual) processes and policies are in place.

☐ Users may exchange, share, trade authentication credentials/tokens. This attack is not countered, but instead the risk is accepted knowing that at all times there is at maximum just one token.

Besides security interests of the content owners, also end-users have security interests. This relates to privacy as discussed in section 2.3, but also to convenience and protection of value. Attacks and countermeasures are:

☐ A malicious user registers his device at a domain and accesses the associated content. The countermeasure here consists of introducing the concept of a domain owner. This domain owner implicitly or explicitly must agree with such device registration. Here, it is required that the ADMCore token is within direct proximity of the device to be added.

☐ A malicious user, e.g. on the same network, deregisters somebody's device from his domain. To counter this attack the concept of device owner is introduced, whose implicit or explicit consent is required. In this case user consent consists of operating the procedure from the device or pressing a button on the device. Alternatively, user authentication may be used, but this requires a pairing of a device and a user.

6 Conclusions

We have presented the PED-DRM concept and an implementation architecture. The implementation architecture specifically targets a deployment with a domain manager running on a token.

The PED-DRM concept is characterized by (1) content is bound to persons, (2) a person has a number of permanent domain devices on which (3) his content can be rendered, and (4) it can be rendered on devices after user authentication for the length of the authentication session. PED allows a user to enjoy his content any time, anywhere and on any device. PED further allows sharing of content with relatives or friends by sharing devices that can belong to multiple domains. By means of the domain policy content proliferation is strictly controlled. The domain policy defines the maximum number of devices in a domain, proximity based authentication and the length of an authentication session.

Person-based DRM, and PED-DRM in particular, put the user in a central position. PED-DRM enables the user to determine what to do with his devices, content and domains. Evaluation of alternative DRM concepts including PED-DRM leads to the conclusion that PED-DRM combines the strong points of device-based AD and person-based DRM.

PED-DRM is practical to implement, although it has a prerequisite on an identity and authentication infrastructure. This infrastructure includes support for and management of authentication tokens. An option is to introduce this infrastructure as part of the DRM system, for example using smartcards. However, ideally existing infrastructures are reused leveraging identity management technology. This also fits well with the foreseen application of the PED-DRM concept in online service oriented architectures such as OMA DRM.

Acknowledgements

We would like to thank our colleagues for their comments and help in the design of the PED-DRM system. Furthermore, we would like to thank the reviewers for their valuable comments on draft versions of this paper.

References

[1] Apple (2005) iTunes Music Store: Authorizing your computer. http://www.apple.com/support/itunes/musicstore/authorization/

[2] Conrado C, Petkovic M, Jonker W (2004) Privacy-Preserving DRM. In: Secure Data Management, 2004. Lecture Notes in Computer Science, vol 3178, Springer, Berlin

[3] Dierks T, Allen C (1999) RFC2246: The TLS Protocol (version 1)

[4] Eskicioglu AM, Delp EJ (2000) An overview of multimedia content protection in consumer electronic devices. Signal Processing: Image Communication 16:681-699

[5] Gildred J, Andreasyan A, Osawa R, Stahl T (2003) Protected Entertainment Rights Management (PERM): Specification Draft v0.54. Pioneer Research Center USA Inc, Thomson

[6] Gooch R (2003) Requirements for DRM systems. In: Digital Rights Management: Technological, Economic, Legal and Political Aspects, Lecture Notes in Computer Science, vol 2770, Springer, Berlin

[7] Guth S (2003) A Sample DRM System. In: Digital Rights Management: Technological, Economic, Legal and Political Aspects, Lecture Notes in Computer Science, vol 2770, Springer, Berlin

[8] Heuvel SAFA van den, Jonker W, Kamperman FLAJ., Lenoir PJ (2002) Secure Content Management in Authorised Domains. In: IBC Conference Publication, Amsterdam, pp467-474

[9] Iannella R (2003) Open Digital Rights Language (ODRL) Version 1.1

[10] Jonker W, Linnartz JP (2004) Digital Rights Management in Consumer Electronics Products. IEEE Signal Processing Magazine, Special Issue on Digital Rights Management 21:82-91

[11] Liberty Alliance Project (2005) Liberty ID-FF Architecture Overview, version 1.2

[12] Microsoft (2004) Next Generation Windows Media DRM for Consumer Electronics Devices. In: WinHEC2004

[13] Microsoft (2004) Windows Media Connect - Connectivity Solution for Networked Media Players. In: WinHEC2004

[14] Microsoft (2005) Windows Media Digital Rights Management. http://www.microsoft.com/windows/windowsmedia/drm/default.aspx

[15] Open Mobile Alliance (2006) DRM Architecture: Approved Version 2.0

[16] Open Mobile Alliance (2006) DRM Specification: Approved Version 2.0

[17] Pestoni, F, Lotspiech JB, Nusser S (2004) xCP: peer-to-peer content protection. IEEE Signal Processing Magazine 21:71-81

[18] Petkovic M, Koster RP (2005) User Attributed Rights in DRM. In: First International Conference on Digital Rights Management: Technology, Issues, Challenges and Systems, 31 October - 2 November 2005, Sydney, Australia

[19] Popescu BC, Crispo B, Kamperman FLAJ, Tanenbaum AS (2004) A DRM Security Architecture for Home Networks. In: Proceedings of the 4th ACM Workshop on Digital Rights Management, pp1-10

[20] Rosenblatt B, Trippe B, Mooney S (2002) Digital Rights Management: Business and Technology, M&T Books, New York

[21] Thomson (2003) SmartRight: Technical white paper, version 1.7

[22] Vevers R, Hibbert C (2002) Copy Protection and Content Management in the DVB. In: IBC Conference Publication, Amsterdam, pp458-466

[23] Wegner, S (ed.) (2003) OPERA - Interoperability of Digital Rights Management (DRM) Technologies: An Open DRM Architecture. Eurescom report

Improving Steganalysis by Fusion Techniques: A Case Study with Image Steganography

Mehdi Kharrazi[1], Husrev T. Sencar[2], and Nasir Memon[2]

[1] Department of Electrical and Computer Engineering
[2] Department of Computer and Information Science
Polytechnic University, Brooklyn, NY 11201, USA

Abstract. In the past few years, we have witnessed a number of powerful steganalysis technique proposed in the literature. These techniques could be categorized as either specific or universal. Each category of techniques has a set of advantages and disadvantages. A steganalysis technique specific to a steganographic embedding technique would perform well when tested only on that method and might fail on all others. On the other hand, universal steganalysis methods perform less accurately overall but provide acceptable performance in many cases. In practice, since the steganalyst will not be able to know what steganographic technique is used, it has to deploy a number of techniques on suspected images. In such a setting the most important question that needs to be answered is: What should the steganalyst do when the decisions produced by different steganalysis techniques are in contradiction? In this work, we propose and investigate the use of information fusion methods to aggregate the outputs of multiple steganalysis techniques. We consider several fusion rules that are applicable to steganalysis, and illustrate, through a number of case studies, how *composite* steganalyzers with improved performance can be designed. It is shown that fusion techniques increase detection accuracy and offer scalability, by enabling seamless integration of new steganalysis techniques.

1   Introduction

Steganography refers to the science of "invisible" communication. Unlike cryptography, where the goal is to secure communications from an eavesdropper, steganographic techniques strive to hide the very presence of the message itself from an observer. On the other hand, *steganalysis* techniques are used to detect the presence of hidden messages in an image. The reader is referred to [1] for a review of the field. Essentially there are two approaches to the problem of steganalysis, one is to come up with steganalysis techniques that are specific to a particular steganographic technique. The other is developing universal techniques that are effective over a wide variety of steganographic techniques. [1]

---

[1] *Universality* can be defined to indicate applicability over all embedding techniques and/or the domains of operation. In this work, we use the notion of *universal* as with respect to embedding techniques.

Y.Q. Shi (Ed.): Transactions on DHMS I, LNCS 4300, pp. 123–137, 2006.
© Springer-Verlag Berlin Heidelberg 2006

Specific steganalysis attacks concentrate on image features which are directly modified by the embedding algorithm. For example, F5 [2] embedding algorithm suffers from DCT histogram shrinkage, in which the number of zero DCT coefficients increases after the embedding operation. To exploit this, the specific attack proposed in [3], examines the differences between the histogram of the stego image and it's estimated original. As another example, in the model based embedding technique [4] the crux of the embedding operation lies in fitting a parametric model to the DCT histograms and preserving those models after embedding. The weakness of this approach is that DCT histograms of the cover images do not follow the model precisely. The specific attack proposed in [5] analyzes how well the image's DCT histograms match the fitted model for that image to determine whether the image in question is carrying hidden messages or not. Although such steganalysis techniques would perform well when tested only on the intended embedding method, they are very likely to fail on all other steganographic methods.

Universal steganalysis techniques operate by extracting some inherent *features* of cover images that are likely to be modified when an image undergoes steganographic embedding process. These features are then used to classify the image as either a cover or stego image. There have been a number of universal steganalysis techniques proposed in the literature. These techniques differ in the feature sets they utilize for capturing the characteristics of images. For example, Avcibas et al. [6] calculate several binary similarity measures between the seventh and eighth bit planes of an image. Farid et al. [7,8], obtain a number of statistics from the wavelet transform coefficients of images. On the other hand, Fridrich [9] utilizes DCT coefficient statistics. As observed in [10,6] universal steganalysis techniques do not perform equally over all embedding techniques; Nor are they able to distinguish perfectly between cover and stego images.

Furthermore, the classifier at the heart of each universal steganalyzer needs to be trained using a set of sample cover and stego images. This training process becomes computationally expensive depending on the type of classifier used, sample dataset size, and the separation of cover and stego images in the feature space.

With the availability of different type of steganalyzers (specific and universal) a number of questions would arise:

- What is the performance penalty due to the use of universal (or specific) steganalysis techniques assuming a practical setting of the problem?
- When multiple steganalyzers are used together, how do we deal with contradictory decisions?
- How does detection performance change when multiple embedding techniques are deployed in training the steganalyzer as opposed to using a specific technique, and what is the computational cost for repeating the training process to include new steganographic methods (in the training phase)?
- What is the most efficient strategy to *combine* different steganalyzers?

To answer these questions, we propose the use of *information fusion* techniques to incorporate steganalyzers, specific and universal, together. This approach has two potential advantages, in addition to providing a solution to real-life steganalysis problem. First, it improves the accuracy of distinguishing between a set of cover and stego images when multiple steganalyzers are available for use. Second, it reduces the computation cost associated with re-training a steganalyzer built to detect different *types* of stego images when a new steganographic technique has to be added to the training dataset.

The organization of the paper is as follows. In Section2, we review fusion techniques that are applicable to steganalysis problem. In Section3, we study the design of a composite steganalyzer by fusing a number of steganalysis techniques and provide performance comparison results. In Section4, we study how incorporation of a number of steganalysis techniques could be made scalable, by avoiding the cost associated with re-training steganalyzers. Our discussion of the results and conclusions are given in Section5.

2   Fusion Techniques

At the heart of every steganalyzer is a classifier which, given an image feature or feature vector, decides whether the image at hand contains any secret messages. Therefore, the fusion strategies developed for constructing more sophisticated classifiers can be considered for our purposes as well.

Motivated by [11], we review possible fusion strategies for classifiers as related to our work. Figure 1 summarizes different scenarios and classification stages in

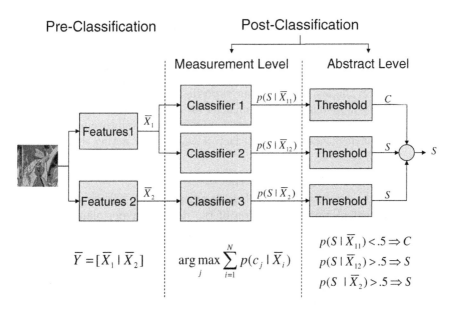

Fig. 1. Different scenarios as well classification stages in which fusion could be applied. For example fusion could be applied among a set of classifier trained using one feature vector, different feature vectors, or a hybrid of the two. Fusion may also be applied at different stages of the classification process (i.e. pre-classification or post-classification).

which fusion could be used. For example, a set of classifiers can be designed using the same feature vector. (I.e., given a feature vector, we could design a linear as well as non-linear classifier and fuse the results together.) On the other hand, fusion could also be applied to a set of classifiers each designed with a separate feature vector. Furthermore the two approaches could be combined into a hybrid approach. But more important is the stage in classification at which fusion is applied. Below, we provide a break up of these stages and discuss how they could be applied to steganalysis techniques.

2.1 Pre-classification

In essence, given an image I, the steganalyst first calculates the feature vector $X_I = [x_1, x_2, x_3, ...]$ from I. The feature vector is then used by a classifier, that was trained on previous observations of X, to output a decision regarding the nature of the image I (i.e., cover or stego). Fusion at this stage could be done by concatenating the feature vectors associated with each steganalysis technique and re-training the classifier with the feature vector Y_I defined as

$$Y_I = [X_{I1}|X_{I2}|X_{I3}...]. \tag{1}$$

But in practice a number of problems arise with such an approach. These are:

- With the increasing number of features, the classifier becomes more susceptible to *curse of dimensionality* problem.
- Correlated and redundant features need to be excluded for better performance.
- Classifier needs to be re-designed every time a new component is added to the feature vector Y_I.
- Different feature compositions may require different designing approaches.

To elaborate on the last point, in our experiments we have observed that some feature vectors show much improvement with more computationally expensive non-linear classifiers, whereas others show very little improvement. Thus one need to take into consideration such factors when constructing the classifier.

2.2 Post-classification

In this case, the classifier is trained using a set of stego and cover feature vectors, thereby calculating the location of the decision hyper-plane in the high-dimensional feature space. Therefore, the trained classifier could be thought of as a function, f_{class}, that computes the perpendicular distance of I, in terms of the extracted features X_I to the decision hyperplane in the feature space. This distance, also called decision value, DV, is used to categorize the image I as either cover or stego. Hence, we have

$$DV_{X_I} = f_{class}(X_I) \tag{2}$$

Below we will discuss two different post-classification levels, with which the obtained decision values are processed. It is after this processing that the decision values obtained from a set of classifiers become comparable, and therefore could be fused.

Measurement Level. The obtained decision values need to be normalized in order to make them comparable among a set of classifiers. This could be done by converting the decision values to a conditional distribution, $P(stego|X_I)$, i.e., the posterior probability of image I represented by feature vector X_I carrying a secret message denoted as

$$P(stego|X_I) = f_{norm}(DV_{XI}) = f_{norm}(f_{class}(X_I)). \tag{3}$$

Since there are only two classes available (i.e. cover or stego), we have

$$P(cover|X_I) = 1 - P(stego|X_I). \tag{4}$$

This is the most widely used stage for fusion. Here, the measurement information obtained from a set of steganalyzers could be either input into a second stage classifier for a final decision, or could be combined using schemes such as the *Mean, Max, Min, Median,* and *Product* rules. In fact, Kittler et al. in [12] conduct a theoretical study of these rules, and show that the *Mean* rule is least susceptible to estimation errors in the conditional probability distributions. Given the results in [12] and based on our preliminary experimental study, we decided to only employ the *Mean* and *Max* rules in our experiments. These two rules are explained below:

- *Mean Rule:*
  $C = argmax_j \sum_{i=1}^{N} P(c_j|X_{Ii})$
  With this rule, the class c_j (for $j = \{stego, cover\}$), assigned to input image I, is the class with which the sum of the conditional probabilities for that class is maximized.
- *Max Rule:*
  $C = argmax_j max_i P(c_j|X_{Ii})$
  Here the class c_j is assigned to input image I with which the maximum conditional probability is obtained.

Abstract Level. Fusion could also be applied at the last stage of classification, in which conditional class distributions are thresholded (or alternatively the decision values are thresholded directly), and a decision is made as to the class of the image I:

$$P(stego|X_I) > .5 \Rightarrow I \in stego \tag{5}$$

$$P(stego|X_I) < .5 \Rightarrow I \in cover \tag{6}$$

In this case, voting rule could be used to obtain a collective decision from a set of steganalyzers. But since this stage is obtained by thresholding the conditional probability distribution values, yielding a binary value, it will provide minimal usable information for fusion.

3   Fusion Based Steganalysis

In a practical setting, the steganalyst will be unsure of the embedding technique being used, if any. Therefore the conventional approach is to employ a universal steganalyzer which could detect, although not perfectly, stego images. But the steganalyst could also have a set of specific steganalyzers at her disposal, that in some cases perform more accurately than the universal techniques, or even alternate universal steganalyzers. In such a scenario, the steganalyst could create a new composite steganalyzer and improve the detection performance by fusing the decision obtained from the available set of universal and/or specific steganalysis techniques as described in Section2.

In what follows, we illustrate through the two possible scenarios, how a new steganalyzer could be built by fusing the results from a select set of steganalyzers. In the first scenario, Section3.1, we investigate the fusion of a number of universal steganalysis techniques, whereas in the second scenario, Section3.2, we investigate the fusion of universal and specific steganalysis techniques.

3.1   Fusing Universal Techniques

We will first study the fusion of three universal steganalysis techniques. Here we employed, binary similarity measures based steganalysis [13] denoted as BSM, wavelet transform coefficient features' based steganalysis [7,8] denoted as WBS, and DCT coefficient features' based steganalysis [9] denoted as FBS. An initial database consisting of 1800 natural images were used [14]. The images were converted to gray-scale and the borders around them were cropped, resulting in images of size 640x480 pixels, after which they were re-compressed with a quality factor of 75.

A stego dataset was created using the LSB and LSB +/- embedding techniques. In the LSB technique, the LSB of the pixels is replaced by the message bits to be sent. Usually the message bits are scattered around the image, by selecting the pixels to be modified in a random walk. Alternatively, LSB +/-, operates by incrementing or decrementing the last bit instead of replacing it. Message size was set as the ratio of bits per pixel in the image, more specifically we used the message sizes of 0.1 (3840 Bytes) and 0.2(7680 Bytes) in creating the stego set. A classifier was built for each message length using the feature vectors obtained by each steganalysis technique.

Fusion of the three steganalysis techniques was done at measurement level, using the *Max* and *Mean* rules discussed earlier in Section2. These rules operate on class conditional probabilities obtained from each steganalysis technique. For example with *Max* rule, the class of an input image is designated by the steganalyzer that has highest confidence in its decision, e.g., yielded the maximum conditional probability. With the *Mean* rule, the class to an input image is assigned so that the sum (or mean) of the conditional probabilities, associated with each steganalyzer, for that class is maximized.

The accuracy of the original steganalysis techniques, as well as the accuracy of the techniques when fused could be seen in terms of ROC curves in figure 2

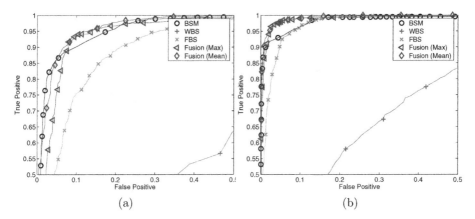

Fig. 2. ROC curves obtained for LSB embedded vs. unmarked images for three different steganalysis as well as two fusion techniques. (a) 0.1 messages size. (b) 0.2 message size.

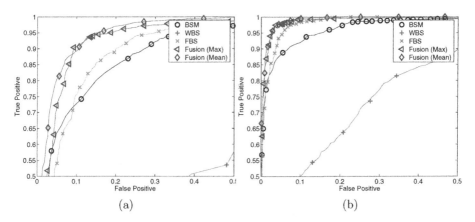

Fig. 3. ROC curves obtained for LSB +/- embedded vs. unmarked images for three different steganalysis as well as two fusion techniques. (a) 0.1 messages size. (b) 0.2 message size.

for the LSB, and in figure 3 for the LSB +/- embedding techniques. As seen in these figures fusion does provide considerable improvement over the three steganalysis techniques. To quantify this improvement the areas under the ROC curves are calculated and given in Table 1. We also observe that from the two fusion rules employed, the *Mean* rule outperforms the *Max* rule, therefore we will only employ the *Mean* rule for the rest of this work.

Here we should note that although the FBS steganalysis technique is proposed for DCT based embedding techniques, it performed satisfactorily on spatial domain embedding technique because of the dataset employed in these experiments. More specifically the original cover images used, were obtained from JPEG images compressed with a quality factor of 75. But, as observed in [15], if we

Table 1. Area under the ROC curves

	BSM	WBS	FBS	Fusion (Max)	Fusion (Mean)
LSB (0.1)	96.62	58.23	91.72	95.58	97.36
LSB (0.2)	98.79	73.97	98.12	99.24	99.54
LSB +/- (0.1)	90.92	59.11	92.09	94.69	96.34
LSB +/- (0.2)	97.51	80.61	98.78	99.14	99.43

use original BMP images as covers, where there exists no JPEG artifacts, the FBS technique is unable to distinguish between cover and LSB embedded stego images.

3.2   Fusing Specific and Universal Techniques

The second scenario we have looked at is one in which the embedder uses two types of embedding techniques, LSB and LSB +/- embedding techniques. We assume the steganalyst has available at her disposal the BSM universal steganalyzer [6], which performs well over both the LSB and LSB +/- embeddings, and the Pair steganalysis [16], which is a specific attack on the LSB embedding technique. From the large data set of gray scale images obtained for our benchmarking study in [10], we obtained about 13000 images with a quality factor of 85 and above and with a minimum width of 1000 pixels. These images were then down-sized to a size of 640x480 and saved as BMP. This was done to minimize the JPEG compression artifacts. We should note that the data set only consists of images that had their aspect ratio preserved after the down sampling operations.

Two BSM steganalyzers were trained independently, using the non-linear SVM [17], with the LSB and LSB +/- stego images. The message size used in creating the stego dataset was set as to the ratio of bits per pixel in the image, where in this case a value of 0.6 was used. Furthermore, in order to obtain the fusion result at different false positive rates (i.e. ROC curve), we opted to choose the output of the pair analysis attack as a feature value to be used by the classifier. This would also allow us to obtain classification confidence values which we will use when fusing the steganalysis techniques. Thus we have four steganalyzers available, including the fused steganalyzer, which was obtained using the *Mean* rule.

The four steganalyzers are tested against the cover dataset and 3 different stego datasets, namely, an LSB dataset, an LSB +/- dataset, and a dataset consisting of equal number of unique LSB and LSB +/- stego images. The obtained ROC curves for each dataset could be seen in figure 4, and the AUR [2] values could be seen in Table 2. From the results we observe that the specific attack works perfectly and has an accuracy of 100% when distinguishing between cover and LSB stego images, and when tested against the LSB +/- dataset the technique fails as expected. But when the pair analysis is tested against the mixed

---

[2] AUR: The area under the ROC curve is generally used to obtain a single comparative performance value for each classifier.

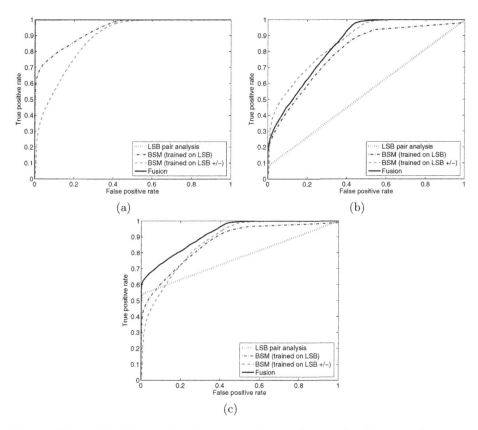

Fig. 4. Obtained ROC curves for the 4 steganalyzers when employed against the same cover but different stego datasets. (a) The stego test images consist of only LSB images. (b) The stego test images consist of only LSB +/- images. (c) The stego test images consist of both LSB and LSB +/- images. Here the number of LSB and LSB +/- stego images is the same, and we have avoided using the same image from both sets.

Table 2. AUR obtained from the ROC curves, when fusing universal and specific steganalysis techniques

	Specific Attack	BSM (LSB)	BSM(LSB +/-)	Fusion
LSB (0.6)	99.96	93.72	88.04	99.06
LSB +/- (0.6)	53.84	79.49	85.72	84.15
Mixed Set	76.94	86.52	86.90	92.07

dataset, its performance reduces since it is only effective in detecting the LSB images and not the LSB +/- images.

The two BSM steganalzyers, one trained with cover and LSB stego images the other with cover and LSB +/- stego images, perform around the same level with all three datasets. But when the outputs of these three steganalyzers (tested against the mixed dataset) are fused together, we observe a 15.3%, 5.55%, and 5.17% performance improvement from the results obtained if we had used only the specific attack, BSM trained with LSB stego images, and BSM trained with LSB +/- stego images, respectively.

It should be noted that we also tried a decision tree approach in which at the root we had placed the pair steganalysis technique. But the results of such fusion technique were poor, due to the inaccuracy of the pair steganalysis technique in identifying LSB +/- stego images.

4   Fusion Based Adaptive Steganalysis

Although in theory universal steganalysis techniques are meant to detect any stego embedding technique, even ones unseen to it at the training stage, in our experiments (as will be discussed later in this section), we have observed otherwise. That is, a trained steganalyzer using embedding technique A, which also performs well when tested on stego images of type A, performs quite inaccurately if it is asked to classify stego image obtained from embedding technique B. This is best illustrated in figure 5, where we show two stego sets denoted as *stego1* and *stego2*.

If the training dataset only consists of *cover* and *stego1* images then the classifiers might have a decision plane following the line A, with which most of *stego2* images will be classified correctly. But if the training dataset consists of *cover* and *stego2* images then the classifiers decision plane will follow line B, with which half of the the *stego1* images will be misclassified as cover images. In order to avoid such a problem, the training set needs to include both *stego1* and *stego2* images so that the classifier's decision plane will follow line C, and it will be able to correctly classify both *stego1* and *stego2* images.

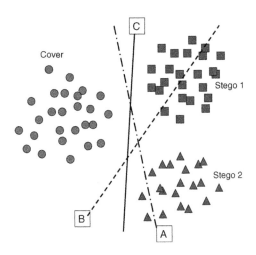

Fig. 5. Effects of training set on the performance of universal steganalysis techniques

Fridrich et al. [18], exploits the above deficiency of the universal steganalysis techniques to address another interesting problem. In their work, a multi-class classifier is designed using cover and stego images created with a number of embedding techniques. Since, presumably, stego images from each embedding technique occupy a unique space in the feature space, the steganalyst, not only differentiates among stego and cover images, but also is able to distinguish between different types of stego images based on the embedding technique used.

We should note that the above problem could potentially be avoided using one-class SVMs, but that approach has its own downsides. One-class SVMs are designed with only one class of images by creating a hyper-sphere in the feature space so that all images that fall inside the hyper-sphere are defined to be cover images and images that fall outside of the hyper-sphere are deemed to be stego images. Hence, the accuracy of such classifiers greatly depends on how well the cover images, represented by a set of extracted features, could be enclosed by a hyper-sphere. Because of the difficulty of this requirement two-class SVM classifiers, which have access to both cover and stego images at the design stage, outperform one-class SVMs.

In universal steganalysis, as the number of stego techniques represented in the training dataset increases the size of the training dataset needs to grow as well. This is so that a minimal number of stego images from each technique could be represented in the dataset. However, this increase in the dataset size also increases the classifier's training cost, thus making this approach unscalable and prohibitive. To show the relationship between the training set size and computational time, we have conducted a simple experiment in which we trained a set of classifiers each using training sets with varying sizes that consist of cover and stego images obtained by Model Based steganoggraphic embedding technique. The images dataset from Section3.2 was used, with the message length set to .08 bits per image pixel. The training set size vs. computational curve is given in figure 6. From the figure, we observe that the computational time increases rapidly as the training set size increases for the linear SVM classifier. This increase is more drastic when we used the superior non-linear SVM classifier. For example if our training set consists of 110000 images, then it would take more than 11 hours to design the non-linear SVM classifier.

The above described problem is further exacerbated due to the fact that the training operation has to be repeated every time with images from a new steganograhic embedding technique are added to the training dataset. The use of fusion strategies, aside from addressing decision aggregation problem, also offers a solution to this problem. This can be realized by designing a separate classifier for each available steganographic technique and then fusing the decisions obtained by testing an image against all available classifiers. Therefore, when a new steganographic technique is introduced or dataset is changed, re-training at a global scale is not needed. But the question to be answered is whether, with fusion, we will be able to obtain accuracy results as well as those obtained from a steganalyzer trained with a dataset containing stego images created with available steganographic techniques.

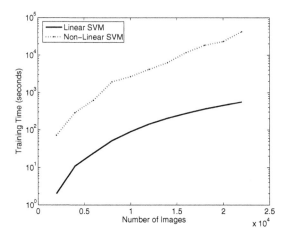

Fig. 6. Computational time for different training set sizes, using the linear and non-linear SVM classifier. Training was done on a machine with a Xeon 2.8GHz processor, and 1GB of memory, running linux. In the case of the non-linear svm, the parameter grid search was done from 2^0 to 2^{15} with steps of 2^3 for parameter c, and from 2^{-10} to 2^5 with steps of 2^3 for parameter g.

To investigate the above question, we obtained a set of cover images, as in Section3.2, and used Outguess (+) [19], F5 [2], and Model Based [4] techniques to create three stego datasets. The message lengths were set to 0.06 bits per image pixel. As for the steganalyzer, we employed the FBS technique. A steganalyzer was trained independently for each of the three cover and stego image pairs. We further designed a steganalyzer using a training set which consists of cover images and a stego dataset compromised of equal number of stego images from all three embedding techniques.

To show the importance of the training set on the performance of the universal steganalyzers, we tested each trained steganalyzer against the same cover but three different stego datasets. The obtained ROC curves are seen in figure 7, and the calculated AURs are presented in Table 3. For example, we observe from these results that the steganalyzer trained solely on the Outguess (+) stego images, when asked to distinguish between cover and Outguess (+) images, obtains an accuracy of 98.49%. But, its accuracy for distinguishing cover images from F5 and Model Based images is 54.37% and 66.45%, respectively.

Afterwards, the output of the three steganalyzers, each trained for one of the three embedding techniques, are fused using the *Mean* rule. Alternatively a steganalyzer is trained using all three available stego images. The obtained results are in figure 7, and the calculated AURs are presented in Table 3. Based on these

---

[3] Outguess (+): The plus sign indicates the usage of the *statistical steganalysis foiling feature* with the Outguess program. With this feature, a set of reserved DCT coefficients are adjusted after the message has been embedded with the aim of preserving the original histogram of DCT coefficients.

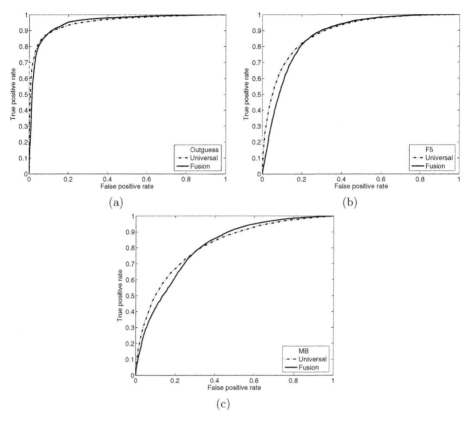

Fig. 7. Obtained ROC curves for the designed steganalyzers when employed against the same cover but different stego datasets. (a) Tested against the Outguess(+) stego set. (b) Tested against the F5 stego set. (c) Tested against the MB stego set.

Table 3. AUR obtained from the ROC curves, when fusing steganalyzers to obtain scalability

	FBS (Out+)	FBS (F5)	FBS (MB)	FBS (Universal)	FBS (Fusion)
Out+	98.49	44.06	86.29	95.36	95.34
F5	54.37	93.12	65.47	88.84	87.16
MB	66.45	63.73	85.22	81.34	80.62

results, we make two observations, first of all, as argued earlier the composition of training set plays an important role on the performance of the steganalyzer. Secondly, we see a performance degradation ranging roughly from 3% to 4% when we test our datasets against the steganalyzer trained with all three stego techniques as opposed to steganlyzers trained with only one stego technique. As evident from the results the fused steganalyzer has performance values very close to the steganalyzer trained with all the three embedding techniques included in its training dataset. Thus, fusion allows us to train steganalyzers only using one embedding technique and then fuse the outputs together, therefore avoiding the re-training of the classifier with new embedding techniques included in the training dataset. We believe that these results will generalize over alternate universal steganalysis techniques, and are not specific to the technique studied here, although the magnitude of the effects may vary.

5   Discussion

With the availability of large number of steganalysis techniques proposed in the literature, one might feel that the steganalyst has a good chance of distinguishing between cover and stego images. But in practice, the steganalyst will have to select one or more techniques which she will employ on a set of suspected stego images. However, the question of what to do when the results produced by various steganalysis techniques are in contradiction was not answered, previously. In this work, we investigated how fusion techniques could be applied in steganalysis to resolve such questions.

As the first application, we illustrated how a new steganalyzer could be created by fusing a number of steganalysis techniques while at the same time improving the detection accuracy. As the second application of fusion, we discussed the importance of the training set for universal steganalysis techniques and argued that incorporation of a new steganographic embedding technique into the an already designed steganalyzer is a costly and unscalable procedure. As an alternative, we proposed fusing decisions from a set of steganalysis technique trained independently using only one embedding technique. We illustrated through experimentation that the obtained accuracy results matches that of a steganalyzer trained with stego images from all embedding techniques studied, while at the same time providing scalability.

We believe that the applications of fusion techniques are not limited to the examples we have studied in this work. For example, as noted earlier, Fridrich et al. [18] illustrate how they could identify between a set of stego images, based on the embedding technique used to create them. In their work, only one steganalysis technique is employed, but with the help of fusion, one could improve and expand the results, by including more steganalyzers. Further more, such approach could be extended to alternate post-steganalysis operations such as estimation of the embedded message length. This form of information would be quite valuable in any forensic analysis of the stego images that intends to recover the hidden message.

References

1. Kharrazi, M., Sencar, H.T., Memon, N.: Image steganography: Concepts and practice. to appear in Lecture Note Series, Institute for Mathematical Sciences, National University of Singapore (2004)
2. Westfeld, A.: F5 steganographic algorithm: High capacity despite better steganalysis. 4th International Workshop on Information Hiding. (2001)

3. Fridrich, J., Goljan, M., Hogea, D., Soukal, D.: Quantitive steganalysis of digital images: Estimating the secret message lenght. ACM Multimedia Systems Journal, Special issue on Multimedia Security (2003)

4. Sallee, P.: Model-based steganography. International Workshop on Digital Watermarking, Seoul, Korea. (2003.)

5. Bhme, R., Westfeld, A.: Breaking cauchy model-based jpeg steganography with first order statistics. 9th European Symposium on Research in Computer Security, Sophia Antipolis, France, September (2004)

6. Avcibas, I., Kharrazi, M., Memon, N., sankur, B.: Image steganalysis with binary similarity measures. To appear in EURASIP Journal on Applied Signal Processing (2005.)

7. Lyu, S., Farid, H.: Detecting hidden messages using higher-order statistics and support vector machines. 5th International Workshop on Information Hiding. (2002.)

8. Lyu, S., Farid, H.: Steganalysis using color wavelet statistics and one-class support vector machines. SPIE Symposium on Electronic Imaging, San Jose, CA, (2004.)

9. Fridrich, J.: Feature-based steganalysis for jpeg images and its implications for future design of steganographic schemes. Proc. 6th Information Hiding Workshop, Toronto, Canada, May 23-25 (2004)

10. Kharrazi, M., Sencar, T.H., Memon, N.: Benchmarking steganographic and steganalysis techniques. EI SPIE San Jose, CA, January 16-20 (2005)

11. Jain, A.K., Nandakumar, K., Ros, A.: Score normalization in multimodal biometric systems. to appear in Pattern Recognition (2005)

12. Kittler, J., Hatef, M., Duin, R., Matas, J.: On combining classifiers. IEEE Transactions on Pattern Analysis and Machine Intelligence **20**(3) (1998) 226–239

13. Avcibas, I., Memon, N., sankur, B.: Image steganalysis with binary similarity measures. IEEE International Conference on Image Processing, Rochester, New York. (September 2002.)

14. Greenspun, P.: Images obtained from. philip.greenspun.com (-)

15. Kharrazi, M., Sencar, T.H., Memon, N.: Benchmarking steganographic and steganalysis techniques. Submitted to the Journal of Electronic Imaging (2006)

16. Dumitrescu, S., Wu, X., Memon, N.: On steganalysis of random lsb embedding in continuous-tone images. IEEE International Conference on Image Processing, Rochester, New York. (September 2002.)

17. Chang, C.C., Lin, C.J.: LIBSVM: a library for support vector machines. (2001) Software available at `http://www.csie.ntu.edu.tw/~cjlin/libsvm`.

18. Fridrich, J., Pevny, T.: Multiclass blind steganalysis for jpeg images. SPIE Electronic Imaging, Photonics West, San Jose,CA (2006)

19. Provos, N.: Defending against statistical steganalysis. 10th USENIX Security Symposium (2001)

Author Index

Adelsbach, André   73

Comesaña, Pedro   41

Dittmann, Jana   1

Herrera-Joancomartí, Jordi   1

Kamperman, Frank   104
Kharrazi, Mehdi   123
Koster, Paul   104

Lang, Andreas   1
Lenoir, Peter   104

Megías, David   1
Memon, Nasir   123

Pérez-Freire, Luis   41
Pérez-González, Fernando   41

Rohe, Markus   73

Sadeghi, Ahmad-Reza   73
Sencar, Husrev T.   123

Troncoso-Pastoriza, Juan Ramón   41

Vrielink, Koen   104

Lecture Notes in Computer Science

For information about Vols. 1–4204

please contact your bookseller or Springer

Vol. 4300: Y.Q. Shi (Ed.), Transactions on Data Hiding and Multimedia Security I. IX, 139 pages. 2006.

Vol. 4292: G. Bebis, R. Boyle, B. Parvin, D. Koracin, P. Remagnino, A. Nefian, G. Meenakshisundaram, V. Pascucci, J. Zara, J. Molineros, H. Theisel, T. Malzbender (Eds.), Advances in Visual Computing, Part II. XXXII, 906 pages. 2006.

Vol. 4291: G. Bebis, R. Boyle, B. Parvin, D. Koracin, P. Remagnino, A. Nefian, G. Meenakshisundaram, V. Pascucci, J. Zara, J. Molineros, H. Theisel, T. Malzbender (Eds.), Advances in Visual Computing, Part I. XXXI, 916 pages. 2006.

Vol. 4283: Y.Q. Shi, B. Jeon (Eds.), Digital Watermarking. XII, 474 pages. 2006.

Vol. 4281: K. Barkaoui, A. Cavalcanti, A. Cerone (Eds.), Theoretical Aspects of Computing - ICTAC. XV, 371 pages. 2006.

Vol. 4279: N. Kobayashi (Ed.), Programming Languages and Systems. XI, 423 pages. 2006.

Vol. 4278: R. Meersman, Z. Tari, P. Herrero (Eds.), On the Move to Meaningful Internet Systems 2006: OTM 2006 Workshops, Part II. XLV, 1004 pages. 2006.

Vol. 4277: R. Meersman, Z. Tari, P. Herrero (Eds.), On the Move to Meaningful Internet Systems 2006: OTM 2006 Workshops, Part I. XLV, 1009 pages. 2006.

Vol. 4276: R. Meersman, Z. Tari (Eds.), On the Move to Meaningful Internet Systems 2006: CoopIS, DOA, GADA, and ODBASE, Part II. XXXII, 752 pages. 2006.

Vol. 4275: R. Meersman, Z. Tari (Eds.), On the Move to Meaningful Internet Systems 2006: CoopIS, DOA, GADA, and ODBASE, Part I. XXXI, 1115 pages. 2006.

Vol. 4273: I.F. Cruz, S. Decker, D. Allemang, C. Preist, D. Schwabe, P. Mika, M. Uschold, L. Aroyo (Eds.), The Semantic Web - ISWC 2006. XXIV, 1001 pages. 2006.

Vol. 4272: P. Havinga, M. Lijding, N. Meratnia, M. Wegdam (Eds.), Smart Sensing and Context. XI, 267 pages. 2006.

Vol. 4271: F.V. Fomin (Ed.), Graph-Theoretic Concepts in Computer Science. XIII, 358 pages. 2006.

Vol. 4270: H. Zha, Z. Pan, H. Thwaites, A.C. Addison, M. Forte (Eds.), Interactive Technologies and Sociotechnical Systems. XVI, 547 pages. 2006.

Vol. 4269: R. State, S. van der Meer, D. O'Sullivan, T. Pfeifer (Eds.), Large Scale Management of Distributed Systems. XIII, 282 pages. 2006.

Vol. 4268: G. Parr, D. Malone, M. Ó Foghlú (Eds.), Autonomic Principles of IP Operations and Management. XIII, 237 pages. 2006.

Vol. 4267: A. Helmy, B. Jennings, L. Murphy, T. Pfeifer (Eds.), Autonomic Management of Mobile Multimedia Services. XIII, 257 pages. 2006.

Vol. 4266: H. Yoshiura, K. Sakurai, K. Rannenberg, Y. Murayama, S. Kawamura (Eds.), Advances in Information and Computer Security. XIII, 438 pages. 2006.

Vol. 4265: N. Lavrač, L. Todorovski, K.P. Jantke (Eds.), Discovery Science. XIV, 384 pages. 2006. (Sublibrary LNAI).

Vol. 4264: J.L. Balcázar, P.M. Long, F. Stephan (Eds.), Algorithmic Learning Theory. XIII, 393 pages. 2006. (Sublibrary LNAI).

Vol. 4263: A. Levi, E. Savas, H. Yenigün, S. Balcisoy, Y. Saygin (Eds.), Computer and Information Sciences – ISCIS 2006. XXIII, 1084 pages. 2006.

Vol. 4261: Y. Zhuang, S. Yang, Y. Rui, Q. He (Eds.), Advances in Multimedia Information Processing - PCM 2006. XXII, 1040 pages. 2006.

Vol. 4260: Z. Liu, J. He (Eds.), Formal Methods and Software Engineering. XII, 778 pages. 2006.

Vol. 4259: S. Greco, Y. Hata, S. Hirano, M. Inuiguchi, S. Miyamoto, H.S. Nguyen, R. Słowiński (Eds.), Rough Sets and Current Trends in Computing. XXII, 951 pages. 2006. (Sublibrary LNAI).

Vol. 4257: I. Richardson, P. Runeson, R. Messnarz (Eds.), Software Process Improvement. XI, 219 pages. 2006.

Vol. 4256: L. Feng, G. Wang, C. Zeng, R. Huang (Eds.), Web Information Systems – WISE 2006 Workshops. XIV, 320 pages. 2006.

Vol. 4255: K. Aberer, Z. Peng, E.A. Rundensteiner, Y. Zhang, X. Li (Eds.), Web Information Systems – WISE 2006. XIV, 563 pages. 2006.

Vol. 4254: T. Grust, H. Höpfner, A. Illarramendi, S. Jablonski, M. Mesiti, S. Müller, P.-L. Patranjan, K.-U. Sattler, M. Spiliopoulou (Eds.), Current Trends in Database Technology – EDBT 2006. XXXI, 932 pages. 2006.

Vol. 4253: B. Gabrys, R.J. Howlett, L.C. Jain (Eds.), Knowledge-Based Intelligent Information and Engineering Systems, Part III. XXXII, 1301 pages. 2006. (Sublibrary LNAI).

Vol. 4252: B. Gabrys, R.J. Howlett, L.C. Jain (Eds.), Knowledge-Based Intelligent Information and Engineering Systems, Part II. XXXIII, 1335 pages. 2006. (Sublibrary LNAI).

Vol. 4251: B. Gabrys, R.J. Howlett, L.C. Jain (Eds.), Knowledge-Based Intelligent Information and Engineering Systems, Part I. LXVI, 1297 pages. 2006. (Sublibrary LNAI).

Vol. 4249: L. Goubin, M. Matsui (Eds.), Cryptographic Hardware and Embedded Systems - CHES 2006. XII, 462 pages. 2006.

Vol. 4248: S. Staab, V. Svátek (Eds.), Managing Knowledge in a World of Networks. XIV, 400 pages. 2006. (Sublibrary LNAI).

Vol. 4247: T.-D. Wang, X. Li, S.-H. Chen, X. Wang, H. Abbass, H. Iba, G. Chen, X. Yao (Eds.), Simulated Evolution and Learning. XXI, 940 pages. 2006.

Vol. 4246: M. Hermann, A. Voronkov (Eds.), Logic for Programming, Artificial Intelligence, and Reasoning. XIII, 588 pages. 2006. (Sublibrary LNAI).

Vol. 4245: A. Kuba, L.G. Nyúl, K. Palágyi (Eds.), Discrete Geometry for Computer Imagery. XIII, 688 pages. 2006.

Vol. 4244: S. Spaccapietra (Ed.), Journal on Data Semantics VII. XI, 267 pages. 2006.

Vol. 4243: T. Yakhno, E.J. Neuhold (Eds.), Advances in Information Systems. XIII, 420 pages. 2006.

Vol. 4242: A. Rashid, M. Aksit (Eds.), Transactions on Aspect-Oriented Software Development II. IX, 289 pages. 2006.

Vol. 4241: R.R. Beichel, M. Sonka (Eds.), Computer Vision Approaches to Medical Image Analysis. XI, 262 pages. 2006.

Vol. 4239: H.Y. Youn, M. Kim, H. Morikawa (Eds.), Ubiquitous Computing Systems. XVI, 548 pages. 2006.

Vol. 4238: Y.-T. Kim, M. Takano (Eds.), Management of Convergence Networks and Services. XVIII, 605 pages. 2006.

Vol. 4237: H. Leitold, E. Markatos (Eds.), Communications and Multimedia Security. XII, 253 pages. 2006.

Vol. 4236: L. Breveglieri, I. Koren, D. Naccache, J.-P. Seifert (Eds.), Fault Diagnosis and Tolerance in Cryptography. XIII, 253 pages. 2006.

Vol. 4234: I. King, J. Wang, L. Chan, D. Wang (Eds.), Neural Information Processing, Part III. XXII, 1227 pages. 2006.

Vol. 4233: I. King, J. Wang, L. Chan, D. Wang (Eds.), Neural Information Processing, Part II. XXII, 1203 pages. 2006.

Vol. 4232: I. King, J. Wang, L. Chan, D. Wang (Eds.), Neural Information Processing, Part I. XLVI, 1153 pages. 2006.

Vol. 4231: J. F. Roddick, R. Benjamins, S. Si-Saïd Cherfi, R. Chiang, C. Claramunt, R. Elmasri, F. Grandi, H. Han, M. Hepp, M. Hepp, M. Lytras, V.B. Mišić, G. Poels, I.-Y. Song, J. Trujillo, C. Vangenot (Eds.), Advances in Conceptual Modeling - Theory and Practice. XXII, 456 pages. 2006.

Vol. 4230: C. Priami, A. Ingólfsdóttir, B. Mishra, H.R. Nielson (Eds.), Transactions on Computational Systems Biology VII. VII, 185 pages. 2006. (Sublibrary LNBI).

Vol. 4229: E. Najm, J.F. Pradat-Peyre, V.V. Donzeau-Gouge (Eds.), Formal Techniques for Networked and Distributed Systems - FORTE 2006. X, 486 pages. 2006.

Vol. 4228: D.E. Lightfoot, C.A. Szyperski (Eds.), Modular Programming Languages. X, 415 pages. 2006.

Vol. 4227: W. Nejdl, K. Tochtermann (Eds.), Innovative Approaches for Learning and Knowledge Sharing. XVII, 721 pages. 2006.

Vol. 4226: R.T. Mittermeir (Ed.), Informatics Education – The Bridge between Using and Understanding Computers. XVII, 319 pages. 2006.

Vol. 4225: J.F. Martínez-Trinidad, J.A. Carrasco Ochoa, J. Kittler (Eds.), Progress in Pattern Recognition, Image Analysis and Applications. XIX, 995 pages. 2006.

Vol. 4224: E. Corchado, H. Yin, V. Botti, C. Fyfe (Eds.), Intelligent Data Engineering and Automated Learning – IDEAL 2006. XXVII, 1447 pages. 2006.

Vol. 4223: L. Wang, L. Jiao, G. Shi, X. Li, J. Liu (Eds.), Fuzzy Systems and Knowledge Discovery. XXVIII, 1335 pages. 2006. (Sublibrary LNAI).

Vol. 4222: L. Jiao, L. Wang, X. Gao, J. Liu, F. Wu (Eds.), Advances in Natural Computation, Part II. XLII, 998 pages. 2006.

Vol. 4221: L. Jiao, L. Wang, X. Gao, J. Liu, F. Wu (Eds.), Advances in Natural Computation, Part I. XLI, 992 pages. 2006.

Vol. 4219: D. Zamboni, C. Kruegel (Eds.), Recent Advances in Intrusion Detection. XII, 331 pages. 2006.

Vol. 4218: S. Graf, W. Zhang (Eds.), Automated Technology for Verification and Analysis. XIV, 540 pages. 2006.

Vol. 4217: P. Cuenca, L. Orozco-Barbosa (Eds.), Personal Wireless Communications. XV, 532 pages. 2006.

Vol. 4216: M.R. Berthold, R. Glen, I. Fischer (Eds.), Computational Life Sciences II. XIII, 269 pages. 2006. (Sublibrary LNBI).

Vol. 4215: D.W. Embley, A. Olivé, S. Ram (Eds.), Conceptual Modeling - ER 2006. XVI, 590 pages. 2006.

Vol. 4213: J. Fürnkranz, T. Scheffer, M. Spiliopoulou (Eds.), Knowledge Discovery in Databases: PKDD 2006. XXII, 660 pages. 2006. (Sublibrary LNAI).

Vol. 4212: J. Fürnkranz, T. Scheffer, M. Spiliopoulou (Eds.), Machine Learning: ECML 2006. XXIII, 851 pages. 2006. (Sublibrary LNAI).

Vol. 4211: P. Vogt, Y. Sugita, E. Tuci, C. Nehaniv (Eds.), Symbol Grounding and Beyond. VIII, 237 pages. 2006. (Sublibrary LNAI).

Vol. 4210: C. Priami (Ed.), Computational Methods in Systems Biology. X, 323 pages. 2006. (Sublibrary LNBI).

Vol. 4209: F. Crestani, P. Ferragina, M. Sanderson (Eds.), String Processing and Information Retrieval. XIV, 367 pages. 2006.

Vol. 4208: M. Gerndt, D. Kranzlmüller (Eds.), High Performance Computing and Communications. XXII, 938 pages. 2006.

Vol. 4207: Z. Ésik (Ed.), Computer Science Logic. XII, 627 pages. 2006.

Vol. 4206: P. Dourish, A. Friday (Eds.), UbiComp 2006: Ubiquitous Computing. XIX, 526 pages. 2006.

Vol. 4205: G. Bourque, N. El-Mabrouk (Eds.), Comparative Genomics. X, 231 pages. 2006. (Sublibrary LNBI).